Informix Database Specialist

Learning Tree International Certifications

Certified Lotus Specialist

Microsoft Certified Professional

Microsoft Certified Professional + Internet

Microsoft Certified Systems Engineer

Microsoft Certified Systems Engineer + Internet

Microsoft Certified Solution Developer

Microsoft Certified Trainer

Microsoft Office Expert

Novell Internet Business Strategist

Certified Novell Administrator

Certified Novell Engineer

Master Certified Novell Engineer

Certified Novell Instructor

Oracle Certified Database Administrator

Prosoft/Net Guru Technologies Certified Internet Webmaster

Santa Cruz Organization (SCO) Advanced Certified Engineer

Silicon Graphics Certified IRIX 6.*x* System and Network Administrator

Sun Certified Java Programmer

Sun Certified Solaris Administrator and Network Administrator

Sybase Certified Database Administrator

USWeb Learning Certified Specialist and Architect

Xylan Certified Switch Specialist and Expert

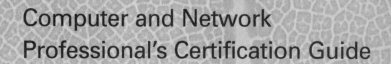

Computer and Network
Professional's Certification Guide

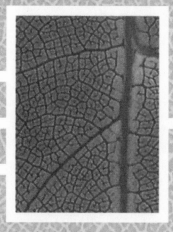

Computer and Network Professional's Certification Guide

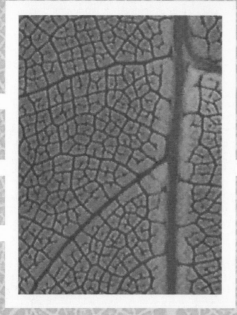

J. Scott Christianson
and Ava Fajen

San Francisco • Paris • Düsseldorf • Soest

Associate Publisher: Guy Hart-Davis
Contracts and Licensing Manager: Kristine Plachy
Acquisitions & Developmental Editor: Krista Reid-McLaughlin
Editor: Davina Baum
Book Designers: Patrick Dintino, Kris Warrenburg Design
Desktop Publisher: Kris Warrenburg Design
Production Coordinator: Eryn L. Osterhaus
Indexer: Nancy Guenther
Cover Designer: Archer Design
Cover Illustrator/Photographer: FPG International

Library of Congress Card Number: 98-84266
ISBN: 0-7821-2260-4

Manufactured in the United States of America

10 9 8 7 6 5 4 3 2 1

To Allie and Cass,
Thanks for your love and companionship.

—Scott and Ava

Acknowledgments

Sybex did an excellent job of guiding us through the process of writing this book. Special thanks go to Krista Reid-McLaughlin and Davina Baum for their advice and patience. We would also like to thank Guy Hart-Davis, Neil Edde, and Kristine Plachy, and our production team of Eryn Osterhaus and Kris Warrenburg for helping to make this book a reality.

We would not have been able to complete this book without the help of numerous individuals and companies who provided and verified information about their certification programs, including:

Kathryn Alderman (Borland), Kristi An (Gallager Marketing), Ginnie Babbet (Silicon Graphics), Jay Bender (DRI), Judi Bernstein (Banyan), Ann Bontatibus (Centura), Paula Cassano (CNX), Jullie CeCe (Silicon Graphics), Eva Chase (Bay Networks), Tony Croes (Compaq), Karen Cunningham (Hewlett-Packard), Valerie Danzey (Ascend), Guy DiBianca (Xylan), Sharon Frank (ICCP), Gay Groom (Learning Tree International), Kisa Harris (Adobe), Holly Heath (Microsoft), Dianne Horton (Compaq), Edward Johnson (Unisys), Linda Kennedy (Lotus), Angela Kinney (CompTIA), Diane Knight (Bay Networks), Carrie Lynden (Adobe), Tammy McBride (SCO), John Monaco (Unisys), Kimberly Moore (Wichita State University), Leslie Owens (Ascend), Uday O. Pabrai (Prosoft/Net Guru Technologies), Imran Qureshi (Cisco), Kathryn Rand (Computer Associates), Tim Rondeau (Bay Networks), Barbara Sandro (Compaq), Dian Schaffhauser (OfficeCert.Com magazine), Jacqueline Schick (Lotus), Dee Sheetz (IBM), Cary Snowden (Microsoft), Jill Suarez (Sybase), Dana Testa (Adobe), Linda Walden (US Web), Shannon Walner (Informix), Jay Warnke (BICSI), Mike Witherel (Business and Technology Review), and Fiazz Wulji (Corel).

And a special thanks to John Monaco for writing our foreword.

Foreword

When the authors first contacted me and asked me to write the foreword for this publication, I was in the midst of preparing a comprehensive review of Unisys Corporation's global network service capabilities for one of our best-of-breed technology partners, Cisco Systems. As busy as I was, I couldn't turn down an opportunity to acknowledge the importance of the work the authors have done in compiling the information contained in this book.

Not a day goes by at my office without someone in my organization, or someone in a customer's organization, asking me how many certified professionals for a given product or technology Unisys has on staff. Why? Quite simply, the right information technology certifications have become the "table stakes" a company needs to compete successfully in the rapidly growing information services marketspace. End users (clients) always request two things from a potential service provider like Unisys: first, what training programs/certifications do your people have, and second, what other clients do you have who are in our industry and use the same technology?

Two factors have contributed to this situation: the less-than-spectacular success rate for large client/server systems integration projects, and the diversity and complexity of the technologies and products that comprise today's corporate enterprise networks. Corporate executives are demanding better returns on information technology investments. Information systems managers see certified professionals as a way to increase their chances of completing projects successfully—i.e., on time and within budget.

The only problem with this situation is that there aren't enough certified professionals to go around. I currently require that every one of my Network Integration Service Engineers in Unisys North America has, at a minimum, one recognized industry certification to join the team. Right now, service providers like Unisys Corporation have an advantage over other companies in that we can offer these highly trained people higher salaries and then leverage that knowledge investment over many projects at different customer sites across the country and—for some of the rarer technical certifications—even across the planet!

Let's face it, a company of average size is at a great disadvantage when it comes to helping their information technology professionals keep up with today's technology. Their staff can only become familiar with, and support, the technologies the company has implemented. Thus, when they need to acquire new technology, they also have to acquire new training. Sometimes the people, time, and money costs associated with new information technology training is so great that companies are forced to "go outside" and hire assistance. Professionals that have both experience and certification with the technologies that are in demand will always be the first ones hired.

But—*if a company can attract and retain certified professionals*— the potential rewards for the typical business employer are many. Certified information technology employees are more efficient, and they make their non-certified team members more efficient, as well. Like a good free safety in football, the non-certified employees know the certified professional can "back them up" on complex problems. Certified employees can also mentor and educate less experienced or knowledgeable staff members.

There are tangible rewards for the information technology product providers, as well. Any Original Equipment Manufacturer (OEM) seeking market share for their hardware or software products must ensure that information technology support personnel are capable of adequately supporting the technical needs of the OEM's users. At the very least, developing a support services training program and marketing it with a certificate sends the industry the message that the OEM's product can be supported in the field, not just in the laboratory.

The personal computing industry has significantly impacted multi-vendor service companies and their technical employees. Companies such as Unisys must maintain a geographically dispersed technical workforce of personnel that have OEM certification. The reasons a service provider wants their employees to have these OEM certifications are two-fold: first, to validate to potential customers their service capability. Second, certification is required to recover any warranty fees or defective parts recovery claims associated with servicing the OEM's products.

At Unisys, we have an on-going skill and technical certification process for all of our technical employees. In 1993, we developed a core competency curriculum for each of our technical job categories. This curriculum identifies mandatory technical skill requirements and OEM certifications. Our core competency curriculum has been customized to ensure Unisys employees have the appropriate skills and certifications to meet the contractual service obligations we have in place with our customers. Throughout the year, we continuously review our technical capabilities against the requirements articulated by our current and potential customers, and make adjustments as needed.

To sum up, the information on information technology product and technology certifications described in this book can:

- Serve as a guide for professionals in computing and networking fields, as well as for those wishing to enter these fields by obtaining a professional certification

- Provide a resource for HR departments about the certifications that they should be looking for in information technology employees

- Help consultants find information on ways they can differentiate themselves from their competitors and validate their abilities to help potential clients

Books like this one may also encourage prospective information technology professionals—especially those just graduating from high school and junior college—to pursue certifications as part of their formal education. By doing so, graduates provide hiring managers with another dimension for evaluating their capabilities. For example, certification validates their commitment to the profession and the industry, and it provides evidence of their desire—and ability—to continue to learn. The latter is essential, given the constantly accelerating pace of change in the technology.

Add this book to your list of *must have* references for your information technology library. It definitely will get a lot of use!

John Monaco
Director, Service Sales Support
Global Customer Services
Unisys Corporation

John Monaco began his career with Unisys Corporation in 1973 as a field engineer and has moved to positions of increasing responsibility within the organization over the past 25 years. John was one of the original members of the first Unisys multivendor network integration group formed in 1989, and he became a Certified Novell Engineer that same year. As Director of Service Sales Support, John is currently responsible for technology skills development, network integration tools, test equipment standards, and the business processes for developing and implementing Unisys global information technology service solutions.

Contents at a Glance

Table of Contents

Part IV　Appendices

Introduction

Professional certification has quickly become the *de facto* credential for computer and networking professionals. The widespread popularity of professional certification in the computer industry began with Novell and Microsoft in the late 1980s and early 1990s. In recent years, the number of certification programs has mushroomed. Today, nearly every major hardware and software manufacturer offers, or shortly will offer, a certification program.

While certification is accepted by many within the computer and networking world as an effective means of proving competence, the sheer number of certification programs available has left both computer professionals and employers confused about the significance and value of these various certifications. Although there are literally hundreds of books on the market to help you study for specific vendor-based certification exams, this book is the only up-to-date, comprehensive guide that presents information on all the most important computing and networking certifications.

Who Needs This Book?

In these pages, we present the latest information on over sixty certification programs. We have organized information about these programs into logical subject-based groupings and have also provided general information about the emergence of the certification phenomenon, how certification can be helpful to you, and your options for obtaining training and certification. It is our hope that this book will serve as a useful guide for professionals in the computing and networking fields as well as for those wishing to enter these fields by obtaining a professional certification. This book can also be a valuable resource for:

- Employers and personnel departments that need a good overview of the competencies validated by particular certifications

- Training centers and technical schools that want to offer test-preparation courses

- Career planning and placement centers that need an up-to-date resource on certification programs for advising their clients on the selection of training courses and computer and networking career paths

Who Needs Certification?

In the computer and networking fields, certification programs have become the roadmap that many people use to chart their careers. The primary reason for the popularity of certification is that it provides an up-to-date, performance-based assessment of a person's knowledge and skills in a particular area. Traditional credentials, such as a university degree, offer a measure of the number of hours spent sitting in a classroom, but may provide little indication of an individual's current job-related skills. In addition, because of its targeted instruction and frequent updating of content, certification is the only credentialling method that can begin to keep pace with the rapid changes in the computing and networking industry. Certification offers job-related benefits to both employer and employee: the employer knows what a person can do, and an employee can demonstrate their computer and networking knowledge and skills without investing the money and time it takes to gain a university degree. A more thorough discussion of the benefits of certification is provided in Chapter 1.

Why Is This Book the One for You?

Getting reliable, clear information about current certifications is, unfortunately, not always easy. Often a company's Web site only lists partial or out-of-date information on their certification programs. And a Web search on the topics "certification" and "computer and networking" will yield links to a number of programs that no longer exist.

We have researched the available computer and networking certification programs—on the Web, in the literature, by phone, and by fax—to make sure that our information is complete and organized in a way that will help you make sense of what is out there. A lot of the information included in this guide cannot be found on the Web or even in company literature. In addition, we provide information in a standard organizational format so you can easily compare and contrast different certification programs. And we have identified, classified, and described them in a way that helps you decide what certifications are right for you.

We have provided information on the most relevant and credible certification programs available today. However, you may find references to other certification programs—in magazine articles and on the Web—that are not included here. If a certification has been omitted, it may have been left out for one of several reasons. Some certification programs are only designed to be used internally within a company. For example, Motorola has several certification programs for its employees that are not available to the general public. You may find several certification programs advertised on the Web whose exams are not really available yet. We included only those programs that are actually up and running. Finally, some programs may not really certify an individual's ability or training. For example, a certification may simply "certify" that you attended a conference or paid membership to an organization. Such a certification is not an assessment of knowledge or abilities; these have been omitted as well.

Keeping Updated

It can be difficult to keep up with the changes in various certification programs. Company mergers, changes in product lines and management, and a number of other variables cause some companies to rapidly change, add, or delete specific certifications within their certification programs. In order to make sure that you are apprised of the latest changes to these certification programs, we have set up the Certification Update Web site (`http://www.certification-update` `.com`) as a supplement to this book. This companion Web site provides information on new certifications and changes to existing certifications. You will find links to information on the certifications listed in this guide and a section on job-hunting resources for the computer and networking professional. Several vendors plan to contact us directly before the release of new certifications and tests; by accessing the Web site, you will have first access to this information.

We have made every effort to ensure that the information in this book is complete and up-to-date at the time of release. However, due to the large number of certification programs covered and the dynamic nature of the certification field, the text may contain minor inaccuracies. Also note that telephone numbers and exam costs apply to tests taken in the United States. Once you have selected a particular certification to pursue, we recommend you check the Certification Update Web site or contact the sponsoring vendor or organization to confirm details, particularly costs.

How Is This Book Organized?

The first part of this book, "Introduction to Certification," consists of two important chapters that will guide you through the rationale behind professional certification and how you can choose the appropriate certification to meet your career objectives. Chapter 1, *Why Become Certified?*, outlines the benefits that certification can provide for employers, employees, and independent contractors. Chapter 2, *Choosing the Right Certification for You*, presents a cross reference for all the certifications listed in this guide, along with tips on how you can match career objectives with certification programs.

The second part of the book, "Certification Programs and Requirements," consists of ten chapters that describe the certification programs, organized according to discipline. We have ordered these subject-based chapters in a progression that begins with the most basic aspects of computing (computing hardware and operating systems) and proceeds to the more abstract or higher levels of computing and networking (Internet/intranets and network management). The certification programs are organized into the following chapters:

- Chapter 3: Hardware Certifications

- Chapter 4: Operating Systems Certifications

- Chapter 5: Software Certifications

- Chapter 6: Networking Hardware Certifications

- Chapter 7: Networking Operating Systems Certifications

- Chapter 8: Client/Server and Database System Certifications

- Chapter 9: Internet Certifications

- Chapter 10: Instructor and Trainer Certifications

- Chapter 11: Other Vendor-Based Certifications

- Chapter 12: Organization-Based Certifications

See Chapter 2 for more information on selecting the chapters that cover the certifications that will best meet your needs.

Each chapter follows the same basic motif in presenting information on a set of certification programs. The certification programs are listed in alphabetical order by the name of the certifying entity—a vendor, organization, or consortium. Within each subsection of the chapter you will find information about the certifying entity and about the certification program's recertification or maintenance requirements, and the benefits provided to certified individuals. This will be followed by one or more sections that describe each of the relevant certification programs offered by that vendor. Each description of a certification starts with an overview of the program, and then includes the following sections that answer your questions on the details of that certification program.

Who Needs It   Is this certification relevant to you and your career goals?

Requirements for Certification   What do you have to do to attain this certification? What tests, courses, or other requirements must be met?

Administrator   Who is responsible for administering tests or giving courses? How do you contact them?

Fee   What are the costs associated with the required tests or courses?

Format   What is the length and format of any required tests?

Resources   How can you get more information on this certification program? What study guides, sample tests, or other preparatory materials are available?

The third part of the book, entitled "Preparing for and Taking Certification Tests," provides general information and ideas on resources and strategies to use when preparing to take certification tests. Chapter 13, the first chapter in this section, discusses the value of instructor-led courses for test preparation, while Chapter 14 covers developing a self-study program. The final chapter, Chapter 15, provides valuable information and tips for taking certification tests.

Finally, the book provides three appendices. Appendix A presents information about a few more specialized technical certification programs that may also be of interest to computer and networking professionals. Appendix B provides a listing of retired certification programs for your reference, and Appendix C provides information on how to access the Certification Update Web site.

Copyrights and Trademarks

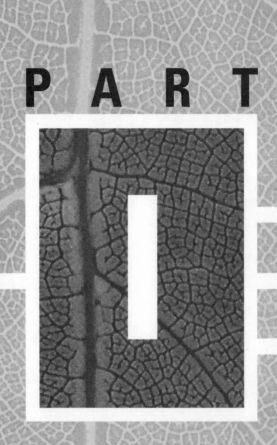

PART

I

Introduction
to Certification

CHAPTER

1

Why Become Certified?

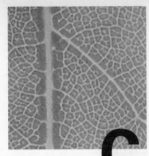

Computer and networking professionals are in demand across the employment spectrum, from business and industry to government and education. And the current high level of demand for information technology professionals—whether highly experienced or newly certified—is expected to continue and even accelerate in the years to come. This chapter outlines some of the many benefits that certification can offer you as a computer or networking professional, including jobs, promotions, professional credibility, and financial rewards. A number of these benefits offer advantages for employers and customers as well.

Open Job Market for Information Technology Professionals

The present shortage of information technology workers in the United States has been well documented. What's more, estimates of the extent of this shortage are quickly being revised upward. As recently as February, 1997, the Information Technology Association of America (ITAA) had estimated that 190,000 such positions were unfilled; by January of 1998, ITAA's second annual workforce study reported a shortage of 346,000 individuals—including programmers, systems analysts, and computer engineers—in the US information technology work force ("Help Wanted: The IT Workforce Gap at the Dawn of a New Century," ITAA report, February, 1997; and

"Help Wanted: A Call for Collaborative Action for the New Millenium," report by ITAA and Virginia Polytechnic Institute, January 1998).

Similarly, estimates of the number of information technology personnel that will be needed in the future have recently been revised upward. In October, 1997, the Office of Technology Policy (OTP) warned that the United States was not keeping up with the demand for new information technology workers and predicted that an average of 95,000 new jobs would open in the field annually; by January, 1998 an updated report already had been issued, projecting a need for almost 140,000 information technology workers each year until the year 2006 ("America's New Deficit: The Shortage of Information Technology Workers" October, 1997, Office of Technology Policy, US Department of Commerce; Update Report, OTP, January, 1998).

Meanwhile, the number of college students graduating with bachelor's degrees in computer science dropped from a peak of 41,889 per year in 1986 to 24,200 per year in 1994, a decrease of 42 percent (*Digest of Education Statistics*, Department of Education, 1996). Universities are clearly not training the numbers of information technology workers that will be needed to meet the demands of the marketplace.

It is anticipated that the shortage of information technology workers will have broad-ranging effects, not just in the computer industry, but in business and industry in general, as well as education and the government. The ITAA and OTP reports suggest that a competent skilled workforce in information technology is crucial to the nation's economy. The ITAA urges industry, education, government, and professional associations to undertake a collaborative effort to head off this shortage. More and more, the information industry is turning to certification programs to fill the gap.

New Avenues to High-Skilled Jobs

To address the shortage of information technology professionals, some companies—Microsoft and Novell, for example—are actively taking their certification programs to higher education partners and even to high schools. Jackson Hole High School in Wyoming was the first high school to offer its students the opportunity to become Microsoft Certified Professionals (see Chapter 4 for more information on MCP certification). Other businesses are reaching out to train new workers as well. In 1997, 23 seniors at Ballou High School in Washington, D.C. took special courses on network administration. The students were trained on computers donated by technology companies in the area, and those who passed standard certification exams were guaranteed jobs at starting salaries of $25,000 to $30,000 (Peter Behr, "Hire Education at Ballou" *Washington Post,* March 7, 1997).

Through its Skills 2000 program, Microsoft has additional strategies in place to encourage new entrants in the information technology field, including a new loan program that lets people pay off training and related costs over time; a partnership with the Green Thumb organization to train adults 55 and over to be software developers, support specialists, and network administrators; reduced-cost programs to help practicing technical professionals keep their skills updated; and a number of new strategies for linking up qualified applicants with available jobs. According to Microsoft's Web page, the company provided training for 1,230,000 information technology workers in 1997, and certified 118,000. Microsoft indicates that their certification programs are growing by 100 percent annually.

Benefits for Individuals

Many people pursue computer and networking certifications because they expect to receive increased salaries, promotions, or job offers. Evidence does indicate that having the right certification at the right time can have excellent salary and promotion potential. Magazines are full of stories about newly certified individuals with little or no experience who have snagged high-paying jobs.

But certification offers other benefits as well. It provides a portable credential that validates your knowledge and abilities, and it shows others that you are willing to do what it takes to keep your knowledge and skills current. As a result, certification improves your marketability and increases your options, whether you seek regular employment or want to promote your skills and abilities as an independent contractor.

Although the effort and cost involved in attaining some certifications is considerable, it is generally much less than the time and expense involved in obtaining a college degree. And, in many situations, an employer will carry the financial burden for certification training and testing. A 1995 study by Dataquest, Inc., a research unit of Dun & Bradstreet, reported that computer companies were paying for more than 80 percent of certification training for their employees (Bob Filipczak, "Certifiable!" *Training* magazine, August, 1995). In addition, a number of certification programs can help you accumulate college credit at the same time as you are earning a certification.

Increased Salary

A number of surveys have documented the financial benefits of certification. Salaries of Microsoft certified professionals have been tracked for several years now, and these figures offer persuasive evidence of the impact of certification on salaries. Between February, 1997 and February, 1998, salaries for individuals with the entry-level Microsoft

Certified Professional (MCP) credential went up by $3,900 to $61,200 annually, while average 1998 salaries were $77,700 for Microsoft Certified Trainers (MCTs) and $67,600 for Microsoft Certified Systems Engineers (MCSEs), according to Linda Briggs's third annual salary survey in *Microsoft Certified Professional* magazine (February, 1998). These salaries were for persons with an average total of five and a half years of experience in information technology (for more information on the MCP, MCSE, and MCT certification programs, see Chapters 4, 7, and 10, respectively). Survey results also indicated that 58 percent believed that their certifications had resulted in salary increases. Briggs estimates that earning an MCSE credential can add approximately $11,000 per year to a previously uncertified individual's salary.

Jobs and Promotions

Certification provides employers with objective evidence that you have a defined set of skills and abilities. Job-seekers and independent contractors alike find that having the right certification can get them preference in the hiring process. Certification can open doors for individuals who have the initiative to seek out new knowledge and skills, but have limited on-the-job experience. Certification can also help experienced computer and networking professionals move up within their current organizations or get good job offers elsewhere. In Linda Briggs's survey, 42 percent of Microsoft-certified respondents received a promotion as a result of attaining certification. Some businesses have actually incorporated vendor certification programs into their internal company certification programs.

Improved Professional Credibility

Potential employers or clients respond well when a computing or networking professional can offer clear evidence of having the skills needed to get the job done. Having relevant, current certifications on your resume gives you an important advantage in this regard; college degrees or years of experience on the resume may not tell an employer whether you have the specific abilities they seek.

A 1995 evaluation of the Microsoft Certified Systems Engineer credential found that more than 90 percent of the 89 MCSEs surveyed felt that obtaining certification was useful in improving their professional credibility, and 70 percent rated certification as "very useful" in that regard ("Evaluation of the Microsoft Systems Engineer Certification" report by the Applied Experimental Psychology Group at SIU-Carbondale in conjunction with Applied Research Consultants, July, 1995).

Education

The recent surge of interest in certification programs coincides with a trend toward performance-based assessment that can be seen across the educational spectrum. From kindergarten through college, an emphasis on competency-based assessment of knowledge and skills is beginning to replace the traditional focus on seat-time and rote memorization. For example, the new Western Governor's University—a nonprofit, independent corporation being developed by the Western Governor's Association—will provide distance-learning courses and programs to people in 15 western states and Guam. These courses and programs will be provided by both traditional providers and corporations and will feature competency-based assessment of knowledge and experience.

Certification programs have increasingly incorporated more sophisticated assessment methods to measure and certify learning and competency. A number of certification programs have established a level of quality and reliability that has made them eligible to provide college credit to their participants. For example, it is possible to obtain college credit for Learning Tree International certifications or courses.

The American Council of Education (ACE) in Washington, D.C. has determined college course equivalencies for Learning Tree International's courses and certifications. As a general rule, ACE will recommend two college credit hours for each four-day Learning Tree course. The ICCP Certified Computing Professional exams also have been approved by ACE for college credit. Approximately 1,500 colleges and universities in the United States will accept ACE recommendations for college credit.

Other opportunities for getting college credit exist as well. A number of community and technical colleges in the United States offer college credit for courses that are part of the Microsoft curriculum. Vendors have partnered with colleges and universities in some interesting ways. For example, at North Carolina's High Point University, computer information system majors can graduate with both a degree and certification in Visual Basic, Windows NT, and Microsoft Office. Lord Fairfax Community College in Virginia offers a popular 15-credit Network Engineer Certificate Program that gives students hands-on experience in installing and configuring servers and workstations, implementing network security, and planning for disaster recovery. At Seattle Pacific University in Washington, the Microsoft Certified Engineer curriculum implemented in 1996 attempts to ensure the quality of its graduates by incorporating an experience requirement—students must have either a degree or industry experience to be admitted to the program. If you are interested in college credit, look for similar opportunities in your area.

Benefits for Employers

In the world of computers and networking, both hardware and software change quickly. Technologies and programs that are cutting edge this year may be considered outdated by next year. In this environment of fast-paced change, traditional resume credentials may not provide an employer much information about whether an individual has up-to-date knowledge and skills. How can an employer know whether a prospective employee will be competent to use, implement, or support the most current technologies and programs? For many employers today, certification is the answer.

Hiring

Many employers and human resources managers don't have the information technology background they would need in order to be able to quickly assess an individual's abilities by reading a resume. In addition, many hiring managers find that a person's years of computer-related experience are not always an indication that an individual has the specific technical knowledge that is needed. For these reasons, employers may view certification as an objective measure for evaluating the abilities of applicants. If an employer needs someone to set up a system for secure, online commerce, for example, he or she needs to know that a potential hire or independent consultant has some pretty specific skills. A variety of certifications that provide evidence of these skills are now available (see Chapter 9 for information on relevant certification programs).

While certification may not guarantee that an individual knows all there is to know about a certain piece of hardware or software, it does provide information that employers value. It indicates that a person has at least a basic knowledge of a product—a core level of knowledge that can be the foundation for additional learning. It indicates that an individual is interested in learning about new technologies or products and maintaining up-to-date skills. And it can—depending on the comprehensiveness and rigor of the certification program—indicate an advanced level of knowledge and skill with a particular system, or even the ability to manage complex, heterogeneous company networks.

Employers admit that they sometimes use the presence of relevant certifications as a screening device when reviewing job applications.

When interviewed for the August, 1996 issue of *Training* magazine, Candace Sutherland of Digital Storagework put it like this: "Yes, I would take someone who has been certified more seriously than someone who hasn't. It's not official policy, but I'll pull that resume out of the stack."

Certified Employees Get the Job Done

Certifications help employers identify individuals with proven knowledge and skill levels. As we have noted, this is certainly important in hiring. But certification has other benefits and uses for employers. Many employers are encouraging their current employees to get certified. Companies need to have individuals with specific skills on staff, and many have found that certification programs offer the verifiable skills and knowledge their employees need.

Employers who send staff for training want concrete results. Certifications that use performance-based exams measure a candidate's ability to perform specific tasks on the job. Since such exams are designed with the help of computer and networking professionals, they measure skills that are directly applicable to the workplace. As a result, certification programs that involve performance-based testing give employers independently verified results that demonstrate the value of their training investments.

Research indicates that certification increases employee productivity and effectiveness. A 1995 study by Dataquest, Inc., a research unit of Dun & Bradstreet, reported that "managers feel that certified employees provide higher levels of service, learn new technologies faster, and are generally more productive." (Bob Filipczak, "Certification!" *Training* magazine, August, 1995). Other studies confirm these results. A 1996 survey of managers who supervise individuals with the Microsoft Certified Solution Developer credential found that managers considered their certified employees to have a significantly higher level of competence on those tasks that were key to their job effectiveness than did non-certified employees under their supervision ("The Value of Certification for Solution Developers," report by the Applied Experimental Psychology Group at SIU-Carbondale, August 1996).

In 1995, IDC Consulting, a Massachusetts research firm, surveyed managers on the benefits of certification. They found that managers felt certification gave their employees a reliable level of skill and expertise. Managers said that with certified information technology professionals on staff, a company could operate a more complex and decentralized information technology environment without hiring additional employees. Further, the IDC survey reported that managers found the average payback time for certification costs was only nine months. Having certified employees resulted in increased network availability and more effective technical support. These improvements were judged to be worth approximately $14,000 per year to the company per trained employee ("Benefits and Productivity Gains Realized Through IT Certification," IDC Report 1995).

Benefits to Customers and Clients

Hiring and supporting certified employees gives resellers and service firms a competitive advantage. In the current market, having a staff that has earned respected certifications in a variety of relevant computing and networking technologies can be crucial to getting clients. When companies outsource their information technology management needs, they expect a service provider to have employees with in-depth knowledge and proven competency with a variety of systems. Service firms with certified employees can provide clients with high-quality, consistent services; many organizations know this and hire only contractors who offer certified staff.

Even companies that are not specifically in the business of providing information technology services to others are likely to find that they can provide higher quality service to their customers by having certified employees on staff. Certification improves user support, whether for internal or external purposes. Employees with certified technical skills can provide effective support for other employees and facilitate quick resolution of problems that impede customer service.

Employees Value Career Growth Opportunities

In today's volatile business environment, companies are unable to guarantee their employees lifetime job security and generous pension plans. Some companies that want to keep their employees happy have begun offering them meaningful career development opportunities instead. Some employers are fearful that paying for training and certification will help employees find better jobs outside their company. Such employers, however, may find themselves losing out anyway, as their employees move to different companies that support their employees in maintaining up-to-date, marketable credentials.

At the same time that career growth increases employees' job capabilities and enhances their marketability, it can also lead to higher morale and job commitment. Employees appreciate the opportunity to maintain current job skills. As a result, employers that support their employees in obtaining certification may see improved employee morale and job satisfaction at the same time as the company benefits from improved productivity and customer service.

Criticisms of Certification

Certification is not without its detractors. Some critics assert that a single multiple-choice test can't tell you whether a person can handle real-world problems using a particular product. It is true that not all certification programs involve hands-on, performance-based testing. Many programs do, however, and the general trend is to move certification programs in that direction. Furthermore, the multiple-choice tests that vendors use are typically designed—by teams of practicing information technology professionals and skilled prometricians (professionals in testing and measurement)—to assess knowledge and abilities as they will be needed in real-world applications.

In addition, some critics have observed that there are certification programs available that do not actually require either any experience or any testing. Such programs are not covered in this book. It is true that certification programs vary widely in their level of difficulty. Some programs don't offer much challenge, while others—such as Cisco's CCIE program, or Sun's Java Developer certification—have gained notoriety for their difficulty. In addition, some of the more rigorous certification programs require documentation of a specified number of months or years of relevant on-the-job experience as a prerequisite to even entering the program.

Other critics of vendor-based certification assert that the vendors are the primary beneficiaries of certification programs because they generate vendor income, create product loyalty, and improve customer satisfaction (because the availability of certified personnel gives customers improved access to qualified product support). While some of this skepticism is undoubtedly justified, those who reject certification outright because it benefits vendors will miss out on the many benefits that certification offers to individuals, employers, and customers. Further, many of the criticisms leveled against vendor-based certification programs are not applicable to organization- or association-based programs, which tend to offer substantive, comprehensive, standards-based training at a reasonable cost.

Other detractors remind us that good customer service requires more than technical skill. There is an important lesson here as well. Without a doubt, the individuals who reap the most success in the information technology field are those who combine high levels of product-related skill and knowledge with strong interpersonal skills.

Importance of Recertification

An issue that will take on increasing importance over time is the need for recertification. Many certification programs are brand new, or less than a year or two old, while others have been revamped recently. But any certification will have a limited useful life.

Many certification programs are tied to specific versions of certain products. Certification programs that are tied to specific versions of products typically do not offer recertification on that product version. An individual who wants to have current credentials will need to obtain certification on new versions as they are released. Programs that do offer recertification options vary widely in the effort required for maintaining certification. Some require testing or extensive continuing education coursework; in other programs, the effort needed to maintain certification is relatively trivial. Alternatively, the issuance of a new software version may be a time when an individual reassesses which certifications to maintain; it will be important to periodically decide whether you want to adhere to the same certification path you have been following or whether it's time to target different technologies or product lines instead.

It is important to keep in mind the fact that, in the field of information technology, your need to seek new education opportunities will be ongoing. Because skills and knowledge can become outdated more quickly today than ever before, the most successful computer and networking professionals are those who commit themselves to lifelong learning. An eagerness to learn new technologies and products as they emerge will keep you highly employable for many years to come.

CHAPTER

2

Choosing the Right Certification for You

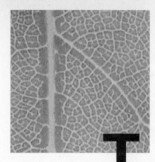

The decision to pursue a certification should be made with forethought. It can take months or years, and a good amount of money, to reach your goal. You want to be certain that the certification(s) you obtain will help you meet your career goals. There may be advantages to obtaining almost any certification related to your career, but taking the time to define your goals and outline a career development plan will allow you to maximize your return on your certification investment.

This chapter offers suggestions on how to go about selecting a certification program, a set of questions that will help you plan specific steps and a timeline for attaining your certification, and concludes with a comprehensive overview of the certification programs covered in this book.

Selecting a Certification Program

Matching your career goals with a specific certification program can be challenging. One of the main reasons that certification is so popular is because it attempts to keep pace with the rapid changes in the computer and networking industry; certification programs are rapidly being developed and changed to accommodate the latest technology. This can make a certification goal into a moving target for the candidate. At the same time, as new technologies emerge and evolve, your own career goals may change rapidly as well.

There are a number of things you may want to consider in choosing your certification path. Relevant questions include: Do you need to establish a new set of skills or do you have evidence of your core skills and just want something recent to add to your resume? Will you have to pay for all tests and required courses or will your employer pay? Are you looking for a comprehensive knowledge base in a certain area or do you need vendor-specific product knowledge?

The latter sections of this chapter offer you an introduction to all the certification programs covered in this book. As you consider which certification programs may be of most interest to you, use the tables in this chapter to get a feel for the options that are available within certain general categories. Then consult Chapters 3 to 12 for more detailed information on the specific programs that interest you.

If you are just beginning your career, we suggest that you try to obtain a respected entry-level certification that covers a wide variety of skills. For example, if you are not yet in the computer networking field and you want certification in order to get a networking job at a company that uses Novell NetWare, you might choose to obtain the Certified Novell Administrator (CNA) certification. The CNA program requires only one test, which covers general knowledge of Novell's network operating system. This might be a more logical starting point than the Certified Novell Engineer certification, which, while more impressive, involves six tests that require a very detailed working knowledge of the product.

In addition, you may want to consider selecting a certification program that has multiple levels (see the tables later in this chapter for examples). Once you attain the entry-level certification, you have the option of building on that certification by taking it to the next higher level or pursuing a different product certification in order to diversify your credentials.

For some, the choice of which certification program to pursue will be easier. If you have set your sights on a job or a promotion that requires a specific certification, your goal is very clear. But it never hurts to think ahead as well. See if you can meet the certification requirement in a way that will help you add on other certifications later. For example, if you decide to get the Microsoft Certified Professional credential, make sure that the test you take can also be applied to a more advanced certification, such as the Microsoft Certified Systems Engineer or Microsoft Certified Solutions Developer, whichever would be more appropriate for you.

We also recommend that you take time to study the job market. Even if you are not ready to make an immediate move, following developments in the market can be extremely valuable. It will be worth your while to notice the directions the computer and networking industry is taking, and to track current salary ranges, duties, and requirements for jobs that are of interest. A surefire way to make your certification efforts pay off is to notice what technology or product is just getting hot and make sure that you are one of the first people to get credentials in that area.

Reaching Your Certification Goals

Once you have selected a certification goal, it's important to make a definite plan for achieving your goal. A lot of folks never develop a concrete plan for attaining their goals, and, as a result, never reach them. For example, we have a friend who passed one Novell test 3 years ago and is not officially certified, but always claims to be "working on my CNE." Don't let yourself get caught in certification limbo. First write down your goals, next outline specific steps that will help you accomplish them, and then develop a strategy for taking those steps within a reasonable timeframe.

The questions that follow will help you to chart a plan for meeting your goals. Use Figure 2.1, "Mapping Your Certification Goals" to answer the questions. To get a bigger form with more space for completing each section, check out the online version of this form at the certification Update Web site (`http://www.certification-update.com`). If you are working toward more than one certification, complete a separate form for each one.

- **Certification goal** Title of the certification program you have selected.

- **Purpose of certification** How will attaining this certification help you meet your job or career goals?

- **Deadline for attaining certification** When will you be certified? This can be a self-imposed deadline, or there may be a time limitation imposed by your employer or the certification program itself. For example, some programs demand that you meet all the requirements for a certification within one year of taking your first certification test.

- **What I need to know** Take a look at the exam objectives. Are you already proficient in any of the content areas? Take any available sample tests to check your knowledge. Determine what areas you need to focus on, what topics you will need to review, and what hands-on experience you will need.

- **Hands-on time** How will you gain hands-on experience with the product or technology? Are you currently using it every day? If not, can you make special arrangements with a friend who has it, or will you need take a course?

- **Self-study opportunities** What opportunities exist for self-study? Are books, CD-ROMs, or Internet courses available that are specifically designed for this certification? What study guides and resources are available from the certifying entity? Will you will able to learn all that you need to know from these resources? If not, how will you address these areas?

- **Courses and other opportunities** What formal courses are available that would help you? Be sure to check with area community colleges and high schools for any continuing education courses that might address the topics you need to learn. Is there a friend or colleague that you can go to for help or mentoring? Can you form a study group with others who are pursuing this certification? Consult Chapter 13 for more information on taking instructor-led training to prepare for certification exams and Chapter 14 for more information on self-study resources.

- **Study plan timeline** After you have collected the information above, construct a detailed timeline for completing your certification. List the specific steps you plan to take to get the education and training you need. We suggest that you mark your timeline in terms of weeks, noting what you will be studying, courses or tests you will be taking, and topics that you will be reviewing each week. Some certification programs may require longer time-frames; in this case, months or quarters would be appropriate markers.

The purpose of a timeline is not to make you feel bad if you miss a deadline, but to allow you to chart your progress toward your goal and to keep moving forward. If find that you need extra time, simply revise your timeline as you go along.

FIGURE 2.1:   Mapping your goals

Mapping Your Certification Goals

Certification Goal:

Purpose of Certification:

Deadline:

What I Need to Know:

Hands-On Time:

Self-Study Opportunities:

Courses and Other Opportunities:

Study Plan Timeline (add more rows as needed):

Step	Start Date	End Eate	Learning Objective or Task	Resources Needed
1				
2				
3				
4				
5				

After you have selected the certification track that meets your professional development and career goals, you may also want to contact the organization or vendor that awards the certification you seek. In this way, you can find out more about the company that will be providing the certification that you are counting on to make a difference in your career. By talking to the certification staff, you may gain additional insight into the long-term value of attaining this particular certification, and learn about any imminent changes to the program.

Finally, before taking your exam, consult Chapter 15 for test-taking tips and information about types of tests and testing centers.

 Before you start pursuing a certification, check with the Certification Update Web site or the certifying entity to make sure that the ID numbers and costs for the required tests and/or courses are still correct.

Certifications

This book presents information on a wide variety of certification programs, organized by general subject area. The rest of this chapter provides an overview of the content of the chapters in Part II, "Certification Programs and Requirements." The sections that follow describe what certifications are covered in each chapter and present tables to help you compare the number of required tests, the test format, the approximate costs of taking the test(s), number of required courses, costs of any required courses, and the relative difficulty of the certification program. Use the cost information as a general guideline; since things change rapidly in the world of certification programs, once you have selected a specific course of action you may want to double-check the costs. See Chapter 15 for an explanation of the test formats.

We rated the difficulty of attaining particular certifications by sorting them into three categories—Moderate, Challenging, and Extremely Challenging—based on the number of required tests and courses, and the relative difficulty of those tests or lab exams. These ratings are approximate and are offered simply as a general guide to help the reader distinguish between entry-level programs and those that require more advanced skill and knowledge. This rating scale assumes that one has experience with the product or technology and has studied the appropriate subject content before attempting the exams.

Chapter 3: Hardware Certifications

This chapter focuses on certification programs that validate an individual's ability to set up, maintain, and troubleshoot computer hardware. Compaq and IBM have programs to certify professionals who have knowledge and experience with their product lines. Learning Tree International, a training organization, has developed its own vendor-independent hardware certification program. The other certification program listed in this chapter—offered by the Disaster Recovery Institute International—involves training to ensure that a company can survive a disaster or natural catastrophe.

TABLE 2.1:   Hardware Certifications

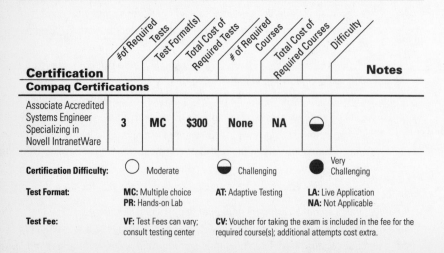

Certification	# of Required Tests	Test Format(s)	Total Cost of Required Tests	# of Required Courses	Total Cost of Required Courses	Difficulty	Notes
Compaq Certifications							
Associate Accredited Systems Engineer Specializing in Novell IntranetWare	3	MC	$300	None	NA	◒	

Certification Difficulty:	○ Moderate	◒ Challenging	● Very Challenging
Test Format:	**MC:** Multiple choice **PR:** Hands-on Lab	**AT:** Adaptive Testing	**LA:** Live Application **NA:** Not Applicable
Test Fee:	**VF:** Test Fees can vary; consult testing center	**CV:** Voucher for taking the exam is included in the fee for the required course(s); additional attempts cost extra.	

TABLE 2.1 (CONTINUED):   Hardware Certifications

Certification	#of Required Tests	Test Format(s)	Total Cost of Required Tests	# of Required Courses	Total Cost of Required Courses	Difficulty	Notes
Compaq Certifications (continued)							
Associate Acredited Systems Engineer Specializing in Microsoft Windws NT	3	MC	$300	None	NA	◒	
Acredited Systems Engineer Specializing in Novell Intranetware	None	NA	NA	None	NA	●	You must first obtain certification at the Associate level and must hold current certification as a Certified Novell Engineer (CNE).
Accredited Systems Engineer Specializing in Microsoft Windows NT	None	NA	NA	None	NA	●	You must first obtain certification at the Associate level and must hold current certification as a Microsoft Certified Systems Engineer (MCSE).
Disaster Recovery Institute International Certifications							
Associate Business Continuity Planner (ABCP)	1	MC	$250	None	NA	○	
Certified Business Continuity Planner (CBCP)	None	NA	NA	None	NA	◒	You must first be an Associate Business Continuity Planner and have two years of experience in the field. $100 application fee.

Certification Difficulty: ○ Moderate   ◒ Challenging   ● Very Challenging

Test Format: **MC:** Multiple choice   **AT:** Adaptive Testing   **LA:** Live Application
PR: Hands-on Lab   **NA:** Not Applicable

Test Fee: **VF:** Test Fees can vary; consult testing center   **CV:** Voucher for taking the exam is included in the fee for the required course(s); additional attempts cost extra.

TABLE 2.1 (CONTINUED): Hardware Certifications

Certification	#of Required Tests	Test Format(s)	Total Cost of Required Tests	# of Required Courses	Total Cost of Required Courses	Difficulty	Notes
Disaster Recovery Institute International Certifications (continued)							
Master Business Continuity Planner (MBCP)	None	NA	NA	None	NA	●	You must first be a Certified Business Continuity Planner, have five years of experience and complete a case study or independent research project. $200 application fee.
IBM Certifications							
Professional Server Specialist (PSS)	1	MC	CV	1	$750	○	
Professional Server Expert (PSE): Novell NetWare	1	MC	CV	1	$600	●	You must first obtain PSS certification and hold current certification as a Certified Novell Engineer (CNE).
Professional Server Expert (PSE): OS/2 Warp Server	1	MC	CV	1	$600	●	You must first obtain PSS certification and hold current certification as an OS/2 Warp Server Engineer.
Professional Server Expert (PSE): Windows NT Server	1	MC	CV	1	$600	●	You must first obtain PSS certification and hold current certification as a Microsoft Certified Systems Engineer (MCSE).

Certification Difficulty: ○ Moderate ◐ Challenging ● Very Challenging

Test Format: **MC:** Multiple choice **AT:** Adaptive Testing **LA:** Live Application
PR: Hands-on Lab **NA:** Not Applicable

Test Fee: **VF:** Test Fees can vary; consult testing center **CV:** Voucher for taking the exam is included in the fee for the required course(s); additional attempts cost extra.

TABLE 2.1 (CONTINUED):   Hardware Certifications

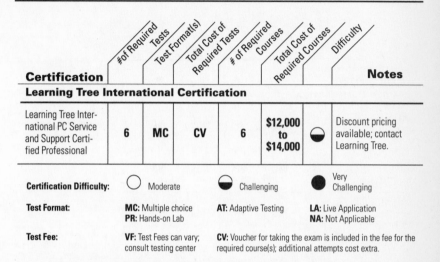

Certification	#of Required Tests	Test Format(s)	Total Cost of Required Tests	# of Required Courses	Total Cost of Required Courses	Difficulty	Notes
Learning Tree International Certification							
Learning Tree International PC Service and Support Certified Professional	6	MC	CV	6	$12,000 to $14,000	◖	Discount pricing available; contact Learning Tree.

Certification Difficulty:	○ Moderate	◖ Challenging	● Very Challenging
Test Format:	**MC:** Multiple choice **PR:** Hands-on Lab	**AT:** Adaptive Testing	**LA:** Live Application **NA:** Not Applicable
Test Fee:	**VF:** Test Fees can vary; consult testing center	**CV:** Voucher for taking the exam is included in the fee for the required course(s); additional attempts cost extra.	

Chapter 4: Operating Systems Certifications

This chapter covers certifications offered by several makers of UNIX-based operating systems—IBM, Santa Cruz Organization, Silicon Graphics, and Sun—as well as Learning Tree International's vendor-independent UNIX certification. In addition, IBM offers certifications related to its AS/400 systems and two certification programs on OS/2, IBM's PC-based operating system. Finally, Microsoft offers the Microsoft Certified Professional credential for technical professionals who are proficient in either Windows 95 or Windows NT.

TABLE 2.2: Operating Systems Certifications

Certification	#of Required Tests	Test Format(s)	Total Cost of Required Tests	# of Required Courses	Total Cost of Required Courses	Difficulty	Notes
IBM AIX Certifications							
IBM Certified AIX User	1	MC	VF	None	NA	◯	Designed for AIX users rather than technical specialists
IBM Certified Specialist: AIX System Administrtaion	1	MC	VF	None	NA	◯	
IBM Certified Specialist: AIX Support	1	MC	VF	None	NA	◯	
IBM Certified Advanced Technical Expert: RS/6000 AIX	3	MC	VF	None	NA	●	You must first be an IBM Certified Specialist in AIX System Administration or Support.
IBM AS/400 Certifications							
IBM Certified Specialist: AS/400 Associate System Operator	1	MC	VF	None	NA	◯	
IBM Certified Specialist: AS/400 Professional System Operator	1	MC	VF	None	NA	◯	
IBM Certified Specialist: AS/400 Associate System Administrator	1	MC	VF	None	NA	◯	

Certification Difficulty: ◯ Moderate   ◐ Challenging   ● Very Challenging

Test Format: **MC:** Multiple choice **AT:** Adaptive Testing **LA:** Live Application
PR: Hands-on Lab **NA:** Not Applicable

Test Fee: **VF:** Test Fees can vary; consult testing center **CV:** Voucher for taking the exam is included in the fee for the required course(s); additional attempts cost extra.

TABLE 2.2 (CONTINUED): Operating Systems Certifications

Certification	#of Required Tests	Test Format(s)	Total Cost of Required Tests	# of Required Courses	Total Cost of Required Courses	Difficulty	Notes
IBM AS/400 Certifications (continued)							
IBM Certified Specialist: AS/400 Professional System Administrator	1	MC	VF	None	NA	◑	
IBM OS/2 Certifications							
IBM Certified Systems Expert: OS/2 Warp	4	MC	VF	None	NA	◑	Covers OS/2 Warp version 3
IBM Certified Systems Expert: OS/2 Warp 4	3	MC	VF	None	NA	◑	
Learning Tree International Certification							
Learning Tree International UNIX Systems Certified Professional	6	MC	CV	6	$12,000-$14,000	◑	Discount pricing available; contact Learning Tree.
Microsoft Certification							
Microsoft Certified Professional	1	MC	$100	None	NA	○	
Santa Cruz Organization (SCO) Certifications							
Santa Cruz Organization Advanced Certified Engineer (SCO ACE): Server Track	4	MC	VF ($500-$640)	None	NA	◑	
SCO ACE: Open Server Release 5 Track	3	MC	VF ($375-$540)	None	NA	◑	

Certification Difficulty: ○ Moderate   ◑ Challenging   ● Very Challenging

Test Format: **MC:** Multiple choice   **AT:** Adaptive Testing   **LA:** Live Application
                    PR: Hands-on Lab   **NA:** Not Applicable

Test Fee: **VF:** Test Fees can vary; consult testing center   **CV:** Voucher for taking the exam is included in the fee for the required course(s); additional attempts cost extra.

TABLE 2.2 (CONTINUED): Operating Systems Certifications

Certification	# of Required Tests	Test Format(s)	Total Cost of Required Tests	# of Required Courses	Total Cost of Required Courses	Difficulty	Notes
Santa Cruz Organization (SCO) Certifications (continued)							
SCO ACE UNIXWare 2.1 Track	3	MC	VF ($375–$540)	None	NA	◒	
Silicon Graphics Certifications							
Silicon Graphics Certified IRIX 6.x System Administrator	2	MC	VF	None	NA	◒	
Silicon Graphics Certified IRIX Network Administrator	1	MC	VF	None	NA	●	You must first be a Silicon Graphics Certified IRIX 6.x Systems Administrator.
Sun Certifications							
Sun Certified Solaris Administrator	2	MC	$300	None	NA	◒	
Sun Certified Solaris 2.5 Network Administrator	1	MC	$150	None	NA	●	You must first be a Sun Certified Solaris Administrator.

Certification Difficulty:	○ Moderate	◒ Challenging	● Very Challenging
Test Format:	**MC:** Multiple choice **PR:** Hands-on Lab	**AT:** Adaptive Testing	**LA:** Live Application **NA:** Not Applicable
Test Fee:	**VF:** Test Fees can vary; consult testing center	**CV:** Voucher for taking the exam is included in the fee for the required course(s); additional attempts cost extra.	

Chapter 5: Software Certifications

This chapter contains a number of certifications that are of interest to all computer users. Adobe offers the Adobe Certified Expert certification for a number of its products. Baan, a maker of business intelligence software, offers both basic and advanced certifications. Corel's certification program includes two levels of certification on its Word-Perfect, Quattro Pro, and Presentations programs. Lotus offers a wide variety of certifications on its software. In addition, Microsoft offers several levels of certification on its Microsoft Office and related software products.

TABLE 2.3:   Software Certifications

Certification	# of Required Tests	Test Format(s)	Total Cost of Required Tests	# of Required Courses	Total Cost of Required Courses	Difficulty	Notes
Adobe Certification							
Adobe Certified Expert	1	MC	$150	None	NA	○	Available on: Illustrator 7.0, Acrobat 3.0, AfterEffects 3.1, Framemaker 5.5, Pagemaker 6.5, PageMill 2.0, Photoshop 4.0
Baan Certifications							
Baan Basic Certification	1	MC	$300	None	NA	○	
Baan Advanced Certification in Enterprise Logistics	1	MC	$300	None	NA	◐	You must first obtain the Baan Basic Certification.

Certification Difficulty:	○ Moderate	◐ Challenging	● Very Challenging
Test Format:	**MC:** Multiple choice **PR:** Hands-on Lab	**AT:** Adaptive Testing	**LA:** Live Application **NA:** Not Applicable
Test Fee:	**VF:** Test Fees can vary; consult testing center	**CV:** Voucher for taking the exam is included in the fee for the required course(s); additional attempts cost extra.	

TABLE 2.3 (CONTINUED): Software Certifications

Certification	# of Required Tests	Test Format(s)	Total Cost of Required Tests	# of Required Courses	Total Cost of Required Courses	Difficulty	Notes
Baan Certifications							
Baan Advanced Certification in Enterprise Finance	1	MC	$300	None	NA	◒	You must first obtain the Baan Basic Certification.
Baan Advanced Certification in Enterprise Tools	1	MC	$300	None	NA	◒	You must first obtain the Baan Basic Certification.
Baan Advanced Certification in Enterprise Modeler	1	MC	$300	None	NA	◒	You must first obtain the Baan Basic Certification.
Corel Certifications							
Corel WordPerfect 7 Certified Resource	1	MC	$55	None	NA	○	
Corel Quattro Pro 7 Certified Resource	1	MC	$55	None	NA	○	
Corel Presentations 7 Certified Resource	1	MC	$55	None	NA	○	
Corel WordPerfect 7 Certified Expert	1	MC	$80	None	NA	◒	$55 application fee (currently waived)
Corel Quattro Pro 7 Certified Expert	1	MC	$80	None	NA	◒	$55 application fee (currently waived)
Corel Presentations 7 Certified Expert	1	MC	$80	None	NA	◒	$55 application fee (currently waived)

Certification Difficulty: ○ Moderate   ◒ Challenging   ● Very Challenging

Test Format: **MC:** Multiple choice   **AT:** Adaptive Testing   **LA:** Live Application
                   PR: Hands-on Lab   **NA:** Not Applicable

Test Fee: **VF:** Test Fees can vary; consult testing center   **CV:** Voucher for taking the exam is included in the fee for the required course(s); additional attempts cost extra.

TABLE 2.3 (CONTINUED): Software Certifications

Certification	#of Required Tests	Test Format(s)	Total Cost of Required Tests	# of Required Courses	Total Cost of Required Courses	Difficulty	Notes
Lotus Certifications							
Certified Lotus Specialist (CLS)	1	MC	$90	None	NA	○	
Certified Lotus Professional (CLP): Application Developer	3	MC or LA	$270	None	NA	◑	
Certified Lotus Professional (CLP): Principal Application Developer	1	MC or LA	$90	None	NA	●	You must first be a CLP Application Developer.
Certified Lotus Professional (CLP): System Administrator	3	MC or LA	$270	None	NA	◑	
Certified Lotus Professional (CLP): Principal System Administrator	1	MC or LA	$90	None	NA	●	You must first be a CLP System Administrator.
Certified Lotus Professional (CLP): cc:Mail System Administrator	2	MC	$90	None	NA	◑	
Microsoft Certifications							
Microsoft Office Proficient Specialist	1	LA	VF (suggested fee is $50)	None	NA	○	Available for Word 95, Word 97, Excel 95, and Excel 97.

Certification Difficulty: ○ Moderate ◑ Challenging ● Very Challenging

Test Format: **MC:** Multiple choice **PR:** Hands-on Lab **AT:** Adaptive Testing **LA:** Live Application **NA:** Not Applicable

Test Fee: **VF:** Test Fees can vary; consult testing center **CV:** Voucher for taking the exam is included in the fee for the required course(s); additional attempts cost extra.

TABLE 2.3 (CONTINUED):   Software Certifications

Certification	#of Required Tests	Test Format(s)	Total Cost of Required Tests	# of Required Courses	Total Cost of Required Courses	Difficulty	Notes
Microsoft Certifications (continued)							
Microsoft Office Expert Specialist	1	LA	VF (suggested fee is $50)	None	NA	◖	Available for Access 97, Excel 95, Excel 97, FrontPage 97, Outlook 97, PowerPoint 95, PowerPoint 97, Word 95, Word 97
Microsoft Office Expert	1	LA	VF (suggested fee is $50)	None	NA	●	You must first be a Microsoft Office Expert Specialist in five core Office 97 applications (Word, Excel, Access, PowerPoint, and Outlook).

Certification Difficulty: ○ Moderate   ◖ Challenging   ● Very Challenging

Test Format: **MC:** Multiple choice   **AT:** Adaptive Testing   **LA:** Live Application
PR: Hands-on Lab   **NA:** Not Applicable

Test Fee: **VF:** Test Fees can vary; consult testing center   **CV:** Voucher for taking the exam is included in the fee for the required course(s); additional attempts cost extra.

Chapter 6: Networking Hardware Certifications

This chapter covers certifications from the major manufacturers of networking equipment. Ascend offers a certification for its product line, which includes remote access and switching equipment. Bay Networks and Cisco are both well-known for their routers, but are also big players in remote access and switching technology. Bay Networks offers two levels of certification in a number of different types of technology. Cisco's Certified Internetworking Expert (CCIE) program has recently expanded to included three specializations. Learning Tree International offers vendor-independent certification programs in local area networking, wide area networking, and internetworking. Finally, Xylan offers two new certifications in its switching technology product line: the Xylan Switch Specialist and the Xylan Switch Expert.

TABLE 2.4: Networking Hardware Certifications

Certification	# of Required Tests	Test Format(s)	Total Cost of Required Tests	# of Required Courses	Total Cost of Required Courses	Difficulty	Notes
Ascend Certification							
Ascend Certified Technical Expert	3	MC, PR	$1250	None	NA	●	
Bay Networks Certifications							
Bay Networks Certified Specialist: Hub Technology	1	MC	$125	None	NA	○	
Bay Networks Certified Expert: Hub Technology	2	MC, PR	$550	None	NA	●	You must first be a Certified Specialist in Hub Technology.
Bay Networks Certified Specialist: Router Technology	1	MC	$125	None	NA	○	
Bay Networks Certified Expert: Router Technology	2	MC, PR	$650	None	NA	●	You must first be a Certified Specialist in Router Technology.
Bay Networks Certified Specialist: Network Management Technology	1	MC	$125	None	NA	○	

Certification Difficulty: ○ Moderate   ◐ Challenging   ● Very Challenging

Test Format: **MC:** Multiple choice   **AT:** Adaptive Testing   **LA:** Live Application
PR: Hands-on Lab   **NA:** Not Applicable

Test Fee: **VF:** Test Fees can vary; consult testing center   **CV:** Voucher for taking the exam is included in the fee for the required course(s); additional attempts cost extra.

TABLE 2.4 (CONTINUED): Networking Hardware Certifications

Certification	# of Required Tests	Test Format(s)	Total Cost of Required Tests	# of Required Courses	Total Cost of Required Courses	Difficulty	Notes
Bay Networks Certifications (continued)							
Bay Networks Certified Expert: Network Management Technology	2	MC, PR	$800	None	NA	●	You must first be a Certified Specialist in Network Management Technology.
Bay Networks Certified Specialist: Switching Technology	1	MC	$125	None	NA	○	
Bay Networks Certified Expert: Remote Access Technology	1	MC	$125	None	NA	○	
Cisco Certifications							
Cisco Certified Internetworking Expert (CCIE): WAN Switching Expert	2	MC, PR	$1200	None	NA	●	
Cisco Certified Internetworking Expert (CCIE): Internet Service Provider Dial Expert	2	MC, PR	$1200	None	NA	●	
Cisco Certified Internetworking Expert (CCIE): Routing and Switching Expert	2	MC, PR	$1200	None	NA	●	

Certification Difficulty: ○ Moderate   ◑ Challenging   ● Very Challenging

Test Format: **MC:** Multiple choice   **AT:** Adaptive Testing   **LA:** Live Application
PR: Hands-on Lab   **NA:** Not Applicable

Test Fee: **VF:** Test Fees can vary; consult testing center   **CV:** Voucher for taking the exam is included in the fee for the required course(s); additional attempts cost extra.

TABLE 2.4 (CONTINUED): Networking Hardware Certifications

Certification	#of Required Tests	Test Format(s)	Total Cost of Required Tests	# of Required Courses	Total Cost of Required Courses	Difficulty	Notes
Learning Tree International Certifications							
Learning Tree International Local Area Networks Certified Professional	5	MC	CV	5	$12,000-$14,000	◗	Discount pricing available; contact Learning Tree.
Learning Tree International Wide Area Networks Certified Professional	5	MC	CV	5	$12,000-$14,000	◗	Discount pricing available; contact Learning Tree.
Learning Tree International Internetworking Certified Professional	5	MC	CV	5	$12,000-$14,000	◗	Discount pricing available; contact Learning Tree.
Xylan Certifications							
Xylan Certified Switching Specialist (XCSS)	1	MC	$100	None	NA	○	
Xylan Certified Switching Expert (XCSE)	1	MC	$200	None	NA	◗	You must first be a Certified Switching Specialist.

Certification Difficulty: ○ Moderate   ◗ Challenging   ● Very Challenging

Test Format: **MC:** Multiple choice   **AT:** Adaptive Testing   **LA:** Live Application
                    PR: Hands-on Lab   **NA:** Not Applicable

Test Fee: **VF:** Test Fees can vary; consult testing center   **CV:** Voucher for taking the exam is included in the fee for the required course(s); additional attempts cost extra.

Chapter 7: Networking Operating Systems Certifications

There are currently four certification programs related to network operating systems. Banyan's certification program concentrates on the Vines network operating system, which is used primarily to link UNIX servers with a variety of clients. IBM offers certifications on its PC-based network operating systems—OS/2 Warp Server and OS/2 LAN server. Novell's certification program, initiated in 1987, offers four levels of certification on the Novell NetWare, IntranetWare and GroupWare products. The Microsoft Certified Systems Engineer credential certifies individuals on Microsoft's network operating system, Windows NT Server.

TABLE 2.5: Network Operating Systems Certifications

Certification	# of Required Tests	Test Format(s)	Total Cost of Required Tests	# of Required Courses	Total Cost of Required Courses	Difficulty	Notes
Banyan Certifications							
Certified Banyan Specialist (CBS)	3	MC	$360	None	NA	○	
Certified Banyan Specialist (CBS): Windows NT	3	MC	$340	2	$3,300	◓	
Certified Banyan Engineer (CBE)	2	MC	$240	2	$4,500	●	You must first be a Certified Banyan Specialist.
IBM Certifications							
IBM Certified Specialist: OS/2 Warp Server Administration	1	MC	VF	None	NA	○	

Certification Difficulty: ○ Moderate	◓ Challenging	● Very Challenging
Test Format: **MC:** Multiple choice **PR:** Hands-on Lab	**AT:** Adaptive Testing	**LA:** Live Application **NA:** Not Applicable
Test Fee: **VF:** Test Fees can vary; consult testing center	**CV:** Voucher for taking the exam is included in the fee for the required course(s); additional attempts cost extra.	

TABLE 2.5 (CONTINUED): Network Operating Systems Certifications

Certification	# of Required Tests	Test Format(s)	Total Cost of Required Tests	# of Required Courses	Total Cost of Required Courses	Difficulty	Notes
IBM Certifications (continued)							
IBM Certified Expert: OS/2 Warp Server	3	MC	VF	None	NA	◖	
IBM Certified Specialist: OS/2 LAN Server 4.0 Administration	1	MC	VF	None	NA	○	
IBM Certified Expert: OS/2 LAN Server 4.0	6	MC	VF	None	NA	●	
Microsoft Certification							
Microsoft Certified Systems Engineer (MCSE)	6	MC	$600	None	NA	●	Pick your elective test carefully and you can obtain MCP + Internet at the same time.
Novell Certifications							
Certified Novell Administrator (CNA)	1	AT, MC	$85	None	NA	○	Available in either NetWare 3, Intranet-Ware, GroupWise 4 or GroupWise 5
Certified Novell Engineer (CNE)	7	AT, MC	VF	None	NA	●	Available in either NetWare 3, Intranet-Ware, GroupWise 4 or GroupWise 5
Master Certified Novell Engineer (MCNE)	4 to 6	AT, MC	VF	None	NA	●	Available to current CNEs. MCNE specialties are Management, Connectivity, Messaging, Internet/Intranet Solutions, AS/400 Integration, UNIX Integration, or Windows NT Integration.

Certification Difficulty: ○ Moderate   ◖ Challenging   ● Very Challenging

Test Format: **MC:** Multiple choice   **AT:** Adaptive Testing   **LA:** Live Application
PR: Hands-on Lab   **NA:** Not Applicable

Test Fee: **VF:** Test Fees can vary; consult testing center   **CV:** Voucher for taking the exam is included in the fee for the required course(s); additional attempts cost extra.

Chapter 8: Client/Server and Database System Certifications

This chapter covers several highly specialized certification programs designed by vendors that make database and client/server products. Borland, Centura, Informix, Oracle, and Sybase all offer certifications on their database products. These certifications focus on the tasks involved in administering and managing large databases for a variety of purposes.

TABLE 2.6: Client/Server Certifications

Certification	# of Required Tests	Test Format(s)	Total Cost of Required Tests	# of Required Courses	Total Cost of Required Courses	Difficulty	Notes
Borland Certification							
Delphi 3 Certified Developer	1	MC	$150	None	NA	○	
Centura Certifications							
Centura Database Developer	1	MC	$120	None	NA	○	
Centura Database Administrator	1	MC	$120	None	NA	○	
Informix Certifications							
Database Specialist: Informix Dynamic Server	2	MC	$500	None	NA	◒	

Certification Difficulty: ○ Moderate   ◒ Challenging   ● Very Challenging

Test Format: **MC:** Multiple choice   **AT:** Adaptive Testing   **LA:** Live Application
PR: Hands-on Lab   **NA:** Not Applicable

Test Fee: **VF:** Test Fees can vary; consult testing center   **CV:** Voucher for taking the exam is included in the fee for the required course(s); additional attempts cost extra.

TABLE 2.6 (CONTINUED): Client/Server Certifications

Certification	#of Required Tests	Test Format(s)	Total Cost of Required Tests	# of Required Courses	Total Cost of Required Courses	Difficulty	Notes
Informix Certifications (continued)							
System Administration: Informix Dynamic Server	2	MC	$500	None	NA	◓	
INFORMIX-4GL Certified Professional	2	MC	$500	None	NA	◓	
Oracle Certifications							
Certified Database Administrator	4	MC	$500	None	NA	●	
Certified Application Developer for Developer/2000	5	MC	$625	None	NA	●	
Sybase Certifications							
Certified Power-Builder Developer Associate	2	MC	VF	None	NA	◓	
Certified Power-Builder Developer Professional	1	LA	VF	None	NA	●	You must first be a PowerBuilder Developer Associate.
Certified Database Administrator	2	MC	VF	None	NA	◓	
Certified Performance and Tuning Specialist	1	MC	VF	None	NA	●	You must first be a Certified Database Administrator.

Certification Difficulty: ○ Moderate   ◓ Challenging   ● Very Challenging

Test Format: **MC:** Multiple choice **AT:** Adaptive Testing **LA:** Live Application
PR: Hands-on Lab **NA:** Not Applicable

Test Fee: **VF:** Test Fees can vary; consult testing center **CV:** Voucher for taking the exam is included in the fee for the required course(s); additional attempts cost extra.

Chapter 9: Internet Certifications

This chapter covers both vendor-based and vendor-independent certification programs that address Internet strategies, procedures, and protocols. The IBM Certified Solutions Expert: Net.Commerce addresses security for financial transactions on the Internet, while the IBM Certified Solution Expert: Firewall targets technical professionals who install secure links between company networks and the Internet. The vendor-independent Learning Tree International certification program covers TCP/IP protocols for setting up and administering intranets and Internet connections. The two new Microsoft certifications covered in this chapter—Microsoft Certified Professional + Internet and Microsoft Certified Systems Engineer + Internet—are focused on the implementation of intranet and Internet solutions using Microsoft products. Novell offers a number of brand new certifications for Internet professionals. Prosoft/Net Guru Technologies offers certification programs in all aspects of the Internet, from Web site design and business strategies to server administration and TCP/IP security. Finally, USWeb Learning offers two vendor-neutral certifications that focus on broadly applicable fundamentals and principles of Web development.

TABLE 2.7: Internet Certifications

Certification	# of Required Tests	Test Format(s)	Total Cost of Required Tests	# of Required Courses	Total Cost of Required Courses	Difficulty	Notes
IBM Certifications							
Certified Solutions Expert: Net. Commerce	1	MC	VF	None	NA	○	

Certification Difficulty:	○ Moderate	◖ Challenging	● Very Challenging

Test Format:	**MC:** Multiple choice	**AT:** Adaptive Testing	**LA:** Live Application
	PR: Hands-on Lab		**NA:** Not Applicable

Test Fee:	**VF:** Test Fees can vary; consult testing center	**CV:** Voucher for taking the exam is included in the fee for the required course(s); additional attempts cost extra.

TABLE 2.7 (CONTINUED): Internet Certifications

Certification	#of Required Tests	Test Format(s)	Total Cost of Required Tests	# of Required Courses	Total Cost of Required Courses	Difficulty	Notes
IBM Certifications (continued)							
Certified Solutions Expert: Firewall Resources	1	MC	VF	None	NA	○	
Learning Tree International Certification							
Learning Tree International Internet/ Intranet Certified Professional	5	MC	CV	5	$12,000-$14,000	◐	Discount pricing available; contact Learning Tree.
Microsoft Certifications							
Microsoft Certified Professional + Internet	3	MC	$300	None	NA	◐	
Microsoft Certified Systems Engineer + Internet	9	MC	$900	None	NA	●	
Novell Certified Internet Professional Certifications							
Internet Business Strategist	1	MC	VF	None	NA	○	
Web Designer	4	MC	VF	None	NA	◐	
Intranet Manager	5	MC	VF	None	NA	◐	
Internet Architect	5	MC	VF	None	NA	◐	

Certification Difficulty: ○ Moderate   ◐ Challenging   ● Very Challenging

Test Format: **MC:** Multiple choice   **AT:** Adaptive Testing   **LA:** Live Application
PR: Hands-on Lab   **NA:** Not Applicable

Test Fee: **VF:** Test Fees can vary; consult testing center   **CV:** Voucher for taking the exam is included in the fee for the required course(s); additional attempts cost extra.

TABLE 2.7 (CONTINUED):   Internet Certifications

Certification	# of Required Tests	Test Format(s)	Total Cost of Required Tests	# of Required Courses	Total Cost of Required Courses	Difficulty	Notes
Prosoft/Net Guru Technologies Certified Internet Webmaster Certifications							
Designer	1	MC	CV	3	$995	◓	
Developer I	1	MC	CV	2	$2275	◓	
Developer II	1	MC	CV	2	$2275	◓	
Administrator	1	MC	CV	2	$2440	◓	
Network Professional	1	MC	CV	2	$2275	◓	
Security Professional	1	MC	CV	4	$4400	●	
ECommerce Professional	2	MC	CV	1	$1445	◓	
USWeb Learning Certifications							
Certified Specialist	2	MC	VF	3-4	VF	◓	
Certified Architect	3	MC	VF	5	VF	●	

Certification Difficulty:	○ Moderate	◓ Challenging	● Very Challenging
Test Format:	**MC:** Multiple choice **PR:** Hands-on Lab	**AT:** Adaptive Testing	**LA:** Live Application **NA:** Not Applicable
Test Fee:	**VF:** Test Fees can vary; consult testing center	**CV:** Voucher for taking the exam is included in the fee for the required course(s); additional attempts cost extra.	

Chapter 10: Instructor and Trainer Certifications

This chapter covers a number of certification programs for instructors and trainers who want to provide "authorized training" for specific vendors, including Adobe, Banyan, Borland, Corel, IBM, Lotus, Microsoft, Novell, and Prosoft/Net Guru Technologies. The vendor-independent Certified Technical Trainer credential offered by the Chauncey Group is also covered. This widely respected certification program is a required component of several of the vendor-based training certifications.

TABLE 2.8: Instructor/Trainer Certifications

Certification	# of Required Tests	Test Format(s)	Total Cost of Required Tests	# of Required Courses	Total Cost of Required Courses	Difficulty	Notes
Adobe Certification							
Adobe Certified Instructor	None	NA	NA	None	NA	◖	Your must be a Certified Technical Trainer and be an Adobe Certified Expert on the product you will teach.
Banyan Certifications							
Certified Banyan Instructor (CBI)	None	NA	NA	1	VF	●	Must be a CBE. Must also be a CTT, have vendor instructor certification, or take an approved instructional skills course.
CBI: Problem Solving for Vines Networks Authorizatation	None	NA	NA	1	VF	●	Obtain CBI status first.

Certification Difficulty: ○ Moderate   ◖ Challenging   ● Very Challenging

Test Format: **MC:** Multiple choice   **AT:** Adaptive Testing   **LA:** Live Application
PR: Hands-on Lab   **NA:** Not Applicable

Test Fee: **VF:** Test Fees can vary; consult testing center   **CV:** Voucher for taking the exam is included in the fee for the required course(s); additional attempts cost extra.

TABLE 2.8 (CONTINUED): Instructor/Trainer Certifications

Certification	#of Required Tests	Test Format(s)	Total Cost of Required Tests	# of Required Courses	Total Cost of Required Courses	Difficulty	Notes
Borland Certification							
Borland Delphi 3 Certified Trainer	None	NA	NA	1	$1000	◐	You must first be a Delphi 3 Certified Developer.
Chauncey Group International Certification							
Certified Technical Trainer (CTT)	1	MC	$150	None	NA	◐	Also requires a performance video ($135 fee for processing).
Corel Certifications							
Corel WordPerfect Suite 7 Certified Instructor	None	NA	NA	None	NA	◐	You must first be a WordPerfect Certified Expert and a CTT. $200 application fee.
CorelDRAW 5 Certified Instructor	1	MC	VF	None	NA	◐	
IBM Certifications							
IBM Certified Instructor: OS/2 Warp	None	NA	NA	None	NA	◐	Must be a Certified Systems Expert: OS/2 Warp and provide proof of teaching experience.
IBM Certified Instructor: OS/2 LAN Server	None	NA	NA	None	NA	◐	Must be a Certified Systems Expert: OS/2 Warp and provide proof of teaching experience.
IBM Certified Instructor: OS/2 Warp Server	None	NA	NA	None	NA	◐	Must be a Certified Systems Expert: OS/2 Warp and provide proof of teaching experience.

Certification Difficulty: ○ Moderate   ◐ Challenging   ● Very Challenging

Test Format: **MC:** Multiple choice   **AT:** Adaptive Testing   **LA:** Live Application
PR: Hands-on Lab   **NA:** Not Applicable

Test Fee: **VF:** Test Fees can vary; consult testing center   **CV:** Voucher for taking the exam is included in the fee for the required course(s); additional attempts cost extra.

TABLE 2.8 (CONTINUED): Instructor/Trainer Certifications

Certification	# of Required Tests	Test Format(s)	Total Cost of Required Tests	# of Required Courses	Total Cost of Required Courses	Difficulty	Notes
Lotus Certifications							
Certified Lotus Instructor (CLI): Level One	2	MC	$180	3	**VF** ($1500-2000)	○	Must provide proof of instructional experience.
Certified Lotus Instructor (CLI): Level Two	2	MC	$180	3	**VF** ($1500-2000)	◓	Must also have experience teaching Level One courses.
Certified Lotus Instructor (CLI): Advanced Course	None	NA	C	None	NA	●	Must have experience teaching Level Two courses; take courses, and pass tests on what you will teach.
Microsoft Certification							
Microsoft Certified Trainer	None	NA	NA	None	NA	◓	Must prove instructional skills (CTT, instructional course, or other vendor trainer certification).
Novell Certifications							
Certified InfiLearning Instructor	None	NA	NA	None	NA	◓	Must prove instructional skills (CTT or course); attend course and pass test for the course you will teach.
Certified Novell Instructor	None	NA	NA	None	NA	●	Obtain CNE, prove instructional skills (CTT or course); take course and pass test for course you will teach.

Certification Difficulty: ○ Moderate   ◓ Challenging   ● Very Challenging

Test Format: **MC:** Multiple choice   **AT:** Adaptive Testing   **LA:** Live Application
PR: Hands-on Lab   **NA:** Not Applicable

Test Fee: **VF:** Test Fees can vary; consult testing center   **CV:** Voucher for taking the exam is included in the fee for the required course(s); additional attempts cost extra.

TABLE 2.8 (CONTINUED): Instructor/Trainer Certifications

Certification	# of Required Tests	Test Format(s)	Total Cost of Required Tests	# of Required Courses	Total Cost of Required Courses	Difficulty	Notes
Novell Certifications (continued)							
Master Certified Novell Instructor	None	NA	NA	None	NA	●	Obtain Master CNE, prove instructional skills (CTT or course); take course and pass test for course you will teach.
Prosoft/Net Guru Technology Certifications							
Prosoft/NGT Certified Windows NT Instructor	1	MC	CV	2	$3425	◓	
Prosoft/NGT Certified Network Professional Instructor	1	MC	CV	4	$5700	◓	
Prosoft/NGT Certified Security Professional Instructor	3	MC	CV	4	$7775	●	
Prosoft/NGT Certified Internet Web Developer Instructor	3	MC	CV	3	$6645	●	

Certification Difficulty: ○ Moderate   ◓ Challenging   ● Very Challenging

Test Format: **MC:** Multiple choice   **AT:** Adaptive Testing   **LA:** Live Application
PR: Hands-on Lab   **NA:** Not Applicable

Test Fee: **VF:** Test Fees can vary; consult testing center   **CV:** Voucher for taking the exam is included in the fee for the required course(s); additional attempts cost extra.

Chapter 11: Other Vendor-Based Certifications

This chapter covers certification programs on aspects of computing and networking that did not fit neatly into the previous chapters, i.e., security, programming, and network management. Two certification programs concentrate on computer security: the Certified Information Systems Security Professional designation, offered by the International Information Systems Security Certification Consortium, and the Certified Information Systems Auditor credential, offered by Information Systems Audit and Control Association.

Two certifications focus on programming. The Microsoft Certified Solution Developer certification program is designed for computer professionals who develop custom applications using Microsoft products and/or programming languages. The Sun Certified Java Programmer and Developer are two popular certifications offered by the inventors of the Java programming language.

The final two certifications covered in this chapter concentrate on network management software. This type of software is used for large-scale monitoring and troubleshooting of networks that are comprised of equipment and software from multiple vendors. The two network management certifications are Computer Associates' Certified Unicenter Engineer credential and Hewlett-Packard's OpenView Certified Consultant designation.

TABLE 2.9: Other Vendor Certifications

Certification	# of Required Tests	Test Format(s)	Total Cost of Required Tests	# of Required Courses	Total Cost of Required Courses	Difficulty	Notes
International Information Systems Security Certification Consortium							
(ISC)²Certified Information Systems Security Professional	1	MC	$395	None	NA	◒	Three years field experience required
Information Systems Audit and Control Association Certification							
Certified Information Systems Auditor (CISA)	2	MC	$295-$385	None	NA	●	Five years field experience required
Microsoft Certification							
Microsoft Certified Solutions Developer	4	MC	$400	None	NA	●	
Sun Certifications							
Certified Java Programmer: JDK 1.0.2	1	MC	$150	None	NA	◒	
Certified Java Programmer: JDK 1.1	1	MC	$150	None	NA	◒	
Certified Java Developer: JDK 1.0.2	1	MC	$150	None	NA	●	Must complete a programming assignment ($250 fee).
Certified Java Developer: JDK 1.1	1	MC	$150	None	NA	●	Must complete a programming assignment ($250 fee).

Certification Difficulty: ○ Moderate ◒ Challenging ● Very Challenging

Test Format: **MC:** Multiple choice **PR:** Hands-on Lab **AT:** Adaptive Testing **LA:** Live Application **NA:** Not Applicable

Test Fee: **VF:** Test Fees can vary; consult testing center **CV:** Voucher for taking the exam is included in the fee for the required course(s); additional attempts cost extra.

TABLE 2.9(CONTINUED): Other Vendor Certifications

Certification	#of Required Tests	Test Format(s)	Total Cost of Required Tests	# of Required Courses	Total Cost of Required Courses	Difficulty	Notes
Computer Associates Certification							
Certified Unicenter Engineer	2	MC	VF	2	VF	◒	
Hewlett-Packard Certifications							
HP OpenView Certified Consultant: UNIX	2	MC	VF	None	NA	◒	
HP OpenView Certified Consultant: Windows NT	2	MC	VF	None	NA	◒	
HP OpenView Certified Consultant: UNIX and Windows NT	2	MC	VF	None	NA	◒	

Certification Difficulty: ◯ Moderate ◒ Challenging ● Very Challenging

Test Format: **MC:** Multiple choice   **AT:** Adaptive Testing   **LA:** Live Application
PR: Hands-on Lab   **NA:** Not Applicable

Test Fee: **VF:** Test Fees can vary; consult testing center   **CV:** Voucher for taking the exam is included in the fee for the required course(s); additional attempts cost extra.

Chapter 12: Organization-Based Certifications

The certifications in this chapter are offered by organizations or associations, rather than by vendors. These certification programs are well respected in the computer and networking fields because they tend to be comprehensive and standards-based.

BICSI offers the Registered Communications Distribution Designer program, which certifies experts who design and install cabling and networking for new and existing buildings. The Computer Technology Industry Association, or CompTIA, offers two important certifications: the A+ certification for computer service technicians, and the Certified Document Architect for imaging specialists. The Certified Network Professional credential—developed by the Network Professional Association—certifies networking expertise, as does the Certified Network Expert credential, which is offered by a consortium of industry representatives. The Institute for Certification of Computing Professionals (ICCP) was founded in 1973 and offers the Certified Computing Professional credential, which covers many different aspects of computing and networking.

TABLE 2.10: Organization-Based Certifications

Certification	# of Required Tests	Test Format(s)	Total Cost of Required Tests	# of Required Courses	Total Cost of Required Courses	Difficulty	Notes
BICSI Certifications							
Registered Communications Distribution Designer (RCDD)	1	MC	$100	None	NA	◑	Requires annual membership ($100) and two years experience.

Certification Difficulty:	○ Moderate	◑ Challenging	● Very Challenging
Test Format:	**MC:** Multiple choice **PR:** Hands-on Lab	**AT:** Adaptive Testing	**LA:** Live Application **NA:** Not Applicable
Test Fee:	**VF:** Test Fees can vary; consult testing center	**CV:** Voucher for taking the exam is included in the fee for the required course(s); additional attempts cost extra.	

TABLE 2.10 (CONTINUED): Organization-Based Certifications

Certification	#of Required Tests	Test Format(s)	Total Cost of Required Tests	# of Required Courses	Total Cost of Required Courses	Difficulty	Notes
BICSI Certifications (continued)							
RCDD: Local Area Network Specialty	1	MC	$100	None	NA	◒	Must obtain an RCDD.
CompTIA Certifications							
A+ Certification	2	MC	$190-220	None	NA	●	
Certified Document Image Architect (CDIA)	1	MC	$150-165	None	NA	◒	
CNX Consortium Certification							
CNX	1	MC	$250	None	NA	●	Specializations: Token Ring, Ethernet, FDDI, or LAN Cabling
ICCP Certification							
Certified Computer Professional (CCP)	3-4	MC	$350-$400	None	NA	●	
Network Professional Association Certification							
Certified Network Professional (CNP)	1	MC	VF	None	NA	●	

Certification Difficulty: ◯ Moderate   ◒ Challenging   ● Very Challenging

Test Format: **MC:** Multiple choice   **AT:** Adaptive Testing   **LA:** Live Application
PR: Hands-on Lab   **NA:** Not Applicable

Test Fee: **VF:** Test Fees can vary; consult testing center   **CV:** Voucher for taking the exam is included in the fee for the required course(s); additional attempts cost extra.

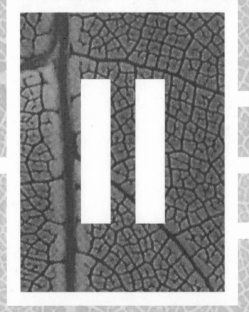

PART II

Certification Programs and Requirements

CHAPTER

3

Hardware Certifications

FEATURING

- Compaq Certifications

- Disaster Recovery Institute International Certifications

- IBM Certifications

- Learning Tree International Certification

For the sheer amount of frustration and panic it can generate, working with hardware problems is probably unbeatable. Most of the truly critical problems with computers are hardware-related; if the hardware doesn't work, nothing else will. Advanced knowledge about a certain software package or programming language is moot if you're dead in the water because your computer's hard disk needs replacing, or you can't get your network card to work correctly.

A solid understanding of how to install and maintain hardware is invaluable to computer and networking professionals and to the organizations that employ them. And if you're into being the computer hero in your organization, just watch the accolades you'll receive after resurrecting your boss's computer from the dead, just in time for an important report to go out.

Unfortunately, because working with hardware is often seen as a mundane task, there are not a lot of certifications available in this field. Compaq and IBM have programs to certify professionals who have knowledge and experience with their product lines. Learning Tree International, a training organization, has developed its own vendor-independent hardware certification program. The other certification program listed in this chapter—offered by the Disaster Recovery Institute International—involves preparation to ensure that a company can survive a disaster or natural catastrophe; this obviously involves a lot of issues, but recovering a company's information infrastructure is a major concern.

Professionals seeking or holding the certifications covered in this chapter run the gamut from service technicians for computer dealers to chief information officers at major corporations. To be sure, the knowledge and skills learned by achieving any one of these certifications will be valuable in your career in information technology. Those who may be interested in pursuing these certifications include:

- Help desk personnel

- Service technicians

- Field engineers

- System administrators

- Information specialists, information planners, and information officers

- Technology coordinators

 If your expertise and interest lie in computer hardware, check out the Computing Technology Industry Association (CompTIA) A+ certification program detailed in Chapter 12. This vendor-independent credential is probably the most widely-recognized hardware certification.

Compaq Certifications

Compaq makes several lines of workstations and servers based on Intel's microprocessors (Pentium, Pentium II, etc.). Compaq was one of the first makers of a PC "clone" in the early 1980s. They earned a reputation for making a clone computer that was much better and cheaper than the original design. Today Compaq is a multi-billion dollar business and a leading manufacturer of servers.

The Compaq Accredited Systems Engineer (ASE) program was developed in 1991 to evaluate and recognize expertise in installing and administering Compaq workstations and servers operating in both Novell IntranetWare and Microsoft Windows NT networking environments. There are two levels to this program—the ASE and the

Associate ASE—as well as specializations in Novell or Microsoft networking. Most Associate ASEs go on to complete the full certification program. There are currently 150 Compaq Associate ASEs and 1,800 fully accredited Compaq ASEs.

Because ASEs can obtain information from Compaq that has not yet been released for public consumption, all ASEs are required to submit a confidentiality and nondisclosure agreement and cannot be employed by a competitor of Compaq.

Recertification or Maintenance Requirements   Compaq requires ASEs to participate in periodic training to maintain their certifications, but there is no set standard for this training. The amount of training required in a given year is based on what new products Compaq releases, and whether Compaq feels that additional training is required for an ASE to successfully install and maintain these products.

Benefits of Certification   Associate ASEs receive the following benefits:

- Access to every technical tool and subscription available from Compaq
- Toll-free access to the Compaq ASE Forum, where ASEs can share information with other ASEs around the world
- Toll-free access to Compaq's technical databases
- Access to private training events on upcoming Compaq products and technologies
- Invitation to the Compaq systems engineering conference
- Use of the ASE logo for stationery and business cards
- Special discounts on selected Compaq products

In addition to the benefits above, full ASEs receive the following benefits:

- A free subscription to Compaq SmartStart, a CD-ROM resource that includes an intelligent program for integrating hardware configuration and software installation into a single automated process

- Free priority access to Compaq technical support

Associate Accredited Systems Engineer Specializing in Novell IntranetWare

To attain certification as an Associate ASE, one must pass three tests. The Compaq Systems Technologies test measures basic knowledge and understanding of PC architecture and operation. The Compaq Integration and Performance test measures the ability to install Novell IntranetWare server and clients on Compaq servers and workstations. Finally, the Compaq Systems Management test measures the advanced troubleshooting and management of Compaq servers and workstations.

Who Needs It This Associate ASE certification is an excellent way to show potential employers that you can install and manage Novell IntranetWare on a Compaq server. This credential can also be of value to systems engineers who do independent consulting and want to validate their expertise for clients.

Requirements for Certification The certification process requires the following steps:

1. Pass the Compaq Systems Technologies test.

2. Pass the Compaq Integration & Performance test for Novell IntranetWare.

3. Pass the Compaq Systems Management test.

4. Submit an ASE application, confidentiality and nondisclosure agreement, and copies of the three examination score reports to Compaq.

An ASE candidate must complete the three Compaq tests within a six-month period.

Administrator   Call Sylvan Prometric at (800) 366-3926 to register for a Compaq exam. (See Chapter 15 for detailed information on taking tests from Sylvan.)

Fee $100 per test

Format   Each of the three tests consists of 50 questions. To pass, you must answer 30 questions correctly within the one-hour time limit.

Associate Accredited Systems Engineer Specializing in Microsoft Windows NT

To attain certification as an Associate ASE, one must pass three tests. The Compaq Systems Technologies test measures basic knowledge and understanding of PC architecture and operation. The Compaq Integration and Performance test measures the ability to install Windows NT Server and Workstation on Compaq computers. Finally, the Compaq Systems Management test measures the advanced troubleshooting and management of Compaq servers and workstations.

Who Needs It   This Associate ASE certification is an excellent way to show potential employers that you can install and manage Microsoft Windows NT on a Compaq server. This credential can also be of value to systems engineers who do independent consulting and want to validate their expertise for clients.

Requirements for Certification The certification process requires the following steps:

1. Pass the Compaq Systems Technologies test.

2. Pass the Compaq Integration & Performance test for Windows NT.

3. Pass the Compaq Systems Management test.

4. Submit an ASE application, confidentiality and nondisclosure agreement, and copies of the three examination score reports to Compaq.

As an ASE candidate, you must complete the three Compaq tests within a six-month period.

Administrator Call Sylvan Prometric at (800) 366-3926 to register for a Compaq exam. (See Chapter 15 for detailed information on taking tests from Sylvan.)

Fee $100 per test

Format Each of the three tests consists of 50 questions. To pass, you must answer 30 questions correctly within the one-hour time limit.

Accredited Systems Engineer Specializing in Novell IntranetWare

The Compaq ASE designation in IntranetWare indicates that the holder has completed the three exams for Compaq Associate ASE certification and also has completed certification as a Certified Novell Engineer (CNE) or a Master CNE.

Who Needs It This ASE certification is the highest credential awarded to systems engineers who sell, support, integrate, plan, or optimize Compaq platforms using Novell IntranetWare. This credential can be a great way to get a higher-paying position within your current company or elsewhere.

Requirements for Certification   The certification process requires the following steps:

1. Attain certification as a Compaq Associate ASE (Accredited Systems Engineer) specializing in Novell IntranetWare.

2. Obtain/maintain certification as a Certified Novell Engineer or a Master Certified Novell Engineer. (See Chapter 7 for details on these certifications.)

3. Submit an ASE application, confidentiality and nondisclosure agreement, copies of the three examination score reports, and proof of Novell certification to Compaq.

Accredited Systems Engineer Specializing in Microsoft Windows NT

The Compaq ASE designation in Windows NT indicates that the holder has completed the three exams for Compaq Associate ASE certification and also has completed certification as a Microsoft Certified System Engineer (MCSE).

Who Needs It   This ASE certification is the highest credential awarded to systems engineers who sell, support, integrate, plan, or optimize Compaq platforms using Microsoft Windows NT. This credential can be a great way to get a higher-paying position within your current company or elsewhere.

Requirements for Certification   The certification process requires the following steps:

1. Attain certification as a Compaq Associate ASE (Accredited Systems Engineer) specializing in Microsoft Windows NT.

2. Obtain/maintain certification as a Microsoft Certified Systems Engineer. (See Chapter 7 for details on this certification.)

3. Submit an ASE application, confidentiality and nondisclosure agreement, copies of the three examination score reports, and proof of Microsoft certification to Compaq.

Resources

Compaq offers several resources to help you prepare for their certification exams. Compaq ASE Self-Assessment Guides provide information about the topics covered on the exams. The Assessment Guides are free and can be downloaded from Compaq's Web site. In addition, Compaq offers training courses that cover the topics addressed on each of the tests. These courses include:

-   Course 397: Compaq Systems Technologies

-   Course 422: Compaq Integration & Performance, Windows NT

-   Course 423: Compaq Integration & Performance, Novell IntranetWare

-   Course 293: Compaq Systems Management

Each of these two-day courses costs $600 and is offered at several locations throughout the United States and Canada. For more information on this organization's certification program and courses, contact Compaq at:

Web   `http://www.compaq.com/ase`

Mail   ASE Program Manager
            Compaq Computer Corporation
            Mailstop 100103
            PO Box 692000
            Houston, TX 77269-2000

Phone   (800) 732-5741

Fax   (281) 514-6039

Faxback   (800) 345-1518, Option 1

Disaster Recovery Institute International Certifications

The Disaster Recovery Institute International (DRII) is a non-profit organization that was founded in 1988 to establish a base of common knowledge and professional practices in business continuity/ disaster recovery planning. DRII also certifies professionals in this field. This certification is not related exclusively to computer hardware; it involves preparation to ensure that a company can survive a disaster or natural catastrophe. Preserving and recovering a company's information infrastructure is clearly a major concern in this type of training. DRII provides professionals with the skills to guarantee that critical data is never lost and downtime is minimized in the event of a major catastrophe.

DRII offers three levels of certification: Associate Business Continuity Planner (ABCP), Certified Business Continuity Professional (CBCP), and Master Business Continuity Professional (MBCP). Professionals who have found it useful to obtain these DRII certifications include independent consultants and information technology professionals in large corporations.

Recertification or Maintenance Requirements Both CBCPs and MBCPs are required to maintain their certification by participating in continuing education. CBCPs must obtain 12 continuing education units (CEUs) on related topics every three years, and MBCPs must obtain eight CEUs every two years. In addition, there is an annual recertification fee of $50 for CBCPs and $75 for MBCPs.

Benefits of Certification While DRII certification does not offer some of the incidental benefits provided with vendor-based certifications (logos, coffee cups, etc.), there can be a great benefit in job security and/or advancement for individuals obtaining any of these three certifications. As more companies invest their future in information infrastructures, having an employee on staff who can plan for and deal with any contingency becomes crucial.

Associate Business Continuity Planner (ABCP)

The one test required for this certification covers basic information on business continuity planning and disaster recovery. To help you prepare for this test, DRII offers related course work and study guides (see the Resources section that follows for more information).

Who Needs It This certification is great for individuals who have not yet acquired the necessary experience to become a CBCP. The ABCP is an important step in building your credentials as a continuity planner for your company's computing resources.

Requirements for Certification The certification process requires only one step:

1. Pass the written qualifying exam with a score of 75 percent.

Administrator Contact DRII for the location nearest you.

Fee $250; candidates who fail may retake the exam within 12 months for only $50.

Format Consists of approximately 125 questions. Candidates for the ABCP and CBCP certifications must score a minimum of 75 percent, while those seeking the MBCP need to pass with an 85 percent score.

Certified Business Continuity Planner (CBCP)

This is the second level of certification for business continuity planners. It uses the same test as the ABCP certification, but also requires related work experience and board certification.

Who Needs It This certification targets individuals who have or desire a high degree of responsibility for business continuity planning and have at least two years of experience in a related field. The CBCP can be an excellent way to prove that you are ready to move up in responsibility within your company or elsewhere.

Requirements for Certification The certification process requires the following steps:

1. Pass the written qualifying exam (described for the ABCP above) with a score of 75 percent.

2. Have at least two years of experience in three of the following areas: project initiation and management, risk evaluation and control, business impact analysis, developing business continuity strategies, emergency response and operations, developing and implementing business continuity plans, awareness and training programs, maintaining and exercising business continuity plans, public relations and crisis communication, and coordination with public authorities.

3. Submit the CBCP application and processing fee.

Administrator Contact DRII for the location nearest you.

Fee There is a $100 fee for processing the CBCP application.

Format Consists of approximately 125 questions. Candidates for the ABCP and CBCP certifications must score a minimum of 75 percent, while those seeking the MBCP need to pass with an 85 percent score.

Master Business Continuity Planner (MBCP)

This is the highest level of certification for business continuity planners. It uses the same test as the ABCP certification, but requires a higher score. To qualify for the MBCP you must have recently (within the past 10 years) had five years of significant experience in business continuity or disaster recovery planning. In addition, the MBCP requires board certification and a case study exam or an independent research effort in the field.

Who Needs It The MBCP is the top-of-the-line certification for business continuity planners. It is an excellent credential for independent consultants in the field.

Requirements for Certification The certification process requires the following steps:

1. Meet the prescribed experience requirement.

2. Pass the written qualifying exam (described for the ABCP above) with a score of 85 or higher.

3. Complete either a case study project or DRII-directed research in the field.

4. Submit the MBCP application and processing fee.

Contact DRII for more information about the criteria for the case study project or DRII-directed research.

Administrator   Contact DRII for the location nearest you.

Fee   There is a $200 fee for processing the MBCP application.

Resources

DRII offers a number of basic, advanced, and specialty courses in business continuity planning and disaster recovery. DRII also provides a free study guide for the basic continuity planning test. For more information on this organization's courses and certification programs, or to request a study guide, contact DRII at:

Web   `http://www.dr.org`

E-mail   `bill@dr.org`

Mail   Disaster Recovery Institute International
           810 Craig Road, Suite 125
           St. Louis, MO 63146

Phone   (314) 434-2272

Fax   (314) 434-1260

IBM Certifications

IBM offers a large number of certification program tracks. For a complete listing, check out `http://www.software.ibm.com/os/warp/pspinfo/proroad.htm`.

IBM makes all types of computers, from mainframes to PCs. IBM offers two certifications that are relevant for professionals dealing with PC hardware issues: the Professional Server Specialist and the Professional Server Expert. The Professional Server Expert certification offers three options for server specialization.

Recertification or Maintenance Requirements After initial certification, IBM requires annual update tests for all Professional Server Experts and Professional Server Specialists. These tests can be taken online through the TechConnect Web site at `http://www.pc.ibm.com/techconnect/`. The update test consists of 25 multiple-choice questions. Test takers have 50 minutes to complete the online test and may attempt the test up to three times.

Benefits of Certification IBM offers several valuable support features to those who complete its hardware certification programs. (Some of these features are even offered to those at the novice level; see the information about the TechConnect Associate in the Tip below.)

Professional Server Specialists receive the following benefits:

- A quarterly subscription to the TechConnect CD-ROM, which offers the latest information on IBM PC servers as well as reference materials, white papers, and industry news

- A separate CD filled with the latest drivers and fixes

- Access to the online TechConnect Forum

- *PSS Priority*, a mailing with up-to-date technical information

- Logos for business cards and stationery

- PSS Certificate

Professional Server Experts receive the TechConnect CD-ROM and a CD with the latest drivers and fixes, in addition to the following benefits:

- *PSE Priority*, a large collection of technical materials that may include videos, audio tapes, or CD-ROMs

- Logos for business cards and stationery

- PSE Certificate

- Priority access to the IBM HelpCenter with a personal identification code

- Special electronic access to IBM support

- Access to interactive forums on the IBM PC Company Bulletin Board System

- Invitation to IBM's annual PSE meeting, referred to as IMPACT

IBM also offers the designation TechConnect Associate—which is not a certification, but provides some very nice benefits—to anyone who registers online at http://www.pc.ibm.com/techconnect/. TechConnect Associates receive a quarterly subscription to the TechConnect CD-ROM, which offers the latest information on IBM PC servers, as well as reference materials, white papers, and industry news; a separate CD filled with the latest drivers and fixes; and access to the online TechConnect Forum.

Professional Server Specialist (PSS)

This is the introductory level of IBM hardware certification. The PSS certification program involves taking one required course and passing the test given at the end of that course. The test assesses knowledge of IBM Netfinity and PC server architecture, design, installation, and configuration. If you fail the test at the end of a training course, you can retake the test at a later date.

You must also sign an IBM certification agreement that spells out the terms under which you are authorized to use the IBM certification logos and titles.

Who Needs It The IBM Professional Server Specialist is a key initial certification for computer professionals who will be installing, maintaining, and administering IBM PC Servers.

Requirements for Certification The certification process requires the following steps:

1. Take the three-day IBM Course V5051 (IBM Netfinity and PC Server Technical Training) and pass the test at the end of the course.

2. Submit a signed IBM Certification Agreement.

Administrator The test is administered by IBM at the completion of the required course. IBM courses are offered throughout the world—call IBM or see their Web site for more information.

Fee The course costs $750. There is no additional cost for the test.

Format The test consists of approximately 75 multiple-choice questions.

Professional Server Expert (PSE): Novell NetWare

The PSE certification builds on the PSS program and offers specialization in a particular network operating system. This certification program involves achieving IBM PSS status, attaining the Certified Novell Engineer credential, and then taking one additional required IBM course and passing the test at the end of that course. The course and test cover knowledge of the installation process for Novell Intranetware using IBM Server Guide, and tuning the software and hardware for optimal performance. If you fail the test at the end of a training course, you can retake the test at a later date.

You must also sign an IBM certification agreement that spells out the terms under which you are authorized to use the IBM certification logos and titles.

Who Needs It This certification provides proof of your expertise in installing, administering, and troubleshooting Novell NetWare server software running on IBM PC Server hardware. The PSE certification is especially valuable to field engineers or independent contractors who are responsible for servers at multiple locations.

Requirements for Certification The certification process requires the following steps:

1. Attain PSS certification (see the previous section for details).

2. Take the two-day IBM Course V5052 (IBM Netfinity and Server/NetWare Installation and Performance) and pass the test at the end of the course.

3. Submit proof of Novell CNE certification (see Chapter 7 for details on this certification).

4. Submit a signed IBM Certification Agreement.

Administrator The test is administered by IBM at the completion of the required course. IBM courses are offered throughout the world—call IBM or see their Web site for more information.

Fee The course costs $600. There is no additional cost for the test.

Format The test consists of approximately 75 multiple-choice questions.

Professional Server Expert (PSE): OS/2 Warp Server

The PSE certification builds on the PSS program and offers specialization in a particular network operating system. This certification program involves achieving IBM PSS status, attaining the IBM OS/2 Warp Server Engineer credential, and then taking one additional required IBM course and passing the test at the end of that course. The course and test cover knowledge of the installation process for OS/2 Warp using IBM Server Guide, and tuning the software and hardware for optimal performance. If you fail the test at the end of a training course, you can retake the test at a later date.

You must also sign an IBM certification agreement that spells out the terms under which you are authorized to use the IBM certification logos and titles.

Who Needs It This certification provides proof of your expertise in installing, administering, and troubleshooting OS/2 server software running on IBM PC Server hardware. The PSE certification is especially valuable to field engineers or independent contractors who are responsible for servers at multiple locations.

Requirements for Certification   The certification process requires the following steps:

1. Attain PSS certification (see the previous section for details).

2. Take the two-day IBM Course V5053 (IBM Netfinity and PC Server/Warp Installation and Performance) and pass the test at the end of the course.

3. Submit proof of OS/2 Warp Server Engineer certification (see Chapter 7 for details on this certification).

4. Submit a signed IBM Certification Agreement.

Administrator   The test is administered by IBM at the completion of the required course. IBM courses are offered throughout the world—call IBM or see their Web site for more information.

Fee   The course costs $600. There is no additional cost for the test.

Format   The test consists of approximately 75 multiple-choice questions.

Professional Server Expert (PSE): Windows NT Server

The PSE certification builds on the PSS program and offers specialization in a particular network operating system. This certification program involves achieving IBM PSS status, attaining the Microsoft Certified Systems Engineer credential, and then taking one additional required IBM course and passing the test at the end of that course. The course and test cover knowledge of the installation process for Microsoft Windows NT using IBM Server Guide, and tuning the software and hardware for optimal performance. If you fail the test at the end of a training course, you can retake the test at a later date.

You must also sign an IBM certification agreement that spells out the terms under which you are authorized to use the IBM certification logos and titles.

Who Needs It This certification provides proof of your expertise in installing, administering, and troubleshooting Microsoft Windows NT server software running on IBM PC Server hardware. The PSE certification is especially valuable to field engineers or independent contractors who are responsible for servers at multiple locations.

Requirements for Certification The certification process requires the following steps:

1. Attain PSS certification (see the previous section for details).

2. Take the two-day IBM Course V5055 (IBM Netfinity and PC Server/Windows NT Installation and Performance) and pass the test at the end of the course.

3. Submit proof of Microsoft Certified Systems Engineer certification (see Chapter 7 for details on this certification).

4. Submit a signed IBM Certification Agreement.

Administrator The tests are administered by IBM at the completion of the required course. IBM courses are offered throughout the world—call IBM or see their Web site for more information.

Fee The course costs $600. There is no additional cost for the test.

Format The test consists of approximately 75 multiple-choice questions.

Resources

Test objectives and sample tests are available online or from IBM's faxback service. For more information on these courses and certification programs, contact IBM at:

Web	`http://www.pc.ibm.com/techconnect/`
E-mail	`techconn@us.ibm.com`
Mail	Professional Certification Program
	IBM Corporation, Mail Stop 3013
	11400 Burnet Rd.
	Austin, TX 78758
Phone	(800) 235-4746
Fax	(512) 838-7961
Faxback	(800) 426-4329

Learning Tree International Certification

Learning Tree International is a worldwide training organization that currently offers over 150 computer and networking courses in the United States, Europe, and Asia. As part of their curriculum in information technology, Learning Tree International offers 27 different vendor-independent professional certification programs, one of which is oriented toward PC hardware. (See Chapter 4, 6, and 9 for additional Learning Tree International Cerification programs.)

The Learning Tree International PC Service and Support Certified Professional credential may be useful to PC support staff, service technicians, engineers, system and network administrators, and anyone else involved with the maintenance and support of PC hardware. This certification involves the mastery of a series of hardware service and support courses.

Recertification or Maintenance Requirements There is no recertification requirement for any of Learning Tree International's certification programs.

Benefits of Certification Learning Tree International PC Service and Support Certified Professionals receive the following benefits:

- Framed diploma of Professional Certification

- An official record of the courses that you have completed

- Option to obtain college credit

It is possible to obtain college credit for Learning Tree International certifications or courses. The American Council of Education (ACE) in Washington, D.C. has worked in cooperation with Learning Tree International to determine college course equivalencies for these courses and certifications. Approximately 1,500 colleges and universities in the United States will accept ACE recommendations for college credit. As a general rule, ACE will recommend two college credit hours for each four-day course. Learning Tree International will pay to have your Learning Tree International credentials registered with ACE and you can then request that your transcript be sent from ACE to any college or university. (Check with your college or university registrar to make sure that your institution accepts ACE recommendations for credit.)

Learning Tree International PC Service and Support Certified Professional

This certification program consists of taking four core courses and one elective course and passing the tests given at the end of each course. The courses and exams are designed to teach and test the candidate's ability to disassemble and reassemble a complete PC system; diagnose and fix PC hardware and software problems; install and configure motherboards, adapter cards, and disk drives; recover lost files and directories; solve memory management conflicts; install, configure, optimize, and troubleshoot Windows 95; work with NetWare, Windows for Workgroups, Windows NT Server, and Windows 95; and optimize PC network performance.

Who Needs It   This certification is a good vendor-independent credential for those who want to get a position working with hardware and software from multiple vendors and manufacturers (a situation typical of many organizations). Since the certification program requires comprehensive training classes, Learning Tree International certifications offer a means for those just beginning their computing careers to gain hands-on experience and training that may not currently be available on the job.

Requirements for Certification   The certification process requires the following steps:

1. Complete the four core courses listed below and pass the test given at the end of each course:

Course Number	Length	Course
Course 145	four days	Hands-On PC Configuration and Troubleshooting
Course 150	four days	Advanced PC Configuration, Troubleshooting and Data Recovery, Hands-On

Course Number	Length	Course
Course 153	five days	Windows 95 Support and Networking, Hands-On
Course 253	four days	Hands-On PC Networking

2. Complete one of the elective courses from the following list and pass the test given at the end of the course:

Course Number	Length	Course
Course 208	four days	Integrating Microsoft Office 97
Course 254	four days	Hands-On LAN Troubleshooting
Course 336	four days	UNIX: A Hands-On Introduction
Course 455	five days	Windows NT 4 Workstation and Server, Hands-On
Course 264	five days	Hands-On InternetWare, IntranetWare 4.x Administration
Course 158	four days	UNIX and Windows NT Integration

Administrator Learning Tree International (Call (800) THE-TREE)

Fee At this writing, the prices for Learning Tree International courses are $1295 for a two-day course, $1745 for a three-day course, $2195 for a four-day course, and $2495 for a five-day course. Learning Tree International offers some significant discounts for those taking more than one course and for government employees. There is no additional charge for the tests.

Format   Each exam consists of 40 to 60 questions. If you fail to pass on the first try, Learning Tree International will arrange for you to take a proctored exam at your place of work.

Resources

For more information on this organization's courses and certification programs, contact Learning Tree International at:

Web	http://www.learningtree.com
E-mail	uscourses@learningtree.com
Mail	Learning Tree International 1805 Library Street Reston, VA 20190-5630
Phone	(800) THE-TREE
Fax	(800) 709-6405

CHAPTER

4

Operating
Systems Certifications

FEATURING

- IBM AIX Certifications

- IBM AS/400 Certifications

- IBM OS/2 Certifications

- Learning Tree International Certifications

- Microsoft Certification

- Santa Cruz Organization (SCO) Certifications

- Silicon Graphics Certifications

- Sun Certifications

An operating system brings life to a computer's chips and electrons. It's the basic code that controls access to a computer's resources and manages all the programs running on that computer. Because of its central importance, an incorrectly configured operating system can suck the speed and productivity right out of the fastest processor.

Desktop computers usually have one of three types of operating systems:

- Apple's Macintosh operating system

- A version of UNIX

- Microsoft's DOS or Windows operating system

There are also several vendor-specific operating systems designed for use only on certain machines.

Apple Computer has recently retired its operating system certification program as a result of restructuring within the company (see Appendix B for more information on retired certifications). Certifications offered by several makers of UNIX-based operating systems are covered in this chapter—IBM, Santa Cruz Organization, Silicon Graphics, and Sun—as well as Learning Tree International's vendor-independent UNIX certification. Microsoft offers the Microsoft Certified Professional credential for technical professionals who are proficient in either Windows 95 or Windows NT. In addition, IBM offers certifications related to its AS/400 operating system and two certification programs on OS/2, IBM's PC-based operating system.

UNIX is used both as a workstation operating system and a network operating system. We chose to list UNIX-based certifications in this chapter because UNIX can be considered—at its most basic level—a computer operating system.

Since problems with networking and software operation are often related to a computer's operating system, many technical professionals will benefit from the knowledge and skills gained from operating system certification programs. An operating system certification may be valuable to:

- Help desk personnel

- Technical staff

- System administrators

- Network administrators

- Field personnel

IBM AIX Certifications

The AIX operating system is the IBM version of UNIX designed for the RS/6000 series of computers. The three important certifications related to the AIX operating system include IBM Certified Specialist: AIX System Administration, IBM Certified Specialist: AIX Support, and IBM Certified Advanced Technical Expert: RS/6000 AIX. An introductory-level certification—IBM Certified AIX User—is also offered.

Recertification or Maintenance Requirements The IBM Certified Specialist and Advanced Technical Expert designations apply to specific version numbers of the AIX operating system, so there is no requirement for recertification on a particular version. Since your certification is tied to a certain version of a product, however, you will want become certified on the newer versions, when they become available, if you want to continue to have the most current credential in this area.

Benefits of Certification   IBM Certified Specialists receive these benefits:

- Logo for use on business cards or stationery

- A certificate of completion, an ID card, and a lapel pin

- Your name listed in IBM's directories of certified personnel

- Subscriptions to technical newsletters and magazines, other technical literature, and other special offers

- IBM technical support

IBM offers a large number of certification program tracks. For a complete listing, check out http://www.software.ibm.com/os/warp/pspinfo/proroad.htm.

IBM Certified AIX User

This certification is the most basic certification related to the AIX operating system. It certifies a candidate's understanding of AIX fundamentals and their ability to apply AIX concepts to the effective use and operation of an AIX system. The exam for this certification covers basic file management, using the screen editor, setting up login sessions, controlling print jobs, and using windows.

IBM recommends that those who seek this certification take the IBM hands-on lab course on AIX Version 4 Basics (IBM Course Number: Q1113). An introductory computer-based course on AIX basics is also offered. Further information on these and other AIX courses is available by calling (800) IBM-TEACH.

Who Needs It This certification can help you get your foot in the door at a company that uses AIX. It lets employers know that you have fundamental knowledge and skill in using the AIX operating system.

Requirements for Certification The certification process requires only one step:

1. Pass the IBM AIX User test (Sylvan ID: 000-160).

Administrator Call Sylvan Prometric at (800) 959-3926 to register for an IBM exam. (See Chapter 15 for detailed information on taking tests from Sylvan.)

Fee Fees for IBM tests vary based on test length and format; call Sylvan Prometric at (800) 959-3926 for pricing.

Format Computer-based, multiple-choice test. Call Sylvan Prometric at (800) 959-3926 for current information on the number of questions, time limit, and passing score.

IBM Certified Specialist: AIX System Administration

This certification is designed for technical professionals who will be working with AIX system administration on a daily basis. The test for this certification assesses the candidate's ability to install AIX and to perform a broad range of general system administration tasks. IBM recommends that candidates have at least six months of experience performing these activities on an AIX system prior to taking the test. IBM also highly recommends that those who seek this certification take these two courses:

IBM Course Number	Course
Q1114	AIX Version 4 System Administration
Q1107	AIX Version 4 Configuring TCP/IP & Accessing Internet

IBM suggests that these additional courses may also be helpful: AIX for Users (IBM Course Number: Q1113); AIX Version 4 Advanced System Administration (IBM Course Number: Q1116); Using X Windows and COSE CDE (IBM Course Number: Q1165); AIX V4 Korn Shell Programming (IBM Course Number: Q1121); and AIX Version 4 Performance Management (IBM Course Number: Q1128). Further information on these and other AIX courses is available by calling (800) IBM-TEACH.

Who Needs It   The IBM Certified Specialist: AIX System Administration designation is a great credential for getting a job in AIX support and administration. It lets employers know that you have the knowledge and skills needed to install and administrate AIX systems.

Requirements for Certification   The certification process requires only one step:

1.   Pass one of the following system administration tests:

   • IBM AIX V4.1 System Administration test (Sylvan ID: 000-161)

   • IBM AIX V4.3 System Administration test (Sylvan ID: 000-181)

Administrator Call Sylvan Prometric at (800) 959-3926 to register for an IBM exam. (See Chapter 15 for detailed information on taking tests from Sylvan.)

Fee Fees for IBM tests vary based on test length and format; call Sylvan Prometric at (800) 959-3926 for pricing.

Format Computer-based, multiple-choice test. Call Sylvan Prometric at (800) 959-3926 for current information on the number of questions, time limit, and passing score.

IBM Certified Specialist: AIX Support

This credential is designed for system administrators and others who provide an advanced level of AIX technical support. This exam covers the administration and networking of AIX systems, with an emphasis on the skills needed for problem determination and resolution. IBM recommends that a candidate have at least six months of experience in an AIX support role prior to attempting the test. In addition, IBM highly recommends that those who seek this certification take these four courses:

IBM Course Number	Course
Q1114	AIX Version 4 System Administration
Q1116	AIX Version 4 Advanced System Administration
Q1107	AIX Version 4 Configuring TCP/IP & Accessing Internet
Q1128	AIX Version 4 Performance Management

IBM suggests that these courses may also be helpful: Using X Windows and COSE CDE (IBM Course Number: Q1165); AIX V4 Korn

Shell Programming (IBM Course Number: Q1121); and AIX for Users (IBM Course Number: Q1113).

Who Needs It   The IBM Certified Specialist: AIX Support designation is a great credential for getting a job in AIX support and administration. It lets employers know that you have the knowledge and skills needed to troubleshoot and maintain AIX systems.

Requirements for Certification   The certification process requires only one step:

1.   Pass one of the following AIX support exams:

   • IBM AIX V4.1 Support test (Sylvan ID: 000-169)

   • IBM AIX V4.3 Support test (Sylvan ID: 000-189)

Administrator   Call Sylvan Prometric at (800) 959-3926 to register for an IBM exam. (See Chapter 15 for detailed information on taking tests from Sylvan.)

Fee   Fees for IBM tests vary based on test length and format; call Sylvan Prometric at (800) 959-3926 for pricing.

Format   Computer-based, multiple-choice test. Call Sylvan Prometric at (800) 959-3926 for current information on the number of questions, time limit, and passing score.

IBM Certified Advanced Technical Expert: RS/6000 AIX

This is the most prestigious certification associated with the AIX operating system, and it builds on either of the IBM Certified Specialist designations discussed previously. An individual with this certification has the ability to perform in-depth analyses, apply complex AIX concepts, and provide resolution to critical problems. The three exams for this certification delve into considerable detail on troubleshooting, networking, and optimizing performance.

Who Needs It The IBM Certified Advanced Technical Expert: RS/6000 AIX designation is a great credential for getting a high-level job in AIX support and administration. It lets employers know that you have an advanced level of knowledge and skills in all aspects of AIX.

Requirements for Certification The certification process requires the following steps:

1. Attain certification as an IBM Certified Specialist in AIX System Administration or AIX Support (described previously).

2. Pass three of the following six exams:

Sylvan ID	Exam
000-163	IBM AIX V4.2 Installation & System Recovery
000-164	IBM AIX Performance & System Tuning
000-165	IBM AIX V4.2 Problem Determination Tools and Techniques
000-166	IBM AIX V4.2 Communications
000-167	IBM HACMP for AIX V4.2
000-168	IBM RS/6000 SP & PSSP 2.2

Administrator Call Sylvan Prometric at (800) 959-3926 to register for an IBM exam. (See Chapter 15 for detailed information on taking tests from Sylvan.)

Fee Fees for IBM tests vary based on test length and format; call Sylvan Prometric at (800) 959-3926 for pricing.

Format   Computer-based, multiple-choice test. Call Sylvan Prometric at (800) 959-3926 for current information on the number of questions, time limit, and passing score.

Resources

IBM's Web site offers a number of excellent resources for certification
candidates, including recommended courses, test objectives, study
guides, and sample tests. For more information on these certification
programs and related courses, contact IBM at:

Web	`http://www.rs6000.ibm.com/support/aixcert/`
E-mail	`ialine@us.ibm.com`
Mail	IBM North America 1133 Westchester Avenue White Plains, NY 10604
Phone	(800) IBM-4YOU
Fax	(404) 238-6628
Faxback	(800) 426-4329

IBM AS/400 Certifications

IBM's mid-range AS/400 computers are used by many businesses,
organizations, and government agencies. The four key IBM Certified

Specialist designations related to the AS/400 operating system are AS/400 Associate System Operator, AS/400 Professional System Operator, AS/400 Associate System Administrator, and AS/400 Professional System Administrator.

Recertification or Maintenance Requirements The IBM AS/400 certifications apply to specific version numbers of the AS/400 operating system, so there is no requirement for recertification on a particular version. Since your certification is tied to a certain version of a product, however, you will want become certified on the newest versions, when they become available, if you want to continue to have the most current credential in this area.

Benefits of Certification IBM AS/400 Certified Specialists receive these benefits:

- Logo for use on business cards and literature
- A certificate of completion, an ID card, and a lapel pin
- Your name listed in IBM's directories of certified personnel
- Subscriptions to technical newsletters and magazines, other technical literature, and other special offers
- IBM technical support

IBM offers several other AS/400 certifications that are not covered in this book. Check out `http://www.software.ibm.com/os/warp/pspinfo/proroad.htm` for a complete listing.

IBM Certified Specialist: AS/400 Associate System Operator

To attain certification as an AS/400 Associate System Operator, a candidate must pass one exam. The exam for this certification covers basic AS/400 operational concepts related to object management, saving and restoring files, managing devices, controlling printer output, controlling jobs, and managing messages. IBM recommends that the candidate have hands-on experience with AS/400 system operation and take one of the following courses prior to taking the exam:

IBM Course Number	Course
PS586	AS/400 Getting to Know Your System
S6029	AS/400 System Operator Workshop

Who Needs It   The IBM Certified Specialist: AS/400 Professional System Operator certification can help you get your foot in the door at a company that uses an AS/400 system. It lets employers know that you have fundamental knowledge and skill on AS/400 systems.

Requirements for Certification   The certification process requires only one step:

1.   Pass the IBM AS/400 Associate System Operator exam (Sylvan ID: 000-052).

Administrator   Call Sylvan Prometric at (800) 959-3926 to register for an IBM exam. (See Chapter 15 for detailed information on taking tests from Sylvan.)

Fee   Fees for IBM tests vary based on test length and format; call Sylvan Prometric at (800) 959-3926 for pricing.

Format   Computer-based, multiple-choice test. Call Sylvan Prometric at (800) 959-3926 for current information on the number of questions, time limit, and passing score.

IBM Certified Specialist: AS/400 Professional System Operator

To attain certification as an AS/400 Professional System Operator, a candidate must pass one exam. Like the exam for the AS/400 Associate System Operator certification described previously, the exam for this certification covers basic AS/400 operational concepts related to object management, saving and restoring files, managing the system, managing devices, controlling printer output, and controlling jobs. In addition, this exam covers problem management, starting and stopping the system, and security issues.

IBM recommends that the candidate have hands-on experience with AS/400 system operation and that he or she take one of the following courses prior to taking the exam:

IBM Course Number	Course
PS586	AS/400 Getting to Know Your System
S6029	AS/400 System Operator Workshop

IBM also recommends taking their AS/400 Advanced System Operator Workshop course (IBM Course Number S6041) in preparation for this exam.

Who Needs It   The IBM Certified Specialist: AS/400 Professional System Operator designation is a great credential for getting a job in AS/400 support and administration. It lets employers know that you have the knowledge and skills needed to provide advanced technical support for AS/400 systems and users.

Requirements for Certification   The certification process requires only one step:

1.   Pass the IBM AS/400 Professional System Operator exam (Sylvan ID: 000-053).

Administrator   Call Sylvan Prometric at (800) 959-3926 to register for an IBM exam. (See Chapter 15 for detailed information on taking tests from Sylvan.)

Fee   Fees for IBM tests vary based on test length and format; call Sylvan Prometric at (800) 959-3926 for pricing.

Format   Computer-based, multiple-choice test. Call Sylvan Prometric at (800) 959-3926 for current information on the number of questions, time limit, and passing score.

IBM Certified Specialist: AS/400 Associate System Administrator

To attain certification as an AS/400 Associate System Administrator, a candidate must pass one exam. The exam for this certification covers AS/400 administration concepts related to hardware, system software, operations, and security. IBM recommends that the candidate have hands-on experience with AS/400 system administration prior to taking the exam. IBM also recommends several options for preparatory courses; check their Web site for a complete listing.

Who Needs It   The IBM Certified Specialist: AS/400 Associate System Administrator designation is a great credential for getting a job in AS/400 administration. It lets employers know that you have the knowledge and skills needed to administrate and maintain AS/400 systems.

Requirements for Certification The certification process requires only one step:

1. Pass the IBM AS/400 Associate System Administrator exam (Sylvan ID: 000-054).

Administrator Call Sylvan Prometric at (800) 959-3926 to register for an IBM exam. (See Chapter 15 for detailed information on taking tests from Sylvan.)

Fee Fees for IBM tests vary based on test length and format; call Sylvan Prometric at (800) 959-3926 for pricing.

Format Computer-based, multiple-choice test. Call Sylvan Prometric at (800) 959-3926 for current information on the number of questions, time limit, and passing score.

IBM Certified Specialist: AS/400 Professional System Administrator

To attain certification as an AS/400 Professional System Administrator, a candidate must pass one exam. Like the exam for the Associate System Administrator certification described previously, the exam for this certification covers AS/400 administration concepts related to hardware, system software, operations, and security. In addition, this exam addresses planning issues, such as capacity planning, backup and recovery, and disaster management.

IBM recommends that the candidate have hands-on experience with AS/400 system administration and take one of the following courses prior to taking this exam:

IBM Course Number	Course
S6023	AS/400 Structure, Tailoring and Basic Tuning

IBM Course Number	Course
PS587	AS/400 Work Management and Basic Tuning

IBM also recommends that a candidate take their course on AS/400 Performance Analysis and Capacity Planning (IBM Course Number S6027) in preparation for the test.

Who Needs It   The IBM Certified Specialist: AS/400 Professional System Administrator designation is a great credential for getting a high-level job in AS/400 support and administration. It lets employers know that you have an advanced level of knowledge and skill with AS/400 systems.

Requirements for Certification   The certification process requires only one step:

1.   Pass the IBM AS/400 Professional System Administrator exam (Sylvan ID: 000-055).

Administrator   Call Sylvan Prometric at (800) 959-3926 to register for an IBM exam. (See Chapter 15 for detailed information on taking tests from Sylvan.)

Fee   Fees for IBM tests vary based on test length and format; call Sylvan Prometric at (800) 959-3926 for pricing.

Format   Computer-based, multiple-choice test. Call Sylvan Prometric at (800) 959-3926 for current information on the number of questions, time limit, and passing score.

Resources

IBM's Web site offers a number of excellent resources for certification candidates, including recommended courses, test objectives, study guides, and sample tests. For more information on these courses and certification programs, contact IBM at:

Web	`http://www.ibm.com/certify/proroad.htm`
E-mail	`ialine@us.ibm.com`
Mail	IBM North America 1133 Westchester Avenue White Plains, NY 10604
Phone	(800) IBM-4YOU
Fax	(404) 238-6628
Faxback	(800) 426-4329

IBM OS/2 Certifications

During the 1980s, IBM and Microsoft worked together to develop the OS/2 operating system as a graphical interface for the PC. After a much-publicized breakup of the partnership, IBM continued to develop OS/2 while Microsoft took off in its own direction with Windows.

IBM offers certifications for two versions of its OS/2 operating system. These are IBM Certified Systems Expert: OS/2 Warp and IBM Certified Systems Expert: OS/2 Warp 4. If you are already certified as an IBM

Certified OS/2 Engineer (OS/2 2.1) or an IBM Certified Systems Expert: OS/2 Warp (V3), you can quickly update your certification to OS/2 Warp 4 by taking the OS/2 Warp 4 Update test (Sylvan ID: 000-203).

Recertification or Maintenance Requirements   The IBM OS/2 certifications apply to specific version numbers of this operating system, so there is no requirement for recertification on a particular version. Since your certification is tied to a certain version of a product, however, you will want become certified on the newest versions, when they become available, if you want to continue to have the most current credential in this area.

Benefits of Certification   IBM Certified OS/2 Systems Experts receive these benefits:

- Logo for use on business cards and literature

- A certificate of completion, an ID card, and a lapel pin

- Your name listed in IBM's directories of certified personnel

- Subscriptions to technical newsletters and magazines, other technical literature, and other special offers

- IBM technical support

IBM Certified Systems Expert: OS/2 Warp

Attaining this certification requires passing four tests. The Using OS/2 test covers basic OS/2 Workplace Shell and Desktop features and operation, file systems, installing and running applications, printing, and customizing. The Installing OS/2 exam covers installations, hard disk management, installing and configuring printers and fonts, managing system files, and application support. The Supporting OS/2 exam covers getting information, system booting, video and printer issues, multitasking, recovery tools, and system dumps.

Detailed information on the elective exams is available on IBM's Web site (see the Resources section that follows). IBM recommends that those who seek this certification have fundamental knowledge of DOS and experience with OS/2 Warp before taking the exams.

Who Needs It   This certification can help you get your foot in the door at a company that uses OS/2 (Version 3) systems. It lets employers know that you have the necessary knowledge and skill to maintain OS/2 systems and support OS/2 users.

Requirements for Certification   The certification process requires the following steps:

1. Pass the IBM Using OS/2 test (Sylvan ID: 000-110).

2. Pass the IBM Installing OS/2 test (Sylvan ID: 000-109).

3. Pass the IBM Supporting OS/2 test (Sylvan ID: 000-112).

4. Pass one of these elective tests:

   • REXX for OS/2 (Sylvan ID: 000-015)

   • IBM TCP/IP for Workstations (Sylvan ID: 000-018)

   • OS/2 Warp Connect (Sylvan ID: 000-126)

It is recommended that the tests be taken in the order listed.

Administrator   Call Sylvan Prometric at (800) 959-3926 to register for an IBM exam. (See Chapter 15 for detailed information on taking tests from Sylvan.)

Fee   Fees for IBM tests vary based on test length and format; call Sylvan Prometric at (800) 959-3926 for pricing.

Format   Computer-based, multiple-choice test. Call Sylvan Prometric at (800) 959-3926 for current information on the number of questions, time limit, and passing score.

IBM Certified Systems Expert: OS/2 Warp 4

Attaining this certification requires passing three tests. The OS/2 Warp 4 Fundamentals test covers the basic concepts of planning and installation, customization and usage, and problem determination. The OS/2 Warp 4 Connectivity exam covers TCP/IP and the Internet, network operating system connectivity, remote access and host connectivity, and remote installation. The OS/2 Warp 4 Advanced Concepts and Support exam covers advanced topics, including speech and multimedia, trouble-shooting and support services, performance optimization, application support, and system extensions.

IBM recommends that those who seek this certification have fundamental knowledge of DOS and experience with OS/2 Warp 4 before taking the exams.

Who Needs It This certification can help you get your foot in the door at a company that uses OS/2 (Version 4) systems. It lets employers know that you have the knowledge and skill necessary to maintain OS/2 systems and support OS/2 users.

Requirements for Certification The certification process requires the following steps:

1. Pass the IBM OS/2 Warp 4 Fundamentals test (Sylvan ID: 000-200).

2. Pass the IBM OS/2 Warp 4 Connectivity test (Sylvan ID: 000-201).

3. Pass the IBM OS/2 Warp 4 Advanced Concepts and Support test (Sylvan ID: 000-202).

It is recommended that the tests be taken in the order listed.

Administrator Call Sylvan Prometric at (800) 959-3926 to register for an IBM exam. (See Chapter 15 for detailed information on taking tests from Sylvan.)

Fee Fees for IBM tests vary based on test length and format; call Sylvan Prometric at (800) 959-3926 for pricing.

Format Computer-based, multiple-choice test. Call Sylvan Prometric at (800) 959-3926 for current information on the number of questions, time limit, and passing score.

Resources

IBM's Web site offers a number of excellent resources for certification candidates, including test objectives, study guides, and sample tests. Several computer-based training courses and instructor-led training courses are also offered. Another excellent resource, the *OS/2 Warp 4 Certification Handbook*, is available for $59.95 from either Sylvan Prometric ((800) 959-3926) or Indelible Blue ((800) 776-8284). For more information on these courses and certification programs, contact IBM at:

Web	`http://www.ibm.com/certify/`
E-mail	`ialine@us.ibm.com`
Mail	IBM North America 1133 Westchester Avenue White Plains, NY 10604
Phone	(800) IBM-4YOU
Fax	(404) 238-6628
Faxback	(800) 426-4329

Learning Tree International Certification

Learning Tree International currently offers over 150 computer and networking courses throughout the United States, Europe, and Asia. As part of their curriculum in information technology, Learning Tree International offers 27 different professional certification programs, one of which is a vendor-independent certification program on UNIX operating systems. (See Chapters 3, 6, and 9 for other Learing Tree International certification programs.)

The Learning Tree International UNIX Systems Certified Professional credential will prove useful to UNIX users, system administrators, network managers, system analysts, and anyone else involved in operating a UNIX-based system. Learning Tree International also offers a UNIX programming certification; for more information on this certification, consult the company's Web site (see the Resources section that follows).

Recertification or Maintenance Requirements There is no maintenance requirement for any of Learning Tree International's certification programs.

Benefits of Certification Learning Tree International UNIX Systems Certified Professionals receive these benefits:

- A framed diploma of Professional Certification
- An official record of the courses that you have completed
- Option of obtaining college credit

It is possible to obtain college credit for earning your certification or for taking Learning Tree International courses. The American Council of Education (ACE) in Washington, D.C. has worked in cooperation with Learning Tree International to determine college course equivalencies for these courses and certifications. Approximately 1,500 colleges and universities in the United States will accept ACE recommendations for college credit. As a general rule, ACE will recommend two college credit hours for each four-day course. Learning Tree International will pay to have your Learning Tree International credentials registered with ACE and you can then request that your transcript be sent from ACE to any college or university. (Check with your college or university registrar to make sure that your institution accepts ACE recommendations for credit.)

Learning Tree International UNIX Systems Certified Professional

Attainment of this certification requires taking five courses and passing a test given at the end of each course. The required introductory course covers user services and utilities, use of the X Window system, common desktop environment and applications, and maintenance functions. The workstation administration course covers menu-driven and command-line workstation management, installation and configuration of system and application software, and shared network resources. The server administration course covers all aspects of implementing TCP/IP network services on UNIX platforms. The final required course covers the use of standard and third-party tools and utilities. Detailed descriptions of the elective courses are available on Learning Tree International's Web site (see the Resources section that follows).

After completing this certification program, candidates will be able to install and configure UNIX on a workstation; manage and provide local system resources; create, edit, find, manage, and protect files in the UNIX directory hierarchy; use the UNIX shells, useful commands, scripts and shortcuts; centralize and distribute UNIX resources among appropriate servers; and optimize UNIX server and network performance.

Who Needs It This certification is a good vendor-independent credential for those who want to get a position working with UNIX operating systems from multiple vendors. Since their certification programs require comprehensive training classes, Learning Tree International certifications offer a way for you to gain hands-on experience and training that may not currently be available to you on the job.

Requirements for Certification The certification process requires the following steps:

1. Complete these four core courses and pass the test given at the end of each course:

Course Number	Length	Course
Course 336	four days	UNIX, A Hands-On Introduction
Course 435	four days	UNIX Workstation Administration: Hands-On
Course 436	four days	UNIX Server Administration: Hands-on
Course 396	four days	Hands-On UNIX Tools and Utilities

2. Complete one elective course from the list below and pass the test given at the end of that course:

Course Number	Length	Course
Course 434	four days	KornShell Programming, Hands-On

Course Number	Length	Course
Course 367	four days	Hands-On Introduction to TCP/IP
Course 467	four days	Hands-On Internetworking with TCP/IP
Course 158	four days	UNIX and Windows NT Integration, Hands-On
Course 468	four days	Internet and System Security: Attacks and Countermeasures
Course 433	four days	UNIX System and Network Security, Hands-On
Course 488	four days	Deploying Internet and Intranet Firewalls, Hands-On
Course 333	four days	Hands-On UNIX Programming
Course 363	four days	Hands-On TCP/IP Programming
Course 338	four days	Hands-On C Programming

Administrator   Learning Tree International (see the Resources section for contact information).

Fee   At this writing, the prices for Learning Tree International courses are $1295 for a two-day course, $1745 for a three-day course, $2195 for a four-day course, and $2495 for a five-day course. Learning Tree International offers some significant discounts for those taking more than one course and for government employees. There is no additional charge for the tests.

Format   Each exam consists of 40 to 60 questions. If you fail a test on the first try, Learning Tree International will arrange for you to take a proctored exam at your place of work.

Resources

For more information on this organization's courses and certification programs, contact Learning Tree International at:

Web http://www.learningtree.com

E-mail uscourses@learningtree.com

Mail 1805 Library Street
   Reston, VA 20190-5630

Phone (800) THE-TREE

Fax   (800) 709-6405

Microsoft Certification

The Microsoft Certified Professional designation is an entry-level certification that denotes expertise with at least one Microsoft Windows operating system. Formerly known as the Microsoft Certified Product Specialist, this certification is designed for those who want to demonstrate their proficiency with Microsoft Windows 95, Windows NT, or Windows NT Server.

The Microsoft Certified Professional certification is intended as a stepping stone to one of Microsoft's premium certifications: the Microsoft Certified Systems Engineer (MCSE), MCSE + Internet, or the Microsoft Certified Solution Developer (MCSD). See Chapters 7, 9, and 11, respectively, for more information on these three certifications.

Recertification or Maintenance Requirements   As Microsoft introduces new products and new versions of its operating systems, it retires the tests for previous versions. If your certification is based on a test that Microsoft is retiring, you will be informed by certified mail of the need to take a current test to maintain your certification. You will have at least six months to complete this new test; if you do not take the test your status as a MCP will no longer be valid.

Benefits of Certification   Microsoft Certified Professionals receive the following benefits:

- An MCP certificate

- Access to technical information through a secured MCP-only Web site

- Use of MCP logos on stationery and business cards

- Invitations to Microsoft-sponsored conferences and technical briefings

- A free subscription to *Microsoft Certified Professional* magazine

Microsoft Certified Professional

Attaining this certification requires passing one exam. Candidates have the choice of specializing in Microsoft Windows 95, Windows NT, or Windows NT Server. The test for each operating system covers the basic concepts and skills involved with installing, using, and troubleshooting the system.

The candidate is expected to have hands-on experience with the product prior to attempting the exam. Microsoft's Web site provides exam guidelines, sample tests, and links to authorized training providers (see the Resources section that follows).

Who Needs It The MCP certification is an excellent entry point for technical professionals getting into network and system administration of Microsoft operating systems. This certification is also valuable to support and help desk personnel.

Requirements for Certification The certification process requires only one step:

1. Pass one of the following operating system exams:

Sylvan ID	Exam
70-073	Implementing and Supporting Microsoft Windows NT Workstation 4.02
70-067	Implementing and Supporting Microsoft Windows NT Server 4.0
70-064	Implementing and Supporting Microsoft Windows 95
70-160	Microsoft Windows Architecture I
70-161	Microsoft Windows Architecture II

Administrator Call Sylvan Prometric at (800) 755-3926 to register for a Microsoft exam. (See Chapter 15 for detailed information on taking tests from Sylvan.)

Fee $100

Format Multiple-choice, closed-book tests. The number of questions and time limit depend on the test selected.

Microsoft offers the MCP + Internet certification to MCPs who pass the Implementing and Supporting Microsoft Windows NT Server 4.0 exam and two additional tests. If you think this is a certification you may want in the future, be sure to take the NT Server 4.0 exam as your operating system exam for the MCP certification. (See Chapter 9 for more information on the MCP + Internet certification.)

Resources

For more information on this certification program, contact Microsoft at:

Web `http://www.microsoft.com/mcp/`

E-mail `mcp@msprograms.com`

Mail Microsoft Corporation
One Microsoft Way
Redmond, WA 98052-6399

Phone (800) 636-7544

Fax (206) 936-7329

Santa Cruz Organization Certifications

The Santa Cruz Organization (SCO) makes a UNIX-based operating system called SCO UNIX. The SCO Advanced Certified Engineer (ACE) certification program is for technical professionals who use SCO's version of UNIX. Three SCO ACE program tracks are offered: Server Track, Open Server Release 5 Track, and UNIXWare 2.1 Track.

Recertification or Maintenance Requirements SCO's current policy on recertification is that you can retain your certification indefinitely, although SCO reserves the right to change its recertification policy in the future. So, technically, there is no recertification requirement. If you want to continue to receive the benefits given to SCO ACEs, however, you must take a recertification test every year.

SCO ACE recertification exams are comprehensive two-hour tests that consist of approximately 80 multiple-choice questions. Currently, recertification involves passing one of the following exams: SCO OpenServer Release 5 Recertification (Sylvan ID: 090-153); SCO

Unixware 2.1 Recertification (Sylvan ID: 090-154); SCO Recertification/LMU (Sylvan ID: 090-102); or SCO Recertification/UUCP (Sylvan ID: 090-101).

Benefits of Certification SCO ACEs receive the following benefits:

- A certificate, lapel pin, certification desk trophy, and logo stickers

- Logo for use on business cards and stationery

- A copy of the SCO Support Library on CD-ROM

- Access to SCO online support through the SCO bulletin board

- Companies employing an SCO ACE receive a 10 percent discount on selected products

Santa Cruz Organization Advanced Certified Engineer (SCO ACE): Server Track

Attaining this certification involves passing four tests. SCO offers a preparation course for each exam. These courses are not required, but the content of each of the courses is closely aligned with the corresponding exam. The recommended courses include SCO UNIX V/386 System Administration; Basic Communications: UUCP Administration; Shell Programming for System Administrators; and, finally, SCO TCP/IP and SCO NFS: Administration and Configuration (see the Resources section that follows for more information).

In preparing for the four tests, remember that the exams are open book: It is not important to memorize specific details. Instead, practice using the system and resolving problems. Sample exam questions can be found on SCO's Web site.

Who Needs It The SCO ACE: Server Track certification is designed for system administrators who will be supporting UNIX-based servers. This designation can help you get a job administering UNIX servers and networks, whether they are SCO-based or not.

Requirements for Certification The certification process requires the following steps:

1. Pass the SCO UNIX System Administration test (Sylvan ID: 090-001).

2. Pass the SCO Basic Communications: UUCP Administration test (Sylvan ID: 090-005).

3. Pass the SCO Shell Programming for System Administrators test (Sylvan ID:090-056).

4. Pass the SCO TCP/IP and SCO NFS Administration and Configuration test (Sylvan ID: 090-004).

From the time the first exam is taken, a candidate has one year to successfully complete the remaining SCO ACE requirements.

Administrator Call Sylvan Prometric at (800) 775-3926 to register for an SCO exam. (See Chapter 15 for detailed information on taking tests from Sylvan.)

Fee One-hour exams cost $125; two-hour exams cost $180.

Format The exams are multiple choice. They consist of 40 or 80 questions, and last one or two hours. Passing score on each exam is 80 percent.

SCO exams are open book. SCO allows candidates to take any written materials to the exam, including SCO documentation, notes, and third-party books and documentation. The candidate is prohibited, however, from bringing a laptop computer or removing any notes taken during the exam.

SCO ACE: Open Server Release 5 Track

Attaining this certification requires passing three tests. SCO offers a preparation course for each exam. These courses are not required, but the content of each of the courses is closely aligned with the corresponding exam. SCO recommends the following courses as preparation for the exams listed below: SCO OpenServer Release 5 System Administration I User Services; SCO OpenServer Release 5 System Administration II Installation, Configuration and Maintenance; Shell Programming for System Administrators; and SCO OpenServer Network Administration (see the Resources section that follows for more information).

In preparing for the exams, remember that the exams are open book: It is not important to memorize specific details. Instead, practice using the system and resolving problems. Sample exam questions can be found on SCO's Web site.

Who Needs It   The SCO ACE: OpenServer Track certification is designed for system administrators who will be dealing specifically with release 5 of the SCO OpenServer product. This designation can help you get a job administering and troubleshooting OpenServer Release 5 servers and networks.

Requirements for Certification   The certification process requires the following steps:

1.   Pass the SCO OpenServer Release 5 Administration test (Sylvan ID: 090-052).

2.   Pass the SCO Shell Programming for System Administrators test (Sylvan ID: 090-056).

3. Pass the SCO OpenServer Release 5 Network Administration test (Sylvan ID: 090-054).

From the time the first exam is taken, a candidate has one year to successfully complete the remaining SCO ACE requirements.

Administrator Call Sylvan Prometric at (800) 775-3926 to register for an SCO exam. (See Chapter 15 for detailed information on taking tests from Sylvan.)

Fee One-hour exams cost $125; two-hour exams cost $180.

Format The exams are multiple choice. They consist of 40 or 80 questions, and last one or two hours respectively. Passing score on each exam is 80 percent.

SCO exams are open book. SCO allows candidates to take any written materials to the exam, including SCO documentation, notes, and third-party books and documentation. The candidate is prohibited, however, from bringing a laptop computer or removing any notes taken during the exam.

SCO ACE: UnixWare 2.1 Track

Attaining this certification involves passing three tests. SCO offers a preparation course for each exam. These courses are not required, but the content of each course is closely aligned with the corresponding exam. SCO recommends the following courses as preparation for the exams listed below: SCO UnixWare 2.1 System Administration; SCO UnixWare 2.1 Advanced System Administration; SCO UnixWare 2.1 Installation and Configuration; Shell Programming for System Administrators; and SCO OpenServer Network Administration (see the Resources section that follows for more information).

In preparing for the exams, remember that the exams are open book: It is not important to memorize specific details. Instead, practice using the system and resolving problems. Sample exam questions can be found on SCO's Web site.

Who Needs It   The SCO ACE: UnixWare Track certification concentrates on the UnixWare workstation product. This designation can help you get a job administering and installing SCO UNIX workstations, servers, and networks.

Requirements for Certification   The certification process requires the following steps:

1.   Pass the SCO UnixWare 2.1 Administration test (Sylvan ID: 090-075).

2.   Pass the SCO Shell Programming for System Administrators test (Sylvan ID: 090-056).

3.   Pass the SCO OpenServer Release 5 Network Administration test (Sylvan ID: 090-054).

From the time the first exam is taken, a candidate has one year to successfully complete the remaining SCO ACE requirements.

Administrator   Call Sylvan Prometric at (800) 775-3926 to register for an SCO exam. (See Chapter 15 for detailed information on taking tests from Sylvan.)

Fee   One-hour exams cost $125; two-hour exams cost $180.

Format   The exams are multiple choice. They consist of 40 or 80 questions, and last one or two hours. Passing score on each exam is 80 percent.

SCO exams are open book. SCO allows candidates to take any written materials to the exam, including SCO documentation, notes, and third-party books and documentation. The candidate is prohibited, however, from bringing a laptop computer or removing any notes taken during the exam.

Resources

SCO exam preparation courses—which are two to five days long—are available at SCO Authorized Education Centers (AECs). SCO's Web site offers sample test questions, test objectives and a listing of AECs and training courses. Self-study materials are not available. For more information on this organization's courses and certification program, contact SCO at:

Web   http://www.sco.com

E-mail   aceinfo@sco.com

Mail   Santa Cruz Organization
           400 Encinal
           P.O. Box 1900
           Santa Cruz, CA 95061-1900

Phone   (800) 726-8649

Fax   (800) 709-6405

Silicon Graphics Certifications

Silicon Graphics, founded in 1982, offers a wide range of computing systems and related products. Their computers—from desktop workstations to Cray supercomputers—are used in manufacturing, government, science, telecommunications, and entertainment.

Silicon Graphics's UNIX operating system is called IRIX. The Certified IRIX System Administrator program became available in October, 1997. This certification can be augmented with a specialization in network administration.

Recertification or Maintenance Requirements The IRIX system and network administration designations apply to specific version numbers of the operating system, so there is no requirement for recertification on a particular version. Since your certification is tied to a certain version of a product, however, you will want become certified on the newest versions when they become available, if you want to continue to have the most current credential in this area.

Benefits of Certification Certified IRIX System and Network Administrators receive these benefits:

- Use of certification logo
- Certificate

Silicon Graphics Certified IRIX 6.*x* System Administrator

Attaining this certification involves passing two exams. Silicon Graphics recommends taking three courses in preparation for the exams: Introduction to IRIX; either the System Administration course or the IRIX Specific System Administration course; and Advanced System Administration. The company offers instructor-led, computer-based, and self-paced courses.

Who Needs It   This certification lets employers know that you are proficient in administrating and maintaining Silicon Graphics IRIX systems. It can be valuable for getting a job as a system administrator in a company that uses Silicon Graphics workstations.

Requirements for Certification   The certification process requires the following steps:

1.   Pass the Silicon Graphics IRIX System Administration test.

2.   Pass the Silicon Graphics IRIX Advanced System Administration test.

Administrator   Call Sylvan Prometric at (800) 815-3926 to register for a Silicon Graphics exam. (See Chapter 15 for detailed information on taking tests from Sylvan.)

Fee   Fees for Silicon Graphics tests vary based on test length and format; call Sylvan Prometric at (800) 815-3926 for pricing.

Format   Computer-based, multiple-choice test. Call Sylvan Prometric at (800) 815-3926 for current information on the number of questions, time limit, and passing score.

Silicon Graphics Certified IRIX Network Administrator

This certification builds on the Silicon Graphics Certified IRIX 6.*x* System Administrator certification program described above. To achieve the network administrator certification, a candidate must pass one additional exam. Silicon Graphics recommends taking their Network Administration course in preparation for this exam.

Who Needs It This certification lets employers know that you are proficient in networking and administrating Silicon Graphics IRIX systems. It can be valuable for getting a job as a network administrator in a company that uses Silicon Graphics workstations.

Requirements for Certification The certification process requires the following steps:

1. Achieve certification as a Silicon Graphics Certified IRIX System Administrator (see previous section).

2. Pass the Silicon Graphics IRIX Network Administration exam.

Administrator Call Sylvan Prometric at (800) 815-3926 to register for a Silicon Graphics exam. (See Chapter 15 for detailed information on taking tests from Sylvan.)

Fee Fees for Silicon Graphics tests vary based on test length and format; call Sylvan Prometric at (800) 815-3926 for pricing.

Format Computer-based, multiple-choice test. Call Sylvan Prometric at (800) 815-3926 for current information on the number of questions, time limit, and passing score.

Resources

This company offers instructor-led, computer-based, and self-paced courses to prepare you for their certification exams. For more information on this organization's courses and certification programs, contact Silicon Graphics at:

Web   http://www.sgi.com/

Mail   Silicon Graphics, Inc
          2011 N. Shoreline Blvd.
          Mountain View, CA 94043

Phone   (800) 800-4744

Fax   (650) 932-0309

Sun Certifications

Sun Microsystems, Inc., the originator of the Java programming language, is well known for its high performance computer systems. The Solaris operating system is Sun's version of UNIX. Sun's Certified Solaris Administrator certification program validates technical expertise in using and administering Solaris-based systems. Like other UNIX vendors, Sun also offers a Certified Network Administrator credential that builds on the System Administrator designation.

Recertification or Maintenance Requirements The Solaris system and network administration designations apply to specific version numbers of the operating system, so there is no requirement for recertification on a particular version. Since your certification is tied to a certain version of a product, however, you will want become certified on the newest versions, when they become available, if you want to continue to have the most current credential in this area.

Benefits of Certification Sun Certified Solaris Administrators receive a logo for use on business cards and materials.

Sun Certified Solaris Administrator

Attaining this certification involves passing two exams. These exams cover the basic installation and operation of the Solaris operating system (as of this writing, certification is available for version 2.5).

Sun recommends these two instructor-led courses as preparation for the Solaris 2.5 System Administrator exam: Course SA-135: Solaris 2.x System Administration Essentials ($2195), and Course SA-285: Solaris 2.x System Administration ($2195). Media-based courses are also offered (see the Resources section that follows for contact information).

Who Needs It This certification lets employers know that you are proficient in administrating and maintaining Sun Solaris systems. It can be valuable for getting a job as a system administrator in a company that uses Sun workstations.

Requirements for Certification The certification process requires the following steps:

1. Pass the Solaris 2.5 System Administrator Exam: Part I (Sylvan ID: 310-005).

2. Pass the Solaris 2.5 System Administrator Exam: Part II (Sylvan ID: 310-006).

Administrator Call Sun Educational Services at (800) 422-8020 to purchase an exam voucher. You will receive the voucher by mail, as well as information on how and when to take the exam. The exams are taken through Sylvan Prometric.

Fee $150 per test

Format The Solaris 2.5 System Administrator Exam: Part I has 108 questions and must be completed in 90 minutes; the passing score is 63 percent. The Solaris 2.5 System Administrator Exam: Part II consists of 83 multiple-choice questions which must be completed in 90 minutes; the passing score is 67 percent.

Sun Certified Solaris 2.5 Network Administrator

This certification builds on the Solaris 2.5 Administrator certification. Attaining this certification involves passing one additional exam. The Network Administrator test covers networking and security aspects of Solaris 2.5.

Sun recommends that those who are preparing to take the Solaris 2.5 Network Administrator exam take Course SA-380: Solaris 2.x Network Administrator ($2495).

Who Needs It This certification lets employers know that you are proficient in networking and administrating Sun Solaris systems. It can be valuable for getting a job as a network administrator in a company that uses Sun workstations.

Requirements for Certification The certification process requires the following steps:

1. Become a Solaris 2.5 System Administrator.

2. Pass the Sun Certified Network Administrator Exam for Solaris 2.5 (Sylvan ID: 310-040).

Administrator   Call Sun Educational Services at (800) 422-8020 to purchase an exam voucher. You will receive the voucher by mail, as well as information on how and when to take the exam. The exam is taken through Sylvan Prometric.

Fee $150

Format   The Sun Certified Network Administrator Exam for Solaris 2.5 has 77 questions and must be completed in 90 minutes; the passing score is 70 percent.

Resources

Sun Educational Services offers instructor-led courses for those who are preparing for Solaris certification tests. Each course involves both classroom instruction and lab work. Media-based courses are also available. For more information on this organization's courses and certification programs, contact Sun at:

Web	http://suned.sun.com/suned/
E-mail	who2contact@chocolate.ebay.sun.com
Mail	Sun Microsystems 901 San Antonio Road Palo Alto, CA 94303
Phone	(800) 422-8020
Faxback	(800) 564-4341 (code #250)

CHAPTER

5

Software Certifications

FEATURING

- Adobe Certifications

- Baan Certifications

- Corel Certifications

- Lotus Certifications

- Microsoft Certifications

T his chapter contains a number of certifications that are of interest to all computer users, and not targeted exclusively to the technical professional. The certifications described in this chapter range from those for common word processing and spreadsheet programs—such as the Microsoft Office or the Corel WordPerfect suites of products—to very specialized business applications. These credentials can be invaluable to proficient software users who want to have evidence of their true abilities.

Employers will also want to be aware of these certifications. Too many employers have been burned by hiring a person who claimed to know how to use a certain software product, only to find out later that the new employee had no idea how to start the program, let alone use it! Another benefit for employers and employees is that the programs for these software certifications offer well-defined curricula for in-house training programs and the certification tests provide benchmarks for successful training.

Professionals seeking software certifications might include:

- Office support personnel
- Graphic designers
- Desktop publishing experts
- Electronic imaging professionals
- Web designers
- Financial clerks
- Help desk personnel
- Architects
- Engineers and mechanical designers

A wide array of software certifications is currently available. Adobe offers the Adobe Certified Expert certification for a number of its products. Baan, a maker of business intelligence software, offers both basic and advanced certifications. Corel's certification program includes two levels of certification on its WordPerfect, Quattro Pro, and Presentations programs. Lotus offers a wide variety of certifications on its software. In addition, Microsoft offers several levels of certification on its Microsoft Office products.

Adobe Certifications

Adobe produces a number of excellent page layout and imaging programs used in desktop publishing and for producing Web pages. Adobe's PhotoShop has become the *de facto* standard for creating and manipulating images. Adobe also developed the Portable Document Format, which is a platform-independent file format for preserving page layout information—including graphics—that is widely used on the Web.

Adobe's certification programs—including the Adobe Certified Expert program and the Adobe Certified Instructor credential (see Chapter 10 for more information)—are part of the Adobe Solution Provider Program. Adobe Solution Providers are third-party organizations that partner with Adobe to design, develop, and implement Adobe-based solutions in various types of organizations.

The Adobe Certified Expert program allows users to certify their expertise with a number of Adobe products, including Illustrator 7.0, Acrobat 3.0, After Effects 3.1, FrameMaker 5.5, PageMaker 6.5, PageMill 2.0, and PhotoShop 4.0.

Recertification or Maintenance Requirements Adobe requires Adobe Certified Experts (ACEs) to update their certifications within six months of the release of a new version of the product for which they are certified. Adobe notifies ACEs of new product releases and related exam information by e-mail. As an ACE, you will be eligible for a 25 percent discount when taking a test to update your certification.

Benefits of Certification Adobe Certified Experts receive these benefits:

- Logo for use on business cards and stationery

- Product-specific certificate and wallet certification card

- An Adobe pin

- Discounts on Adobe Press books purchased from Macmillan Computer Publishing

Adobe Certified Expert: Illustrator 7.0

Illustrator 7.0 is the latest version of Adobe's sophisticated illustration and drawing program. The exam for this certification tests the candidate's knowledge of Illustrator concepts and program operation. You will need to know basic Illustrator terms and concepts; how to use filters, pens, and other tools; how to manipulate color; and how to import and export files (see the exam bulletin on the Adobe Web site for more information).

Who Needs It This certification can help you get a job in the production of graphics, art, or technical drawings using Illustrator. This certification may also be valuable to freelance artists and Web page designers.

Requirements for Certification The certification process requires only one step:

1. Pass the Adobe Illustrator 7.0 Certified Expert test (Sylvan ID: 9A0-005).

Administrator Call Sylvan Prometric at (800) 356-3926 to register for a Adobe exam. (See Chapter 15 for detailed information on taking tests from Sylvan.)

Fee $150. If the first attempt is unsuccessful, a 25 percent discount is given on repeat attempts.

Format This test consists of 60–90 multiple-choice questions and must be completed in 85 minutes.

Adobe Certified Expert: Acrobat 3.0

Acrobat 3.0 is a program for creating and publishing documents in the Portable Document Format (PDF). This format allows users to view, print, and annotate documents—independent of any one operating system or page-layout program—while retaining all the page layout information, including graphics and images. The exam for this certification tests the candidate's knowledge of Acrobat concepts and program operation, including the creation and viewing of PDF files.

Who Needs It This certification can help you get a job or independent contract work in desktop publishing.

Requirements for Certification The certification process requires only one step:

1. Pass the Adobe Acrobat 3.0 Certified Expert test (Sylvan ID: 9A0-007).

Administrator Call Sylvan Prometric at (800) 356-3926 to register for a Adobe exam. (See Chapter 15 for detailed information on taking tests from Sylvan.)

Fee $150. If the first attempt is unsuccessful, a 25 percent discount is given on repeat attempts.

Format This test consists of 60–90 multiple-choice questions and must be completed in 85 minutes.

Adobe Certified Expert: After Effects 3.1

After Effects 3.1 is a program for creating digital compositions, 2D animations, and special effects for multimedia programs, the Web, TV, and film. The exam for this certification tests the candidate's knowledge of After Effects concepts and program operation, including animation, motion controls, and advanced special effects (see the exam bulletin on the Adobe Web site for more information).

Who Needs It After Effects certification can help you get a job or independent contract work in Web design or the production of graphic art, TV, or film.

Requirements for Certification The certification process requires only one step:

1. Pass the Adobe After Effects 3.1 Certified Expert test (Sylvan ID: 9A0-010).

Administrator Call Sylvan Prometric at (800) 356-3926 to register for a Adobe exam. (See Chapter 15 for detailed information on taking tests from Sylvan.)

Fee $150. If the first attempt is unsuccessful, a 25 percent discount is given on repeat attempts.

Format This test consists of 60–90 multiple-choice questions and must be completed in 85 minutes.

Adobe Certified Expert: FrameMaker 5.5

Adobe FrameMaker 5.5 is a document authoring and publishing package that includes tools for writing and distributing long, structured, content-rich documents across all major computing platforms. The exam for this certification tests the candidate's knowledge of FrameMaker concepts and program operation, including character and paragraph formatting, tables, document design, and hypertext links (see the exam bulletin on the Adobe Web site for more information).

Who Needs It This certification can help you get a job in publishing, layout design, or electronic document management using Framemaker. This certification may also be valuable to independent publishers.

Requirements for Certification The certification process requires only one step:

1. Pass the Adobe FrameMaker 5.5 Certified Expert test (Sylvan ID: 9A0-004).

Administrator Call Sylvan Prometric at (800) 356-3926 to register for a Adobe exam. (See Chapter 15 for detailed information on taking tests from Sylvan.)

Fee $150. If the first attempt is unsuccessful, a 25 percent discount is given on repeat attempts.

Format This test consists of 60–90 multiple-choice questions and must be completed in 85 minutes.

Adobe Certified Expert: PageMaker 6.5

PageMaker is Adobe's popular desktop publishing program. The exam for this certification tests the candidate's knowledge of Page-Maker concepts and program operation, including working with color, graphics, typestyles, plug-ins, table editors, and book features. Adobe is the only company that currently offers a certification program in desktop publishing.

Who Needs It This certification can help you get a job in publishing or layout design using PageMaker. This certification may also be valuable to independent publishers.

Requirements for Certification The certification process requires only one step:

1. Pass the Adobe PageMaker 6.5 Certified Expert test (Sylvan ID: 9A0-008).

Administrator Call Sylvan Prometric at (800) 356-3926 to register for a Adobe exam. (See Chapter 15 for detailed information on taking tests from Sylvan.)

Fee $150. If the first attempt is unsuccessful, a 25 percent discount is given on repeat attempts.

Format This test consists of 60–90 multiple-choice questions and must be completed in 85 minutes.

Adobe Certified Expert: PageMill 2.0

PageMill is a graphical program for creating and editing HTML (Hypertext Markup Language), the language in which Web documents are created. The program allows the user to create Web pages, import images, and publish Web sites without having to learn how to write in HTML. The exam for this certification tests the candidate's knowledge of PageMill concepts and program operation, creating and editing links, creating tables and frames, and publishing Web documents (see the online Adobe exam bulletin for more information).

Who Needs It This certification can help you get a job or independent contract work in Web page design and publishing.

Requirements for Certification The certification process requires only one step:

1. Pass the Adobe PageMill 2.0 Certified Expert test (Sylvan ID: 9A0-009).

Administrator Call Sylvan Prometric at (800) 356-3926 to register for a Adobe exam. (See Chapter 15 for detailed information on taking tests from Sylvan.)

Fee $150. If the first attempt is unsuccessful, a 25 percent discount is given on repeat attempts.

Format This test consists of 60–90 multiple-choice questions and must be completed in 85 minutes.

Adobe Certified Expert: PhotoShop 4.0

PhotoShop is a popular program for manipulating, creating, and formatting images. It is used in both electronic and traditional publishing. The PhotoShop exam tests the user's ability to apply color correction, use PhotoShop tools, import and export files, and deal with pre-press and publishing issues.

Who Needs It   PhotoShop certification is valuable to anyone in publishing—whether electronic or traditional—as well as professional photographers.

Requirements for Certification   The certification process requires only one step:

1. Pass the Adobe PhotoShop 4.0 Certified Expert test (Sylvan ID: 9A0-006).

Administrator   Call Sylvan Prometric at (800) 356-3926 to register for a Adobe exam. (See Chapter 15 for detailed information on taking tests from Sylvan.)

Fee $150. If the first attempt is unsuccessful, a 25 percent discount is given on repeat attempts.

Format   This test consists of 60–90 multiple-choice questions and must be completed in 75 minutes.

Resources

The Adobe Web site offers exam bulletins that detail the objectives of each exam. Adobe's Web site also offers a listing of Adobe Authorized Learning Providers and Adobe Certified Instructors. For more information on this organization's certifications and courses, contact Adobe at:

Web   http://www.adobe.com/supportservice/
            training/aceprogram.html

E-mail   certification@adobe.com

Mail   Certification Coordinator
            Adobe Systems Incorporated
            Mailstop W07-123
            345 Park Avenue
            San Jose, CA 95110-2704

Phone   (800) 685-4172

Fax   (408) 537-4033

Baan Certifications

The Baan Company makes enterprise and inter-enterprise business software used by major corporations around the world. These software products are used for managing manufacturing, distribution, finance, transportation, services, projects, and organizational structure data. Essentially, Baan does for large companies like General Motors what QuickBooks does for a local "mom and pop" computer store.

The current set of business programs are referred to as the Baan IV suite of programs. Baan offers both basic and advanced levels of certification in Baan IV applications. After completing basic certification, advanced certification can be obtained in one of four specialties: Enterprise Logistics, Enterprise Finance, Enterprise Tools, and Enterprise Modeler. Any company that wants to become a Baan consulting or business partner—a company working closely with Baan to design custom applications and installations—must have at least one person on staff who is Baan-certified in at least one specialty.

Recertification or Maintenance Requirements   The Baan certifications apply to a specific version number of Baan products— the Baan IV suite of programs—so there is no requirement for recertification on that version. Since your certification is tied to a certain version of the product, however, you will want become certified on the newer versions when they become available if you want to continue to have the most current Baan credential.

Baan Basic Certification

Baan Basic Certification is a prerequisite to any Baan Advanced Certification. The exam for this certification covers the basic use and operation of the programs in the Baan IV suite. Baan offers an overview multimedia-based training product to help candidates gain an overall understanding of these programs (see the Resources section that follows for information on how to contact Baan about the availability of this product).

Who Needs It   This certification is valuable to anyone who needs to demonstrate basic proficiency with entering data, developing reports, and tracking data using Baan IV products.

Requirements for Certification   The certification process requires only one step:

1.   Pass the Baan Basic Certification for Baan IV test (Sylvan ID: 1AO-160).

Administrator   Call Sylvan Prometric at (800) 304-2226 to register for a Baan exam. (See Chapter 15 for detailed information on taking tests from Sylvan.)

Fee $300

Format Computer-based, multiple-choice test. Call Sylvan Promet-ric at (800) 304-2226 for current information on the number of ques-tions, time limit, and passing score.

Baan Advanced Certification in Enterprise Logistics

This certification builds on the Basic Baan Certification. The exam for this certification focuses on the Baan IV logistics functions—such as manufacturing and distribution—from a business process perspective. The processes covered include make-to-stock, make-to-order, and assemble-to-order processes.

Who Needs It This certification is valuable to professionals in busi-ness management and finance in large corporations that use Baan products.

Requirements for Certification The certification process requires the following steps:

1. Attain Baan Basic Certification (see previous section).

2. Pass the Baan Enterprise Logistics for Baan IV test (Sylvan ID: 1AO-180).

Administrator Call Sylvan Prometric at (800) 304-2226 to register for a Baan exam. (See Chapter 15 for detailed information on taking tests from Sylvan.)

Fee $300

Format   Computer-based multiple-choice test. Call Sylvan Prometric at (800) 304-2226 for current information on the number of questions, time limit, and passing score.

Baan Advanced Certification in Enterprise Finance

This certification builds on the Baan Basic Certification. The exam for this certification tests the candidate's ability to use the finance modules in Baan IV, including General Ledger, Financial Budgets, Financial Statements, Accounts Receivable, Accounts Payable, Cash Management, Fixed Assets, and Cost Allocation.

Who Needs It   This certification is valuable for financial planners and managers in large corporations that use Baan products.

Requirements for Certification   The certification process requires the following steps:

1. Attain Baan Basic Certification (see previous section).

2. Pass the Baan Enterprise Finance for Baan IV test (Sylvan ID: 1AO-190).

Administrator   Call Sylvan Prometric at (800) 304-2226 to register for a Baan exam. (See Chapter 15 for detailed information on taking tests from Sylvan.)

Fee $300

Format   Computer-based, multiple-choice test. Call Sylvan Prometric at (800) 304-2226 for current information on the number of questions, time limit, and passing score.

Baan Advanced Certification in Enterprise Tools

This certification builds on the Baan Basic certification. The exam for this certification tests the ability to administrate and operate the Baan Tools application. The information covered includes configuring the system; system security; initial setup; submitting jobs; and setting up users, menus, jobs, devices, and databases.

Who Needs It This certification is valuable to professionals that support users of Baan products in large corporations.

Requirements for Certification The certification process requires the following steps:

1. Attain Baan Basic Certification (see previous section).

2. Pass the Tools for Baan IV test (Sylvan ID: 1AO-200).

Administrator Call Sylvan Prometric at (800) 304-2226 to register for a Baan exam. (See Chapter 15 for detailed information on taking tests from Sylvan.)

Fee $300

Format Computer-based, multiple-choice test. Call Sylvan Prometric at (800) 304-2226 for current information on the number of questions, time limit, and passing score.

Baan Advanced Certification in Enterprise Modeler

This certification builds on the Baan Basic Certification. The exam for this certification covers the essential concepts of dynamic enterprise modeling—the process of using business data to create dynamic models of company finances and other inputs and outputs.

Who Needs It This certification is valuable to corporate business managers and financial planners in companies that use Baan products.

Requirements for Certification The certification process requires the following steps:

1. Attain Baan Basic Certification (see previous section).

2. Pass the Enterprise Modeler for Baan IV test (Sylvan ID: 1AO-170).

Administrator Call Sylvan Prometric at (800) 304-2226 to register for a Baan exam. (See Chapter 15 for detailed information on taking tests from Sylvan.)

Fee $300

Format Computer-based, multiple-choice test. Call Sylvan Prometric at (800) 304-2226 for current information on the number of questions, time limit, and passing score.

Resources

For more information on this organization's certification program and courses, contact Baan at:

Web   http://www.baan.com/education/certify/

E-mail	training_info@baan.com
Mail	Baan USA Inc.
	4600 Bohannon Drive
	Menlo Park, California, 94025
Phone	(650) 462-4949

Corel Certifications

Corel® WordPerfect® 7
CERTIFIED
EXPERT

Corel Corporation produces excellent word-processing, spread-sheet, presentation, and drafting programs used in offices around the world. Corel offers two levels of certification on its products. The Corel Certified Resource designation is for software users with a good basic understanding of the features and functions of one or more of the Corel WordPerfect Suite programs. The Corel Certified Expert program is for those with more in-depth knowledge of program operation. Both Resource and Expert certifications are available for the following programs in the Corel WordPerfect Suite: WordPerfect, Quattro Pro, and Presentations.

Recertification or Maintenance Requirements The Corel Certified Resource and Expert designations apply to specific version numbers of Corel software products, so there is no requirement for recertification on a particular version. Since your certification is tied to a certain version of a product, you will want to become certified on the newest versions when they become available if you want to continue to have the most current Corel Certified Resource or Expert credential.

Benefits of Certification   As a Corel Certified Resource, you may use the Corel Certified Resource logo on your stationery and business cards.

Corel Certified Experts receive the following benefits:

- Logo for stationery and business cards

- Certificate

- Opportunity to purchase one copy of each product at a significant discount

Corel WordPerfect 7 Certified Resource

WordPerfect is one of the two most popular word processing programs available. The exam for this certification covers the basic features of WordPerfect; it tests the candidate's ability to perform routine tasks on existing documents and to produce new documents using templates.

Who Needs It   This certification can help you get a position as an office professional by demonstrating your ability to use WordPerfect to create, edit, and print documents.

Requirements for Certification   The certification process requires only one step:

1.   Pass the Corel WordPerfect 7 Certified Resource test (Sylvan ID: 770-010).

Administrator Call Sylvan Prometric at (800) 662-6735 to register for a Corel exam. (See Chapter 15 for detailed information on taking tests from Sylvan.)

Fee $55

Format Computer-based, multiple-choice test. This closed-book exam has 54 questions and lasts one hour.

Corel Quattro Pro 7 Certified Resource

Quattro Pro is Corel's spreadsheet program. The exam for this certification covers the basic features of Quattro Pro; it tests the candidate's ability to perform routine tasks on existing spreadsheets and to produce new spreadsheets using templates.

Who Needs It This certification can help you get a position as an office professional by demonstrating your ability to use Quattro Pro to create and use spreadsheets.

Requirements for Certification The certification process requires only one step:

1. Pass the Corel Quattro Pro 7 Certified Resource test (Sylvan ID: 771-020).

Administrator Call Sylvan Prometric at (800) 662-6735 to register for a Corel exam. (See Chapter 15 for detailed information on taking tests from Sylvan.)

Fee $55

Format Computer-based, multiple-choice test. This closed-book exam has 170 questions and lasts 210 minutes.

Corel Presentations 7 Certified Resource

Corel Presentations is a program for making and presenting computer-based slide shows or presentations. The exam for this certification covers the basic features of Presentations; it tests the candidate's ability to create and edit new presentations using templates.

Who Needs It This certification can help you get a position as an office professional by demonstrating your ability to create slide presentations. This certification is also valuable to professionals in any field who create and deliver their own presentations.

Requirements for Certification The certification process requires only one step:

1. Pass the Corel Presentations 7 Certified Resource test (Sylvan ID: 771-030).

Administrator Call Sylvan Prometric at (800) 662-6735 to register for a Corel exam. (See Chapter 15 for detailed information on taking tests from Sylvan.)

Fee $55

Format Computer-based, multiple-choice test. This closed-book exam has 176 questions and lasts 210 minutes.

Corel WordPerfect 7 Certified Expert

WordPerfect is more than just a basic word-processing program. This Corel Certified Expert certification demonstrates the holder's ability to use WordPerfect's advanced features. The exam for this certification covers the production of complex, non-routine documents requiring features such as graphics, charts, formulas, and tables.

Who Needs It This certification can help you get a promotion or a new position as an office professional by demonstrating your advanced skills in producing high-quality documents with WordPerfect.

Requirements for Certification The certification process requires the following steps:

1. Pass the WordPerfect 7 Certified Expert test (Sylvan ID: 770-011).

2. Submit a completed Corel Certified Expert application form along with a $50 application fee.

Administrator Call Sylvan Prometric at (800) 662-6735 to register for a Corel exam. (See Chapter 15 for detailed information on taking tests from Sylvan.)

Fee $80 for the test. Contact Corel for details on the application fee.

Format Computer-based, multiple-choice test. This closed-book exam has 57 questions and must be completed in one hour.

Corel Quattro Pro 7 Certified Expert

Quattro Pro 7 has a number of advanced features; these are the topics of the expert level certification program. The exam for this certification covers the creation of spreadsheets using advanced Quattro Pro features, including complex equations, linking data between documents, and creating graphs and charts.

Who Needs It This certification can help you get a promotion or a new position as an office professional by demonstrating your advanced skills in using Quattro Pro, including the production of high-quality charts and graphs.

Requirements for Certification The certification process requires the following steps:

1. Pass the Quattro Pro 7 Certified Expert test (Sylvan ID: 771-021).

2. Submit a completed Corel Certified Expert application form along with a $50 application fee.

Administrator Call Sylvan Prometric at (800) 662-6735 to register for a Corel exam. (See Chapter 15 for detailed information on taking tests from Sylvan.)

Fee $80 for the test. Contact Corel for details on the application fee.

Format Computer-based, multiple-choice test. This closed-book exam has 169 questions and must be completed in 210 minutes.

Corel Presentations 7 Certified Expert

The exam for this expert level certification tests the candidate's ability to use the advanced features of the Corel Presentations 7 program, including creating presentations from scratch and integrating images, movies, and sound into presentations.

Who Needs It This certification can help you get a position as an office professional by demonstrating your ability to create top-quality slide presentations. This certification is also valuable to professionals in any field who create and deliver their own presentations.

Requirements for Certification The certification process requires the following steps:

1. Pass the Presentations 7 Certified Expert test (Sylvan ID: 771-031).

2. Submit a completed Corel Certified Expert application form along with a $50 application fee.

Administrator   Call Sylvan Prometric at (800) 662-6735 to register for a Corel exam. (See Chapter 15 for detailed information on taking tests from Sylvan.)

Fee $80 for the test. Contact Corel for details on the application fee.

Format   Computer-based, multiple-choice test. This closed-book exam has 181 questions and must be completed in 210 minutes.

Resources

Exam guidelines are available from the Corel Web site and through the Corel faxback service. For more information on this organization's certification programs, contact Corel at:

Web	`http://www.corel.com/learning/training/`
E-mail	`custserv2@corel.com`
Mail	Corel Corporation 1600 Carling Avenue Ottawa, Ontario K1Z 8R7
Phone	(800) 772-6735
Fax	(613) 761-9176
Faxback	(613) 728-0826, ext. 3080

Lotus Certifications

Lotus was launched in 1982 with the popular spreadsheet program, Lotus 1-2-3. Since that time, Lotus has branched out into several other areas, including business collaboration (Lotus Notes) and the Internet (Lotus Domino). Lotus now offers certification programs related to Lotus Notes, Lotus Domino, and the Lotus e-mail system, cc:Mail. These programs certify technical expertise in system administration or in developing applications using the object-oriented scripting language included with Lotus Notes.

There are two levels of certification: the Certified Lotus Specialist, which is designed for those who have basic technical knowledge of a product, and the Certified Lotus Professional, for those with more in-depth knowledge and experience. To become a Certified Lotus Specialist, an individual must pass one product-specific exam. The Certified Lotus Professional designation follows specific product-related tracks and requires passing several related exams. Certification options include:

- Certified Lotus Specialist

- Certified Lotus Professional Notes Application Developer

- Certified Lotus Professional Principal Notes Application Developer

- Certified Lotus Professional Notes System Administrator

- Certified Lotus Professional Principal Notes System Administrator

- Certified Lotus Professional cc:Mail System Administrator

Recertification or Maintenance Requirements The Certified Lotus Specialist and Certified Lotus Professional designations apply to specific numbers of Lotus software products, so there is no requirement for recertification on a particular release. Since your certification is tied to a certain version of a product, however, you will want to become certified on the newest releases when they become available if you want to continue to have the most current Certified Lotus Specialist or Certified Lotus Professional credential.

Benefits of Certification As a Certified Lotus Specialist or a Certified Lotus Professional you will receive:

- Direct access to technical information
- Welcome kit with certificate, logo sheet, and usage guidelines
- Free subscription to Lotus' bimonthly certification newsletter
- Access to private Lotus Certification Web site
- Invitation to Lotus conferences, technical training, and special events
- Discounts on selected Lotus and IBM events and computer-based training products

Lotus also offers a Certified Lotus Instructor credential for those who want to deliver Lotus education training courses at Lotus Authorized Education Centers. See Chapter 10 for details.

Certified Lotus Specialist (CLS)

Each CLS specializes in one Lotus product and must pass an exam associated with that product. The product options for the CLS certification include Lotus Domino (Web development), Lotus 1-2-3 (spreadsheet), Lotus Notes (collaborative business software), or cc:Mail (e-mail).

The Domino Web Development and Administration exam assesses the candidate's knowledge and skills in developing and deploying Web sites using Domino 4.5. The LotusScript exam tests advanced knowledge of coding and troubleshooting Lotus Script for 1-2-3 applications. The Notes R4 Application Development 1 test and the Notes R4 System Administration 1 tests are described in the "Certified Lotus Professional (CLP)—Application Developer" section that follows. The cc:Mail R6 Systems Administration test is described in the "Certified Lotus Professional (CLP)—cc:Mail System Administrator" section that follows. The Domino Messaging Administration exam tests a candidate's ability to design and deploy Lotus messaging solutions. Some exams are offered in two different formats, as described below.

Who Needs It   The Certified Lotus Specialist credential demonstrates to employers that you can use a particular Lotus product effectively and can be a resource for others in the office. In addition, it is valuable to those in charge of developing Internet- and intranet-based solutions based on Lotus products.

Requirements for Certification   The certification process requires only one step:

1. Pass one of the tests listed below; select the test for the product in which you plan to specialize:

ID	Exam
190-281	Domino Web Development and Administration
190-291	Developing Lotus Script Applications for SmartSuite using 1-2-3 '97
190-271 (multiple-choice)	Notes R4 Application Development 1
190-171 (live-application)	Notes R4 Application Development 1

ID	Exam
190-274 (multiple-choice)	Notes R4 System Administration 1
190-174 (live-application)	Notes R4 System Administration 1
190-251	cc:Mail R6 Systems Administration 1
190-311	Domino Messaging Administration

Administrator   Lotus exams can be taken from Sylvan Prometric (call (800) 745-6887 to register for a Lotus exam) or from CATGlobal (see their Web site at `http://www.catglobal.com/` for registration information). Chapter 15 contains detailed information on taking tests from both Sylvan and CATGlobal.

Fee $90

Format   Some of these tests are offered in two formats: a multiple-choice format or a "live-application" format (a hands-on, performance-based exam in which the candidate performs tasks within the Notes environment). Be sure to ask your testing provider what test format is offered at their centers.

The Developing Lotus Script Applications for SmartSuite using 1-2-3 '97 test is in beta at this writing. Call Lotus for information on the final format of this multiple-choice test.

The Domino Web Development and Administration multiple-choice test consists of 39 questions. The passing score is 82 percent. The Notes Application Development 1 multiple-choice test consists of 37 questions. A score of 75 percent is required to pass. The Notes System Administration 1 multiple-choice test consists of 34 questions. A score of 64 percent is required to pass. The cc:Mail R6 Systems Administration 1 multiple-choice test consists of 36 questions. A score of 77 percent is required to pass. All the tests are one hour long. Tests are revised periodically, so contact Lotus Education for the latest information.

Certified Lotus Professional (CLP): Application Developer

This certification denotes expertise in Notes application architecture, application development, application security, and application documentation. To become a CLP Application Developer, a candidate must pass three tests. The first test is the Notes R4 Application Development 1 test, which assesses the candidate's ability to build a Notes database application. Second, the Notes R4 System Administration 1 test assesses a candidate's ability to set up, operate, and maintain Notes and Domino servers and client workstations. Finally, the Notes R4 Application Development 2 test assesses the candidate's ability to create advanced Notes applications and troubleshoot problems. Each test is offered in two formats, as described below.

Who Needs It   Many employers are eager to hire technical professionals with the CLP designation. The CLP: Application Developer certification demonstrates to employers that you have a high level of competence in developing and troubleshooting complex Lotus Notes applications, and that you can provide high quality support for other Lotus users.

Requirements for Certification   The certification process requires the following steps:

1. Pass the Notes R4 Application Development 1 test: either the multiple-choice test (ID: 190-271) or the live-application test (ID: 190-171).

2. Pass the Notes R4 System Administration 1 test: either the multiple-choice test (ID: 190-274) or the live-application test (ID: 190-174).

   3. Pass the Notes R4 Application Development 2 test: either the multiple-choice test (ID: 190-272) or the live-application test (ID: 190-172).

Administrator Lotus exams can be taken from Sylvan Prometric (call (800) 745-6887 to register for a Lotus exam) or from CATGlobal (see their Web site at `http://www.catglobal.com/` for registration information). Chapter 15 contains detailed information on taking tests from both Sylvan and CATGlobal.

Fee $90 per test

Format These tests are offered in two formats: a multiple-choice format or a "live-application" format (a hands-on, performance-based exam in which the candidate performs tasks within the Notes environment). Be sure to ask your testing provider what test format is offered at their centers.

   The Notes Application Development 1 multiple-choice test consists of 37 questions. A score of 75 percent is required to pass. The Notes System Administration 1 multiple-choice test consists of 34 questions. A score of 64 percent is required to pass. The Notes Application Development 2 multiple-choice test consists of 42 questions. A score of 76 percent is required to pass. All the tests are one hour long. Tests are revised periodically, so contact Lotus Education for the latest information.

Certified Lotus Professional (CLP): Principal Application Developer

The CLP: Principal Application Developer program builds on the CLP: Application Developer certification, and denotes a high level of expertise and ability. The candidate for this level of certification must meet the requirements for the CLP: Application Developer and pass an additional elective test in their selected area of specialization.

Who Needs It   Many employers are eager to hire technical professionals with the CLP designation. The CLP: Principal Application Developer certification demonstrates to employers that you are capable of high-level management of expanding their business solutions by creating workflow and mail-enabled applications.

Requirements for Certification   The certification process requires the following steps:

1. Attain CLP: Application Developer certification (described above).

2. Pass one of the following elective exams:

ID	Exam
190-273	Lotus Script in Notes for Advanced Developers
190-278	Developing Domino Applications for the Web
190-291	Developing LotusScript Applications for SmartSuite Using 1-2-3
190-281	Domino Web Development and Administration

Administrator   Lotus exams can be taken from Sylvan Prometric (call (800) 745-6887 to register for a Lotus exam) or from CATGlobal (see their Web site at http://www.catglobal.com/ for registration information). Chapter 15 contains detailed information on taking tests from both Sylvan and CATGlobal.

Fee $90 per test

Format   The Lotus Script in Notes for Advanced Developers multiple-choice test consists of 39 questions, and must be completed in 60 minutes. A score of 71 percent is required to pass. The Developing Domino Applications for the Web multiple-choice test consists of 38 questions, and must be completed in 60 minutes. A score of 73 percent is required to pass. The Domino Web Development and Administration test has 39 multiple-choice questions and must be completed in 60 minutes. The passing score is 82 percent. The Developing Lotus Script Applications for SmartSuite using 1-2-3 '97 tests is in beta at this writing. Call Lotus for information on the final format of this multiple-choice test.

Certified Lotus Professional (CLP): System Administrator

The CLP: System Administrator certification program covers all aspects of working with Notes servers, managing multiple Notes domains, and controlling Notes communications. Attaining this certification involves passing three tests. This program parallels the CLP: Application Developer program, described previously, and uses two of the same tests. For information on the Notes R4 Application Development 1 and System Administration 1 tests, see the "Certified Lotus Professional (CLP): Application Developer" section. The third required test for this certification—the Notes R4 System Administration 2 test—assesses the candidate's ability to administrate, operate, maintain, and troubleshoot Notes and Domino servers and client workstations.

Who Needs It Many employers are eager to hire technical professionals with the CLP designation. The CLP: System Administrator certification demonstrates to employers that you have a high level of competence in the installation, configuration, maintenance, and operation of Notes servers, and that you can provide high quality support for other Lotus users.

Requirements for Certification The certification process requires the following steps:

1. Pass the Notes R4 Application Development 1 test (see the CLP Application Developer section for details).

2. Pass the Notes R4 System Administration 1 test (see the CLP Application Developer section for details).

3. Pass the Notes R4 System Administration 2 test: either the multiple-choice test (ID: 190-275) or a live-application test (ID: 190-175).

Administrator   Lotus exams can be taken from Sylvan Prometric (call (800) 745-6887 to register for a Lotus exam) or from CATGlobal (see their Web site at http://www.catglobal.com/ for registration information). Chapter 15 contains detailed information on taking tests from both Sylvan and CATGlobal.

Fee $90 per test

Format   These tests are offered in two formats: a multiple-choice format or a "live-application" format (a hands-on, performance-based exam in which the candidate performs tasks within the Notes environment). Be sure to ask your testing provider which test format is offered at their centers.

The Notes Application Development 1 multiple-choice test consists of 37 questions, and must be completed in 60 minutes. A score of 75 percent is required to pass. The Notes System Administration 1 multiple-choice test consists of 34 questions, and must be completed in 60 minutes. A score of 64 percent is required to pass. The Notes Systems Administration 2 multiple-choice test consists of 38 questions, and must be completed in 60 minutes. A score of 76 percent is required to pass.

Certified Lotus Professional (CLP): Principal System Administrator

The CLP Principal System Administrator program builds on the CLP System Administrator certification, and denotes a high level of expertise and ability. The candidate for this level of certification must meet the requirements for the CLP System Administrator and pass an additional elective test in their selected area of specialization.

Who Needs It   Many employers are eager to hire technical professionals with the CLP designation. The CLP: Principal System Administrator certification demonstrates to employers that you are capable of high level management of Lotus Notes, e.g., you can integrate additional technologies into the Lotus Notes environment, and that you can provide high-quality support for other Lotus users.

Requirements for Certification   The certification process requires the following steps:

1.   Attain CLP: System Administrator certification (described previously).

2.   Pass one of the following elective exams:

ID	Exam
190-276	Administrating Specialized Tasks for Domino 4.5
190-251	cc:Mail R6 System Administration

Administrator   Lotus exams can be taken from Sylvan Prometric (call (800) 745-6887 to register for a Lotus exam) or from CATGlobal (see their Web site at http://www.catglobal.com/ for registration information). Chapter 15 contains detailed information on taking tests from both Sylvan and CATGlobal.

Fee $90

Format   The Administrating Specialized Tasks for Domino 4.5 multiple-choice test consists of 39 questions, and must be completed in 60 minutes. A score of 72 percent is required to pass. The cc:Mail R6

System Administration multiple-choice test consists of 36 questions, and must be completed in 60 minutes. A score of 77 percent is required to pass.

Certified Lotus Professional (CLP): cc:Mail System Administrator

The CLP cc:Mail System Administrator certification—the credential for those who work with cc:Mail, the Lotus e-mail system—involves passing two exams. The cc:Mail System Administration 1 test assesses the candidate's ability to set up and operate cc:Mail servers. The cc:Mail System Administration 2 test assesses the candidate's ability to administrate, operate, maintain, and troubleshoot cc:Mail servers and clients. Both tests are available for either cc:Mail R2 or cc:Mail R6.

Who Needs It Many employers are eager to hire technical professionals with the CLP designation. The CLP cc:Mail System Administrator certification demonstrates to employers that you have a high level of competence in the deployment, installation, and configuration of cc:Mail across multiple networks and platforms, and that you can provide high quality support for other Lotus users.

Requirements for Certification The certification process requires the following steps:

1. Pass the cc:Mail R2 System Administration 1 test (ID: 190-051), or the cc:Mail R6 System Administration 1 test (ID: 190-251).

2. Pass the cc:Mail R2 System Administration 2 test (ID: 190-052), or the cc:Mail R6 System Administration 2 test (ID: 190-252).

Administrator Lotus exams can be taken from Sylvan Prometric (call (800) 745-6887 to register for a Lotus exam) or from CATGlobal (see their Web site at `http://www.catglobal.com/` for registration information). Chapter 15 contains detailed information on taking tests from both Sylvan and CATGlobal.

Fee $90 per test

Format The cc:Mail R2 System Administration 1 multiple-choice test consists of 62 questions, and must be completed in 60 minutes. A score of 75 percent is required to pass. The 60-minute cc:Mail R6 System Administration 1 test has 36 multiple-choice questions. Passing score is 77 percent. The cc:Mail R2 System Administration 2 multiple-choice test consists of 50 questions, and must be completed in 60 minutes. A score of 72 percent is required to pass. The 60-minute cc:Mail R6 System Administration 2 test has 39 multiple-choice questions. Passing score is 77 percent.

Resources

For more information on this organization's certification programs, contact Lotus at:

Web	`http://www.lotus.com/`
Mail	Lotus Education Programs
	55 Cambridge Parkway
	Cambridge, MA 02142
Phone	(800) 346-6409 or (617) 693-4436

Microsoft Certifications

The Microsoft Office suite of programs—Word, Excel, Access, Outlook, and PowerPoint—offers an excellent set of tools for business and personal productivity. Microsoft Word is one of the two most popular word processing programs, while the Microsoft Excel spreadsheet program is used by businesses around the world. Access is a database program used by many small businesses. Outlook is an integrated e-mail and communication system. PowerPoint is Microsoft's presentation program.

The Microsoft Office User Specialist (MOUS) designation was introduced in 1997 as a way to certify the skills of users of one or more of the programs offered in the Microsoft Office suite. Three levels of certification are available:

- Microsoft Office Proficient Specialist

- Microsoft Office Expert Specialist

- Microsoft Office Expert

The first two of these certifications can be obtained for Microsoft Office 95 or 97 programs, while the third certification is available only for Office 97.

Recertification or Maintenance Requirements The Microsoft Office User Specialist designations apply to specific version numbers of Microsoft software products, so there is no requirement for recertification on a particular version. Since your certification is tied to a certain version of a product, you will want become certified on the newest versions when they become available if you want to continue to have the most current Microsoft Office User Specialist credential.

Benefits of Certification Microsoft Office User Specialists receive these benefits:

- Use of the Microsoft Office User Specialist logo

- A certificate of accomplishment

Microsoft Office Proficient Specialist

The Proficient Specialist designation is the entry-level certification in the Microsoft Office User series. This level of certification indicates that the holder can perform basic tasks—such as creating new documents, printing and saving documents, basic formatting, and data entry—using a particular Microsoft program. To achieve this certification, the candidate must pass one of the exams listed below. This certification is available for Microsoft Word 95 and 97 and Microsoft Excel 95 and 97 only.

Who Needs It This certification is a great way for office professionals to demonstrate their skills with Word or Excel to current or potential employers. It can be especially valuable to those seeking entry-level office positions.

Requirements for Certification The certification process requires only one step:

1. Pass one of the exams listed below; select the one for the program in which you plan to specialize:

    - Microsoft Word 95 Proficient Specialist

- Microsoft Word 97 Proficient Specialist

- Microsoft Excel 95 Proficient Specialist

- Microsoft Excel 97 Proficient Specialist

Administrator MOUS tests are given at Microsoft Authorized Client Testing (ACT) Centers. Call (800) 933-4493 to register for a test or to locate an ACT center near you.

Fee The suggested price is $50 per test; actual price may vary with location.

Format Performance-based, hands-on test in which you are required to perform a set of basic tasks using the software program for which you are testing. The test takes approximately one hour.

Microsoft Office Expert Specialist

The Expert Specialist designation denotes a higher level of proficiency with a particular Microsoft product than does the Proficient Specialist certification. This certification indicates that the holder can handle more advanced tasks—e.g., advanced formatting and macro creation— using the selected program. This certification also requires passing one exam, and it is not necessary to become a Proficient Specialist before taking the Expert Specialist exam.

This certification level is available for all Office 97 products and some Office 95 products (Excel, PowerPoint and Word only).

Who Needs It This certification is a great way for office professionals to demonstrate to current or potential employers that they have an advanced level of competence with one or more of the Microsoft Office programs.

Requirements for Certification The certification process requires only one step:

1. Pass one of the exams listed below; select the one for the program in which you plan to specialize:

    - Microsoft Access 97 Expert Specialist

    - Microsoft Excel 95 Expert Specialist

    - Microsoft Excel 97 Expert Specialist

    - Microsoft FrontPage 97 Expert Specialist

    - Microsoft Outlook 97 Expert Specialist

    - Microsoft PowerPoint 95 Expert Specialist

    - Microsoft PowerPoint 97 Expert Specialist

    - Microsoft Word 95 Expert Specialist

    - Microsoft Word 97 Expert Specialist

Administrator MOUS tests are given at Microsoft Authorized Client Testing (ACT) Centers. Call (800) 933-4493 to register for a test or to locate an ACT center near you.

Fee The suggested price is $50 per test; actual price may vary with location.

Format Performance-based, hands-on test in which you are required to perform a set of basic tasks using the software program for which you are testing. The test takes approximately one hour.

Microsoft Office Expert

The Expert designation is the highest level of certification in the Microsoft Office User series. This certification indicates that the holder is not only an expert in each of the individual Office 97 products, but is also skilled in using these products in an integrated fashion. For example, a Microsoft Office Expert knows how to use the linking and cross-program abilities of the Microsoft Office Suite to produce Word documents that contain charts and data that are automatically updated when data in the linked Excel spreadsheets is changed.

To attain this certification, the candidate must pass six exams. First, he or she must attain Expert Specialist certification on the five core Microsoft Office 97 products—Word, Excel, Access, Powerpoint, and Outlook. Then the candidate must pass an exam that tests the ability to integrate these products.

Who Needs It   This certification is a great way for office professionals to demonstrate that they have an advanced level of knowledge and skill in using all of the Microsoft Office programs. It can be especially valuable to those seeking office positions with a high level of responsibility.

Requirements for Certification   The certification process requires the following steps:

1.   Attain Expert Specialist status on all five core Office 97 applications (Word, Excel, Access, PowerPoint, and Outlook) as described above.

2.   Pass the Office 97 Integration exam.

Administrator MOUS tests are given at Microsoft Authorized Client Testing (ACT) Centers. Call (800) 933-4493 to register for a test or to locate an ACT center near you.

Fee The suggested price is $50 per test; actual price may vary with location.

Format Performance-based, hands-on test in which you are required to perform a set of basic tasks using the software program for which you are testing. The test takes approximately one hour.

If you want more resources, tips, and suggestions about becoming a Microsoft Office User Specialist (affectionately known as a MOUS), check out *OfficeCert.com* magazine. This magazine is available online at www.OfficeCert.com.

OfficeCert.com provides the latest information on the certification program, tips for passing exams, ideas on how to get your boss to pay for certification, messages from successful candidates, and job listings. In addition, it offers links to training providers, sample tests, and reviews of self-study resources.

Resources

Microsoft Office tests are administered at Microsoft Authorized
Client Testing (ACT) Centers. To register for a test, call (800) 933-
4493 or contact a local ACT Center directly. For more information on
this organization's certifications, contact Microsoft at:

Web	`http://www.microsoft.com/office/train_cert/`
Mail	Microsoft Corporation One Microsoft Way Redmond, WA 98052-6399
Phone	(800) 933-4493
Fax	(425) 936-7329

CHAPTER

6

Networking
Hardware Certifications

FEATURING

- Ascend Certification

- Bay Networks Certifications

- Cisco Certifications

- Learning Tree International Certifications

- Xylan Certifications

I n today's world, if a computer is not networked or capable of connecting to a network in some way, it is like a castway on a desert island—information exchange with the outside world is limited to the occasional floppy in a bottle. Networks have changed many aspects of our daily lives. The Internet, e-mail, and the World Wide Web are what pops into most people's minds when they think of networking, but networks also control electronic credit card transactions, ATMs, electronic card catalogs at the local library, flight control information, medical records and billing, and the telephone system that allows us talk to each other across the world instantaneously.

Just as networks have become vital to business, government, and education, so have the networking professionals who can set up, maintain, and secure networks. Having a good knowledge about networks—and the certification to prove it—is an excellent way to get and keep a good job. Any one of the certifications in this chapter is a valuable credential in the networking field because much the of the knowledge gained in working with a particular product is applicable to products from other vendors.

If you are considering a network-related certification, be sure to also check out Chapter 12 (*Organization-Based Certifications*) for some very important vendor-independent organization-based networking certifications.

Chapter 6 is the first of four chapters that deal with networking. This chapter concentrates on the physical aspects of the network, i.e., the hardware that connects networks together. The following three chapters deal with the operating systems and protocols that run on those networks (Chapter 7), client-server applications and databases (Chapter 8), and, of course, the Internet (Chapter 9).

This chapter covers certifications from the major manufacturers of networking equipment. Ascend offers a certification for its product line, which includes remote access and switching equipment. Bay Networks and Cisco are both well-known for their routers, but are also big players in remote access and switching technology. Bay Networks offers two levels of certification on a number of different types of technology. Cisco's Certified Internetworking Expert (CCIE) program has recently expanded to included three specializations. Learning Tree International offers vendor-independent certification programs in local area networking, wide area networking, and internetworking. Finally, Xylan offers two new certifications in its switching technology product line: the Xylan Switch Specialist and the Xylan Switch Expert.

Networking certifications are in high demand today because of the recent explosive growth of the telecommunications and networking industries. Those who complete networking certification programs will learn how to improve network functionality, maximize network capacity, and promote network stability. Jobs as network designers, network administrators, and a variety of other titles are open to those who obtain these certifications. Persons who might want to pursue certifications described in this chapter include:

- Network administrators

- Internetworking engineers

- Telecommunications consultants

- Local area networking specialists

- Wide area networking designers

- Wide area switching experts

Ascend Certification

Ascend, founded in 1989, is a leading provider of technology and equipment solutions for telecommunications carriers, Internet service providers, and corporate customers worldwide. The company makes devices for remote access, for wide area networking, and for linking telephone switches, network connections, and videoconferencing facilities to phone company networks. Ascend products are used in networks for carrying voice, data, and video information over long distances.

Today, the majority of the leading international telephone companies, global carriers, and network service providers offer Internet access using Ascend equipment. Ascend has installed more than 3,500,000 access concentrator ports (network access points) throughout the world. The MAX WAN access switch family—an Ascend product line—accounts for over 50 percent of the worldwide market share in access concentrators for analog lines, and 62 percent of access concentrators for ISDN PRI lines (The Dell'Oro Group, Quarterly Router and Remote Access Service report for the second quarter of 1997, http://www.delloro.com/).

The Ascend Certified Technical Expert program was developed in 1997 as a way to certify those who have expertise in installing, configuring, and troubleshooting the Ascend remote-access product line. This certification is valuable to technical professionals working with Ascend products. For example, it would be a competitive advantage to Ascend partners who provide remote-access solutions and for technical support staff of Internet service providers using Ascend products.

Recertification or Maintenance Requirements Ascend's program is new and there is currently no announced policy for maintaining certification. However, Ascend is exploring multiple recertification options for Ascend Certified Technical Experts. In addition, Ascend is planning to introduce specialty tracks for the Ascend Certified Technical Expert program, reflecting the specialized roles that technical professionals perform.

Benefits of Certification Ascend Certified Technical Experts receive the following benefits:

- A plaque, lapel pin, and Ascend Certified Technical Expert logos for use on business cards and stationery

- High-level technical service from Ascend

- Access to restricted areas of Ascend's Web site

- Inclusion of your company's name and contact information in a directory of Ascend Certified Technical Experts

Designing the Ascend Certified Technical Expert Certification Program

A company may have a variety of reasons to design a certification program: increased visibility for the company, generation of revenue, or the certification of staff in other companies that represent their products. For Ascend, one of the main reasons for designing the Ascend Certified Technical Expert program was to increase the number of skilled Ascend field personnel (both internal and external). When the skill level of their field personnel is increased, calls to Ascend are less frequent and those calls are usually made by someone who has already done some extensive testing.

Continued on next page

Designing the Ascend Certified Technical Expert Certification Program (continued)

Ascend's decision to include a lab exam was quite deliberate. "We are really looking for the experts, and not just someone who is competent, or at a journeyman level" said Leslie Owens, Ascend's certification program manager, when interviewed recently by phone. "The lab helps us differentiate the borderline person from the real expert. With the written test it is often hard to assess for some issues such as troubleshooting. We really wanted to test real-world expertise. So we felt it was critical to have the lab."

Ascend's biggest challenge in designing this program was to bring together a variety of talented subject-matter experts, both internal and external, to help design the tests and the practical exam. "We relied on subject-matter experts at every step of the way," says Leslie. "Pulling all of this 'people resource' together was the biggest challenge... and a lot of fun."

Ascend Certified Technical Expert

Becoming an Ascend Certified Technical Expert requires passing three tests, the last of which is a hands-on lab test administered at Ascend's headquarters in Alameda, California. The Networking and Telecommunications exam covers advanced networking and telecommunications and explores the technologies on which Ascend products are based. The Remote Access exam covers Ascend's Pipeline, MAX, and Secure Access products. The Technical Expert Troubleshooting lab exam is a two-day test that requires the candidate to configure the Ascend products and third-party management tools, troubleshoot protocol incompatibilities, use debugging and authentication tools, and select and configure bandwidth requirements.

Ascend offers several training courses that can get you started in preparing for the exams. These courses are described in the Resources section. Ascend recommends that candidates have two years of industry experience and three to six months of Ascend product experience prior to attempting certification.

Who Needs It   An Ascend certification is a great credential to get if you are in the field of wide area networking and switching, and have experience with Ascend products. It can help you establish yourself within your organization, or get a new position.

Requirements for Certification   The certification process requires the following steps:

1. Pass the Ascend Networking and Telecommunications test (Sylvan ID: 101).

2. Pass the Ascend Remote Access Exam test (Sylvan ID: 102).

3. Pass the Ascend Certified Technical Expert Troubleshooting lab test.

Administrator   The Networking and Telecommunications (101) and Remote Access (102) tests are administered by Sylvan Prometric. Call (888) 322-ACTE (press option 1), to register for these tests. (See Chapter 15 for additional information on Sylvan Prometric.)

The Certified Technical Expert Troubleshooting lab test is administered by Ascend at their company facilities in Alameda, California, and can be scheduled by calling (888) 322-ACTE (press option 2).

Fee   The first two tests cost $125 each. The two-day lab exam costs $1000.

Format   The networking and telecommunications exam has 75 questions, and must be completed in 90 minutes. The remote access exam has 100 questions, and must be completed in 120 minutes. Both are closed-book, computerized tests.

The lab test is a two-day, hands-on lab exam.

Resources

The primary prerequisite for taking the Ascend Certified Technical Expert tests is extensive hands-on experience with Ascend products. However, Ascend offers several training courses that can help you get started in preparing for the Ascend Certified Technical Expert exams.

The courses Ascend recommends as a first step in preparing for the Remote Access exam are:

- The MAX/Pipeline Course, an instructor-led, three-day course that costs $1200

- The Radius Course, an instructor-led, two-day course that costs $1000

- The Secure Access Course, a $300 CD-ROM–based self-study course

The course recommended as background for the Ascend Certified Technical Expert Troubleshooting lab test is the Advanced Troubleshooting Course, which is an instructor-led, two-day course that costs $1000.

These courses, which are recommended but not required, are offered at Ascend's training centers. Call (888) 322-ACTE (press option 3) to order a self-study course or to register for an instructor-led course. In addition, Ascend's Web site offers a list of test objectives for each exam. For more information on this organization's certification program and courses, contact Ascend at:

Web   `http://www.ascend.com/`

E-mail   `acte@ascend.com`

Mail   Ascend Communications, Inc.
            One Ascend Plaza
            1701 Harbor Bay Parkway
            Alameda, CA 94502

Phone   (888) 322-ACTE

Bay Networks Certifications

Bay Networks is a leader in the worldwide networking market, providing a complete line of products that serve corporate enterprises, service providers, and telecommunications carriers. Bay Networks began in 1994 with the merger of SynOptics Communications, a leading manufacturer of hubs, switches, and network management technology, and Wellfleet Communication, a maker of high-speed routers. Today Bay Networks makes all types of networking devices for corporate networks, Internet service providers and telecommunications carriers. The company offers frame and ATM switches, routers, shared media, remote and Internet Access solutions, IP services and network management applications.

Bay Networks' certification program offers two titles: Bay Networks Certified Specialist and Bay Networks Expert. The Bay Networks Certified Specialist designation recognizes a basic level of technical expertise in one or more Bay Networks technology areas. Currently, Bay Networks offers Specialist-level certifications in Router, Hub, Network Management, Remote Access, and Switching technologies. Bay Networks Certified Experts have demonstrated expertise in building enterprise-wide solutions to network problems. Currently, Bay Networks offers Expert-level certifications in Router, Hub, and Network Management technologies.

Since much of the knowledge gained in these certification programs is independent of the Bay product line, these certifications are valuable not only when dealing with Bay products but also when working with any hub, router, or network management tool. In addition to its certification-related courses, Bay Networks offers a comprehensive curriculum of courses on all aspects of networking.

Recertification or Maintenance Requirements   Certification is specific to a particular version of a product. As a product changes, new certification requirements may be established. Once certified, a candidate will retain their certification status in relation to a specific product release. However, becoming certified on the latest product release ensures that a candidate's product knowledge is accurate and current. In the event that recertification is required, timely notice will be provided by Bay Networks.

Benefits of Certification   Bay Networks Certified Specialists and Experts receive certificates on completion of their training programs, and Bay Networks Certified Experts receive personalized plaques and a Bay Networks gift (different for each technology).

Soon, Bay Networks will be offering the following benefits to Certified Experts:

- Access to technical information on the Web

- Updated technical training via CDs and videos

- Access to second-level support engineers at Bay Networks Technical Support Center, if employed by a Premier Service Provider

Bay Networks Certified Specialist: Hub Technology

Bay Networks Hub Specialist candidates are evaluated and certified based on their knowledge of installing, configuring, and troubleshooting hubs in complex networks. To attain this certification the candidate must pass a hub technology exam, which covers basic knowledge of Bay Networks hub features, connectivity, configuration, and LAN design. Bay Networks recommends these instructor-led courses as preparation for the test: Hub Connectivity (#AV0029196) and FDDI Connectivity (#AV0029031). Self-study courses are also offered; see the Resources section for more information.

Who Needs It   The Bay Networks Certified Specialist: Hub Technology certification is a good way to validate your skills in hub and LAN connectivity. Certification with Bay Networks equipment can be valuable to independent contractors and consultants as well.

Requirements for Certification   The certification process has only one required step:

1. Pass the Bay Networks Hub Specialist electronic test (Sylvan ID: 920-001).

Administrator   This exam is administered by Sylvan Prometric; call (800) 791-3926 to register for Bay Networks tests. (See Chapter 15 for additional information on Sylvan Prometric.)

Fee $125

Format   The Hub Specialist electronic test is a 60-minute multiple-choice test consisting of 77 questions; passing score is 75 percent.

Bay Networks Certified Expert: Hub Technology

This credential builds on the Bay Networks Certified Specialist: Hub Technology certification, and indicates that an individual has in-depth expertise in all of Bay Networks hub technology product lines. To attain this certification, the candidate must pass an additional test administered by Sylvan Prometric, as well as a practical exam delivered at designated Bay Networks corporate sites. The electronic exam covers hub basics, network management, Ethernet network design and troubleshooting, token ring troubleshooting, and features of the supervisory module. The hands-on practical exam evaluates a candidate's ability to design an Ethernet, Token Ring, and FDDI networks and then implement their design using Bay Networks Hubs, Routers, Bridges, and Switches.

Who Needs It   The Bay Networks Certified Expert: Hub Technology certification offers excellent proof of your expertise in designing and managing local area networks. It is a good credential to obtain if you are looking for a way to validate your skills in your current position, or looking for a new position.

Requirements for Certification   The certification process requires the following steps:

1. Attain certification as a Bay Networks Certified Hub Technology Specialist (see previous section).

2. Pass the Bay Networks Certified Hub Expert electronic test (Sylvan ID: 920-005).

3. Pass the Bay Networks Certified Hub practical test (Bay Networks ID: BC0029202).

Candidates seeking this credential must pass all three exams within six months.

Administrator The Hub Expert electronic exam is administered by Sylvan Prometric; call (800) 791-3926 to register for Bay Networks tests. (See Chapter 15 for additional information on Sylvan Prometric.)

Expert practical exams are offered through several worldwide Bay Network corporate locations. To register call (800) 2LANWAN.

Fee The Hub Expert electronic test is $150; the hub practical exam is $400.

Format The Hub Expert electronic test is a 45-minute multiple-choice test consisting of 20 questions; passing score is 75 percent.

The Hub practical exam is a four-hour hands-on exam that may be taken at one of several worldwide Bay Network corporate locations.

Bay Networks Certified Specialist: Router Technology

To become a Bay Networks Certified Specialist: Router Technology, a candidate must pass one test which will evaluate and certify their knowledge of installation and configuration of the Bay Networks Router product family. A Router Specialist candidate must understand basic configurations of the following protocols: LAN using TCP/IP, IPX, RIP, AppleTalk, Transparent Bridge with Spanning Tree, and Source Route Bridge. Knowledge of Site Manager is also required.

To prepare for this test, Bay Networks recommends taking either these two courses—Router Installation & Basic Configuration (#AV0030080) and Router Configuration & Management (#AV0030090)—or this course: Accelerated Router Installation, Configuration and Management (#AV0025110). Self-study courses are also available (see the Resources section for more information).

Who Needs It The Bay Networks Certified Specialist: Router Technology certification is a good way to validate your skill in router installation, configuration, and management. Certification with Bay Networks equipment can also be valuable to independent contractors and consultants.

Requirements for Certification The certification process requires the following steps:

1. Pass the Bay Networks Router Specialist electronic test (Sylvan ID: 920-002).

Administrator This exam is administered by Sylvan Prometric; call (800) 791-3926 to register for Bay Networks tests. (See Chapter 15 for additional information on Sylvan Prometric.)

Fee $125 per test

Format The Router Specialist electronic test is a 60-minute multiple-choice test consisting of 55 questions; passing score is 72 percent.

Bay Networks Certified Expert: Router Technology

This credential builds on the Bay Networks Certified Specialist: Router Technology certification. Candidates are evaluated and certified based on their knowledge of installation and configuration procedures for the Router products with advanced protocols including LAN-Advanced IP, VINES, and DECnet, as well as WAN-Frame Relay, SMDS, X.25, PPP, and Dial Services. To attain the Bay Networks Certified Expert: Router Technology credential, a candidate must pass one exam administered by Sylvan Prometric as well as a practical exam delivered at designated Bay Networks corporate sites.

The Router Expert electronic test covers IP routing and the configuration of LAN and WAN protocols. Bay Networks recommends these courses as preparation for the expert electronic exam: WAN Protocol Implementation (#AV0030131), Advanced IP Routing Technology (#AV0030160), and LAN Protocol Implementation (#AV0030120). The Bay Networks Certified Router practical exam tests the ability to install and configure routers in a multiple protocol environment using Bay Networks site manager. An additional course is recommended as preparation for this exam: Accelerated Router Installation, Configuration and Management (#AV0025110).

Who Needs It The Bay Networks Certified Expert: Router Technology certification offers excellent proof of your expertise with designing and configuring WANs using Bay Networks router technology. It is a good credential to obtain if you are looking for a promotion in your current job, or looking for a job with another company.

Requirements for Certification The certification process requires the following steps:

1. Attain certification as a Bay Networks Certified Specialist: Router Technology (see previous section).

2. Pass the Bay Networks Certified Router Expert Electronic test (Sylvan ID: 920-006).

3. Pass the Bay Networks Certified Router Practical test (Bay Networks ID: BC0030205).

Candidates seeking this credential must pass all three exams within six months.

Administrator The Router Expert electronic test is administered by Sylvan Prometric; call (800) 791-3926 to register for Bay Networks tests. (See Chapter 15 for additional information on Sylvan Prometric.)

Expert practical exams are offered through several worldwide Bay Network corporate locations. To register call (800) 2LANWAN.

Fee The Router Expert electronic test is $150. The router practical test is $500.

Format The Router Expert electronic test is a 60-minute multiple-choice test consisting of 55 questions; passing score is 68 percent.

The Router practical exam is a six-hour hands-on practical exam that may be taken at one of several worldwide Bay Network corporate locations.

Bay Networks Certified Specialist: Network Management Technology

This certification validates an individual's proficiency with network management technology. To become certified as a Bay Networks Certified Specialist: Network Management Technology, the candidate must pass one test. This test covers a variety of network management topics, including performance management, the OSI model, and Bay Networks Optivity management product. Bay Networks recommends the instructor-led Optivity for Windows 6.*x* (#AV00311171) course. Self-study courses are also available (see the Resources section for more information).

Who Needs It The Bay Networks Certified Specialist: Network Management Technology certification is a good way to validate your skill in using the Bay Network Optivity network management product. Certification with Bay Networks equipment can also be valuable to independent contractors and consultants.

Requirements for Certification The certification process requires only one step:

1. Pass the Bay Networks Network Management Technology Specialist electronic test (Sylvan ID: 920-003).

Administrator This exam is administered by Sylvan Prometric; call (800) 791-3926 to register for Bay Networks tests. (See Chapter 15 for additional information on Sylvan Prometric.)

Fee $125 per test

Format The Network Management Technology test is a 90-minute multiple-choice test consisting of 93 questions; passing score is 75 percent.

Bay Networks Certified Expert: Network Management Technology

This credential builds on the Bay Networks Certified Specialist: Network Management Technology certification, and indicates that an individual has in-depth expertise in network management technology. To attain this certification, the candidate must pass an electronic test administered by Sylvan Prometric and a practical exam which is available at various Bay Networks corporate locations.

The Network Management Technology Expert electronic test covers installation and trouble-shooting of LAN and WAN networks, and the use of the Optivity LAN management product. Bay Networks recommends the following preparatory course for the expert electronic exam: Net Management—Optivity Enterprise for UNIX (#AV0025301). The practical exam covers product knowledge and skills, as well as the ability to perform configuration, performance and fault management tasks using Optivity LAN 7.*x* on an Enterprise Network.

Who Needs It The Bay Networks Certified Expert: Network Management Technology certification offers excellent proof of your expertise in managing and troubleshooting LANs and WANs using the Bay Network Optivity network management product. It is a good credential to obtain if you are looking for a promotion in your current job, or looking for a job with another company.

Requirements for Certification The certification process requires the following steps:

1. Attain certification as a Bay Networks Certified Networks Management Technology Specialist (see the previous section).

2. Pass the Bay Networks Network Management Technology Expert electronic test (Sylvan ID: 920-010).

3. Pass the Bay Networks Network Management Technology Expert practical test (Bay Networks ID: BC0031208).

Candidates seeking this credential must pass all three exams within six months.

Administrator The Network Management Technology Expert electronic exam is administered by Sylvan Prometric; call (800) 791-3926 to register for Bay Networks tests. (See Chapter 15 for additional information on Sylvan Prometric.)

Expert practical exams are offered through several worldwide Bay Network corporate locations. To register call (800) 2LANWAN.

Fee The Network Management Technology Expert electronic test is $150. The Network Management Technology practical test is $650.

Format The Network Management Technology Expert electronic test is a 90-minute multiple-choice test consisting of 75 questions; passing score is 75 percent.

The Network Management practical exam is a six-to-eight-hour hands-on test that may be taken at one of several worldwide Bay Network corporate locations.

Bay Networks Certified Specialist: Switching Technology

This certification validates an individual's proficiency with switching technology. To become certified as a Bay Networks Certified Specialist: Switching Technology, the candidate must pass one test, which covers a variety of switching topics, including the 28XXX, 30X, 58K, 350T, and Centillion 100 products. Bay Networks recommends these instructor-led courses as preparation for the test: Centillion (#AV0033193), High-Speed Frame Switching Solutions (#AV0032169), and ATM Technical Tutorial (#AV0025501). Self-study courses are also available (see the Resources section for more information).

Who Needs It The Bay Networks Certified Specialist: Switching Technology certification is a good way to validate your skill with Bay Networks switching products. Certification with Bay Networks equipment can be valuable to independent contractors and consultants as well.

Requirements for Certification The certification process requires only one step:

1. Pass the Bay Networks Switching Technology Specialist electronic test.

Administrator The Bay Networks Switching exam is administered by Sylvan Prometric; call (800) 791-3926 to register for Bay Networks tests. (See Chapter 15 for additional information on Sylvan Prometric.)

Fee $125 per test

Format The Switching Technology Specialist electronic test is a 90-minute multiple-choice test consisting of 75 questions; passing score is 75 percent.

Bay Networks Certified Specialist: Remote Access Technology

This certification validates an individual's proficiency with remote access technology. To become certified as a Bay Networks Certified Specialist: Remote Access Technology, a candidate must pass one test which covers a variety of switching topics, including ISDN, Channel Associated Signaling, PPP, TCP/IP, PPP Multilink, RIP, and RS232. Bay Networks recommends these instructor-led courses as preparation for the test: Introduction to Remote Access with Remote Annex (#AV0025401), and Remote Access Concentrators Solutions (#AV0025402). Self-study courses are also available (see the Resources section for more information).

Who Needs It The Bay Networks Certified Specialist: Remote Access Technology certification is a good way to validate your skill in installing and configuring remote access servers and clients. Certification with Bay Networks equipment can be valuable to independent contractors and consultants as well.

Requirements for Certification The certification process requires only one step:

1. Pass the Bay Networks Remote Access Technology Specialist electronic test (Sylvan ID: 920-012).

Administrator The Bay Networks Remote Access Technology exam is administered by Sylvan Prometric; call (800) 791-3926 to register for Bay Networks tests. (See Chapter 15 for additional information on Sylvan Prometric.)

Fee $125 per test

Format The Remote Access Technology Specialist electronic test is a 90-minute multiple-choice test consisting of 75 questions; passing score is 75 percent.

Resources

Additional information on Bay Networks instructor-led and self-study courses can be found on the company's certification Web site. To register for one of the Bay Networks practical tests, call the Bay Networks Education Services department at (800) 2LANWAN. For more information on this organization's certification programs and courses, contact Bay Networks at:

Web   http://support.baynetworks.com/training/

E-mail   echase@baynetworks.com

Mail   Bay Networks Corporate Headquarters
          4401 Great America Parkway
          Santa Clara, CA 95054

Phone   (978) 916-8357

Cisco Certifications

Cisco is the world's leading manufacturer of routers and internetworking products; over 70 percent of the routers in use today are Cisco products. Cisco was started in 1984 by Stanford professors Leonard Bosack and Sandy Lerner, a husband and wife team who designed and built their own router. Since then, Cisco has grown into a company that sells over $6 billion in networking equipment per year.

The Cisco Certified Internetworking Expert (CCIE) is one of the most coveted vendor-based certifications in the networking field. There are currently only 2000 CCIEs. While there are many benefits to becoming a CCIE, it is not an easy task; 70 percent of those who take the CCIE practical exam fail on their first attempt. As of December 1997, the CCIE designation has been expanded to offer these three areas of specialization: CCIE WAN Switching Expert, CCIE Internet Service Provider (ISP) Dial Expert, and CCIE Routing and Switching Expert.

The CCIE credential is extremely valuable to anyone in the networking field. For some, perhaps the strongest motivation for attempting this certification is that it can be an excellent way to get a job at Cisco.

Recertification or Maintenance Requirements CCIEs are required to maintain their certifications by passing a recertification test and attending a CCIE technical update conference once every 24 months.

Benefits of Certification   Cisco Certified Internetworking Experts receive the following benefits:

- Technical support from senior support engineers in Cisco's Technical Assistance Centers

- Access to CCIE chat forums

- Logo for use on business cards and stationery

- Invitations to special technical training for CCIEs

Cisco Certified Internetworking Expert (CCIE): WAN Switching Expert

To attain this certification, the candidate must first pass a qualification test and then a lab exam. The CCIE: WAN Switching Expert qualifying exam covers general WAN knowledge; time division multiplexing (TDM); knowledge of corporate technologies and applications, including Integrated Services Digital Network (ISDN), Frame Relay, X.25, and Asynchronous Transfer Mode (ATM); knowledge of Cisco-specific technologies; and knowledge of service provider technology. The lab exam requires the candidate to design and implement an ATM network and a frame relay network, troubleshoot an existing WAN switched network, interconnect network nodes, and manage traffic and voice technologies. If a candidate fails the lab exam on the first try, he or she must wait at least 30 days before attempting it again.

Before attempting this certification, Cisco recommends the following preparation: two or more years of internetwork administration, experience with internetwork installation and troubleshooting, extensive experience with Cisco products in a production environment, and familiarity with all Cisco product and service documentation. Cisco offers several training courses for CCIE candidates, and its Web site provides sample tests and detailed information on the test objectives (see the Resources section for more information).

Who Needs It   A CCIE certification is one of the most coveted networking certifications. CCIEs are widely recognized as internetworking experts. Some technical professionals undertake CCIE certification as the first step toward employment with Cisco or with one of their partners.

Requirements for Certification The certification process requires the following steps:

1. Pass the CCIE: WAN Switching Expert qualification exam.

2. Pass the CCIE: WAN Switching Expert lab test.

Administrator The CCIE: WAN Switching Expert qualification exam is administered by Sylvan Prometric; call (800) 204-3926 to register for Cisco tests. (See Chapter 15 for additional information on Sylvan Prometric.)

The CCIE: WAN Switching Expert lab exam is given by Cisco in San Jose, California and London, England. Contact Cisco at (800) 553-NETS (ext. 6387) to schedule your lab test.

Fee The qualification exam costs $200. The lab exam costs $1000.

Format The two-hour, closed-book, computer-based qualification exam has 100 multiple-choice questions; the passing score is 65 percent.

The CCIE: WAN Switching Expert lab exam is a two-day, hands-on practical exam, evaluated by a senior CCIE internetworking engineer. Point values are given for each configuration scenario and problem; an aggregate score of 80 percent is needed to pass.

Cisco Certified Internetworking Expert (CCIE): Internet Service Provider Dial Expert

To attain this certification, the candidate must first pass a qualification exam and then a lab exam. The CCIE: Internet Service Provider Expert qualifying exam covers general ISP dial access knowledge; encryption and authentication technologies; subnetting, static/dynamic, and classless interdomain routing (CIDR) addressing; corporate technologies and services such as Integrated Services Digital Network (ISDN), Multichassis Multilink Point-to-Point Protocol (MMP), virtual private dial network (VPDN); and Cisco-specific dial technologies. The lab exam requires the candidate to implement dial firewall and security, implement all forms of dial-on-demand routing, configure router/access servers, and implement transmission protocols. If a candidate fails the lab exam on the first try, he or she must wait at least 30 days before attempting it again.

Before attempting this certification, Cisco recommends the following preparation: two or more years of internetwork administration, experience with internetwork installation and troubleshooting, extensive experience with Cisco products in a production environment, and familiarity with all Cisco product and service documentation. Cisco offers several training courses for CCIE candidates, and its Web site provides sample tests and detailed information on the test objectives (see the Resources section for more information).

Who Needs It A CCIE certification is one of the most coveted networking certifications. CCIEs are widely recognized as Internetworking experts; this particular CCIE certification is highly sought by Internet Service Providers. Some technical professionals undertake CCIE certification as the first step toward employment with Cisco or with one of their partners.

Requirements for Certification The certification process requires the following steps:

1. Pass the CCIE: Internet Service Provider Dial Expert qualification exam.

2. Pass the CCIE: Internet Service Provider Dial Expert lab test.

Administrator   The CCIE: Internet Service Provider Dial Expert qualification test is administered by Sylvan Prometric; call (800) 204-3926 to register for Cisco tests. (See Chapter 15 for additional information on Sylvan Prometric.)

The CCIE: Internet Service Provider Dial Expert lab exam is given by Cisco in Halifax, Nova Scotia and San Jose, California. Contact Cisco at (800) 553-NETS (ext. 6387) to schedule your lab test.

Fee   The qualification exam costs $200. The lab exam costs $1000.

Format   The two-hour, closed-book, computer-based qualification exam has 100 multiple-choice questions; 65 percent is the passing score.

The CCIE: Internet Service Provider (ISP) Dial Expert lab exam is a two-day, hands-on practical exam, evaluated by a senior CCIE internetworking engineer. Point values are given for each configuration scenario and problem; an aggregate score of 80 percent is needed to pass.

Cisco Certified Internetworking Expert (CCIE): Routing and Switching Expert

To attain this certification, the candidate must first pass a qualification test and then a lab exam. The CCIE: Routing and Switching Expert qualifying exam covers general LAN/WAN knowledge, knowledge of the functionalities and protocols of desktop, WAN, and Internet technologies, and knowledge of Cisco-specific technologies, capabilities, and applications. The lab exam requires the candidate to build, configure, and test complex internetworks to provided specifications, diagnose and resolve network faults, and use Cisco debugging tools. If a candidate fails the lab exam on the first try, he or she must wait at least 30 days before attempting it again.

Before attempting this certification, Cisco recommends the following preparation: two or more years of internetwork administration, experience with internetwork installation and troubleshooting, extensive experience with Cisco products in a production environment, and familiarity with all Cisco product and service documentation. Cisco offers several training courses for CCIE candidates, and its Web site provides sample tests and detailed information on the test objectives (see the Resources section for more information).

Who Needs It   A CCIE certification is one of the most coveted networking certifications. CCIEs are widely recognized as internetworking experts. Some technical professionals undertake CCIE certification as the first step toward employment with Cisco or with one of their partners.

Requirements for Certification   The certification process requires the following steps:

1. Pass the CCIE: Routing and Switching Expert qualifying exam.

2. Pass the CCIE: Routing and Switching Expert lab test.

Administrator   The CCIE: Routing and Switching Expert qualifying exam is administered by Sylvan Prometric; call (800) 204-3926 to register for Cisco tests. (See Chapter 15 for additional information on Sylvan Prometric.)

The CCIE: Routing and Switching Expert lab exam is given by Cisco in San Jose, California; Raleigh, North Carolina; Brussels, Belgium; Halifax, Nova Scotia; Sydney, Australia; and Tokyo, Japan. Contact Cisco at (800) 553-NETS (ext. 6387) to schedule your lab test.

Fee   The qualification exam costs $200. The lab exam costs $1000.

Format   The two-hour, closed-book, computer-based qualification exam has 100 multiple-choice questions; 65 percent is the passing score.

The CCIE: Routing and Switching Expert lab exam is a two-day, hands-on practical exam, evaluated by a senior CCIE internetworking engineer. Point values are given for each configuration scenario and problem; an aggregate score of 80 percent is needed to pass.

Practice Laboratory for Cisco Lab Test

Because the CCIE lab test is known to be a real killer (over half of the candidates fail on their first attempt), Cisco has teamed up with Wichita State University in Kansas to offer a practice laboratory for CCIE candidates.

This lab facility has two stations, each with the following equipment:

- Five 2500 series Cisco Routers (2501, 2511, 2524 (2), 2515)

- Two 4000M Cisco Routers

- Three Ethernet Hubs

- Three Token Ring MAUs

- One Ethernet Patch Panel

- One Serial Patch Panel

- Two ISDN Lines

- Two Modem Lines

- One Server for router configuration and TFTP

Continued on next page

Practice Laboratory for Cisco Lab Test (continued)

It is recommended that participants pass the CCIE qualification exam before attending the practice laboratory. The practice laboratory offers a self-study environment. You can complete a series of lab exercises that are written by Cisco and are similar to what you will encounter on the actual lab exam. The preparation lab fee is currently $500 per day.

To register, or for additional information, see `http://www.engr.twsu.edu/cisco`, or contact:

Kimberly Moore, `kmoore@twsuvm.uc.twsu.edu`
University Conferences and Non-Credit Programs
Wichita State University
1845 Fairmount
Wichita, Kansas 67260-0136
Phone: (800) 550-1306
Fax: (316) 978-3064

Resources

Cisco offers several training courses for CCIE candidates through its Certified Training Partners located throughout the world (see the Cisco Web site for a complete listing). The courses Cisco recommends as preparation for CCIE certification include Introduction to Cisco Router Configuration, Installation and Maintenance of Cisco Routers, Advanced Cisco Router Configuration, Cisco Internetwork Design, and Cisco Internetwork Troubleshooting.

In addition, the Cisco Web site provides sample tests, recommended reading lists, and detailed information on the test objectives. For more information on this organization's certification program and courses, contact Cisco at:

Web   http://www.cisco.com/warp/public/625/ccie/
             index.html

E-mail   ccie_ucsa@cisco.com

Mail   Cisco Systems, Inc.
             170 West Tasman Drive
             San Jose, CA 95134-1706

Phone   (800) 553-6387

Learning Tree International Certifications

Learning Tree International offers over 150 computer and networking courses throughout the United States, Europe, and Asia. As part of their curriculum in information technology, Learning Tree International offers 27 different professional certification programs, three of which are vendor-independent certifications oriented toward networking hardware: Local Area Network (LAN) Certified Professional, Wide Area Network (WAN) Certified Professional, and Internetworking Certified Professional. (See Chapters 3, 4, and 9 for other Learning Tree International certification programs.)

The Learning Tree International Certified Professional credentials may be useful to PC support staff, service technicians, engineers, system and network administrators, and anyone else involved with the maintenance and support of network hardware. This type of certification, which involves taking training courses followed immediately by exams that are based on the objectives of those courses, is especially useful for someone who is just beginning in the field of networking.

Recertification or Maintenance Requirements There is no maintenance requirement for any of Learning Tree International's certification programs.

Benefits of Certification Learning Tree International Certified Professionals receive these benefits:

- Framed diploma of Professional Certification

- An official record of the courses that you have completed

- Option of obtaining college credit

It is possible to obtain college credit for earning your certification or for taking Learning Tree International courses. The American Council of Education (ACE) in Washington, D.C. has worked in cooperation with Learning Tree International to determine college course equivalencies for these courses and certifications. Approximately 1,500 colleges and universities in the United States will accept ACE recommendations for college credit. ACE typically will recommend two college credit hours for each four-day course. Learning Tree International will pay to have your Learning Tree International credentials registered with ACE and you can then request that your transcript be sent from ACE to any college or university. (Check with your college or university registrar to make sure that your institution accepts ACE recommendations for credit.)

Learning Tree International Local Area Networks Certified Professional

This certification program involves taking five courses and passing the associated examinations. Four of the courses are required core courses, while the fifth course is selected from a list of options. The test for each course is given on site at the end of the course.

The courses and examinations in this certification program are designed to teach and test the candidate's ability to design, implement, configure, and interconnect local area networks; install and configure the latest Ethernet technologies; analyze the Ethernet protocol and its impact on network performance; troubleshoot multi-vendor, multiple-protocol LAN environments; develop strategies for LAN monitoring and management; evaluate and select fast LAN technologies, including FDDI, Fast Ethernet, Gigabit Ethernet, ATM, and 100VG-AnyLan.

Who Needs It   This Learning Tree International certification is an excellent path for network administrators and engineers who need general education in LAN technologies.

Requirements for Certification   The certification process requires the following steps:

1.   Complete these four core courses and pass the tests given at the end of each course:

Course Number	Length	Course
Course 352	four days	Local Area Networks: Implementation and Configuration
Course 452	four days	Migrating to Switched and Fast Ethernet LANs, Hands-On

Course Number	Length	Course
Course 254	four days	Hands-On LAN Troubleshooting
Course 259	four days	Fast LAN Technologies

2. Complete one of the following elective courses and pass the test given at the end of the course:

Course Number	Length	Course
Course 258	four days	Designing and Implementing High-Performance Cabling Systems
Course 253	four days	Hands-On PC Networking
Course 153	five days	Windows 95 Support and Networking: Hands-On
Course 367	four days	Hands-On Introduction to TCP/IP
Course 467	four days	Hands-On Internetworking With TCP/IP
Course 364	four days	Introduction to Internetworking: Bridges, Switches and Routers
Course 264	five days	Hands-On IntranetWare: NetWare 4.x Administration
Course 466	four days	Cisco Routers: A Comprehensive Hands-On Introduction

Administrator Learning Tree International (Call (800) THE-TREE)

Fee At this writing, the prices for Learning Tree International courses are $1295 for a two-day course, $1745 for a three-day course, $2195 for a four-day course, and $2495 for a five-day course. Learning Tree

International offers some significant discounts for those taking more than one course and for government employees.

Format Each exam consists of 40 to 60 questions. If you fail to pass on the first try, Learning Tree International will arrange for you to take a proctored exam at your place of work.

Learning Tree International Wide Area Networks Certified Professional

This certification program involves taking five courses and passing the associated examinations. Four of the courses are required core courses, while the fifth course is selected from a list of options. The test for each course is given on site at the end of the course.

The courses and examinations in this certification program are designed to teach and test the candidate's ability to apply fundamental data communications and network concepts to the administration of a wide area network; use ATM, frame relay, X.25, T1, and other services to establish wide area communications; maintain and manage existing voice and data wide area services and plan for future connectivity needs; select wide area services by analyzing traffic volumes, transmission costs, and operating expenses; evaluate and select high-speed WAN services to meet LAN-to-LAN interconnection requirements; and use a wide variety of troubleshooting tools to identify and correct wide area network problems.

Who Needs It This Learning Tree International certification is an excellent path for network administrators and engineers who need general, vendor-independent experience with WAN technologies.

Requirements for Certification The certification process requires the following steps:

1. Complete these four core courses and pass the test given at the end of each course:

Course Number	Length	Course
Course 350	four days	Introduction to Data Communications and Networks
Course 278	three days	Utilizing Frame Relay Networks
Course 456	four days	Hands-On Wide Area Network Troubleshooting
Course 379	four days	High-Speed Wide Area Networks

2. Complete one of the following elective courses and pass the test given at the end of the course:

Course Number	Length	Course
Course 277	three days	Deploying T1 and T3 Services
Course 373	four days	Wide Area Networking and Telecommunications
Course 279	three days	Implementing ATM
Course 378	four days	Mobile Communications and Wireless Networks
Course 364	four days	Introduction to Internetworking: Bridges, Switches and Routers
Course 367	four days	Hands-On Introduction to TCP/IP
Course 374	four days	Hands-On Implementing ISDN Data Networks

Course Number	Length	Course
Course 466	four days	Cisco Routers: A Comprehensive Hands-On Introduction
Course 468	four days	Internet and System Security: Attacks and Countermeasures
Course 464	four days	Hands-On SNMP: From Workgroup to Enterprise Networks

Administrator   Learning Tree International (call (800) THE-TREE)

Fee   At this writing, the prices for Learning Tree International courses are $1295 for a two-day course, $1745 for a three-day course, $2195 for a four-day course, and $2495 for a five-day course. Learning Tree International offers some significant discounts for those taking more than one course and for government employees.

Format   Each exam consists of 40 to 60 questions. If you fail to pass on the first try, Learning Tree International will arrange for you to take a proctored exam at your place of work.

Learning Tree International Internetworking Certified Professional

This certification program involves taking five courses and passing the associated examinations. Four of the courses are required core courses, while the fifth course is selected from a list of options. The test for each course is given on site at the end of the course.

The courses and examinations in this certification program are designed to teach and test the candidate's ability to implement internetworking technologies; segment LANs with bridges and switches; deploy routers to connect LANs into the wide area network; design, implement, and optimize TCP/IP-based Internetworks; add TCP/IP applications and protocols to existing networks; configure detailed router parameters; select appropriate internetworking technologies for your organization; and design scalable networks based on bandwidth, delay, and growth criteria.

Who Needs It This Learning Tree International certification is an excellent path for network administrators and engineers who need a broad education in LAN and WAN integration and internetworking technologies.

Requirements for Certification The certification process requires the following steps:

1. Complete these four core courses and pass the test given at the end of each course:

Course Number	Length	Course
Course 364	four days	Introduction to Internetworking: Bridges, Switches and Routers
Course 367	four days	Hands-On Introduction to TCP/IP
Course 465	four days	IP Routing with OSPF and BGP, Hands-On
Course 453	four days	Data Network Design and Performance Optimization

2. Complete one of the following elective courses and pass the test given at the end of the course:

Course Number	Length	Course
Course 467	four days	Hands-On Internetworking with TCP/IP
Course 463	four days	Migrating to IPv6: Hands-On

Course Number	Length	Course
Course 464	four days	Hands-On SNMP: From Workgroup to Enterprise Networks
Course 355	four days	Computer Network Architectures and Protocols
Course 466	four days	Cisco Routers: A Comprehensive Hands-On Introduction
Course 481	four days	Configuring Cisco Routers: Advanced Hands-On Workshop
Course 468	four days	Internet and System Security: Attacks and Countermeasures
Course 154	four days	Hands-On TCP/IP Internetworking on Windows NT
Course 158	four days	UNIX and Windows NT Integration: Hands-On
Course 488	four days	Deploying Internet and Intranet Firewalls: Hands-On

Administrator   Learning Tree International (call (800) THE-TREE)

Fee   At this writing, the prices for Learning Tree International courses are $1295 for a two-day course, $1745 for a three-day course, $2195 for a four-day course, and $2495 for a five-day course. Learning Tree International offers some significant discounts for those taking more than one course and for government employees.

Format   Each exam consists of 40 to 60 questions. If you fail to pass on the first try, Learning Tree International will arrange for you to take a proctored exam at your place of work.

Resources

For more information on this organization's courses and certification programs, contact Learning Tree International at:

Web http://www.learningtree.com

E-mail uscourses@learningtree.com

Mail Learning Tree International
1805 Library Street
Reston, VA 20190-5630

Phone (800) THE-TREE

Fax (800) 709-6405

Xylan Certifications

Xylan is best known for their ATM and LAN switching equipment. They started with one product in 1993, and have grown rapidly since. Xylan currently offers two professional certification programs: the Xylan Certified Switch Specialist (XCSS) and the Xylan Certified Switch Expert (XCSE).

Recertification or Maintenance Requirements Xylan's program is brand new and there is currently no policy for maintaining certification. However, Xylan is planning to implement an annual recertification process soon (check their Web site for current information).

Benefits of Certification Xylan Certified SwitchExperts receive these benefits:

- Certificate of achievement

- Logo for use on business cards and stationery

- Exclusive technical support access

Xylan Certified Switch Specialist (XCSS)

This certification provides systems engineers with the skills necessary to develop solutions for switched networks. The test for this certification covers the basic concepts of frame and cell switching, the architecture and functionality of Xylan's switching products, and improving network performance and scalability using switching and VLANs.

Xylan recommends—but does not require—that those who seek this certification take three preparation courses (see the Resources section for details) and have hands-on experience with Xylan switching technologies. A sample version of the exam is available on the Xylan Web page.

Who Needs It The Xylan Certified Switch Specialist credential is a good way to demonstrate your skills with managing switched networks. Right now is an excellent time to have a credential of this type—there are many high paying jobs available for network professionals with experience and credentials in switching technologies.

Requirements for Certification The certification process requires only one step:

1. Pass the Xylan Certified Switch Specialist exam (Sylvan ID: XY-001).

Administrator Xylan exams are administered by Sylvan Prometric; call (800) 610-3926 to register for an Xylan test. (See Chapter 15 for additional information on Sylvan Prometric.)

Fee $100 per test. ($150 outside the US and Canada.)

Format 75-minute, multiple-choice exam. Call Sylvan Prometric at (800) 610-3926 for current test information.

Xylan Certified Switch Expert (XCSE)

This certification builds on the XCSS certification described previously. This is Xylan's certification for technical professionals who want to demonstrate their skills in designing, maintaining, and troubleshooting switched networks. Candidates will need to be able to install, configure, and support the OmniSwitch and Xylan products that support ATM switching.

Xylan recommends—but does not require—that those who seek this certification take two additional preparation courses (see the Resources section for details). Hands-on experience with Xylan switching technologies is essential prior to taking the XCSE practical exam.

Who Needs It Switching technology is a rapidly growing segment of the networking field. Obtaining a Xylan Certified Switch Expert certification is a great way to move into this high-paying specialty for those already working in the networking field, or for anyone who wants to certify their skills in designing and supporting switched networks.

Requirements for Certification The certification process requires the following steps:

1. Attain certification as a Xylan Certified Switch Specialist.

2. Pass the Xylan Certified Switch Expert practical exam.

Administrator Xylan Corporation (call (800) 999-9526 ext. 4768)

Fee $300 per test

Format This hands-on practical exam takes six hours.

Resources

Xylan offers courses for those who are preparing for Xylan certification tests. Each course involves both classroom instruction and lab work. The courses are offered at Xylan training centers located in Calabasas, California; Dover, New Hampshire; and Hoofddorp, in the Netherlands. Register online at least three weeks before you plan on taking your test.

These three courses are recommended as preparation for the Xylan Certified Switch Specialist (XCSS) exam:

- Course 101: Introduction to Switching ($50)

- Course: 201 Product Features and Technical Specifications ($400)

- Course 301: Design and Implementation ($400)

Xylan recommends that those who are preparing to take the Xylan Certified Switch Expert (XCSE) exam take the three courses listed above, plus these two:

- Course 401: Installation and Support ($400)

- Course 701: ATM with X-Cell ($600)

A sample version of the XCSS exam is available on Xylan's Web page. For more information on the this organization's certification program and courses, contact Xylan at:

Web `http://www.xylan.com/`

E-mail `training@xylan.com`

Mail Xylan SwitchExpert Training Program
26679 West Agoura Road
Calabasas, CA 91302

Phone (800) 999-9526 ext. 4768

CHAPTER

7

Network Operating
Systems Certifications

FEATURING

■ Banyan Certifications

■ IBM Certifications

■ Microsoft Certification

■ Novell Certifications

Network operating systems—such as Novell's NetWare and Microsoft's Windows NT—have rapidly replaced mainframe computers and mini-computers as the primary medium for sharing files and printers. These systems allow companies to use inexpensive PCs and workstations to provide shared resources to all of their employees—whether in one location or many locations—simultaneously.

There are currently four certification programs related to network operating systems. Banyan's certification program concentrates on the Vines network operating system, which is used primarily to link UNIX servers with a variety of clients. IBM offers several certifications on its PC-based server products—OS/2 Warp Server and OS/2 LAN Server. It was Novell's certification program, initiated in 1987, that really launched the recent explosion of computer and network certification. The Novell certification program, with over 100,000 networking professionals certified, has been wildly successful. Microsoft's program, begun in 1992, also has certified a total of over 100,000 individuals (including Microsoft Certified Professionals, Microsoft Certified Systems Engineers, Microsoft Certified Solutions Developers, and Microsoft Certified Trainers). But there is still plenty of demand.

Even though the average MCSE (Microsoft Certified Systems Engineer) has only 1.7 years of networking experience, the average MCSE salary, as of February 1998, was $67,600. (For the latest data on Microsoft certified professionals, go to http://www.mcpmag.com/ for *Microsoft Certified Professional* magazine's annual salary survey.) Many networking professionals wrestle with the decision about whether to seek certification with Novell or Microsoft. The best option right now may be to do a little of both. See the sidebar in this chapter titled "CNE or MCSE?" for a discussion of some of the issues to consider.

Professionals seeking these certifications include:

- Network administrators

- System administrators

- Field engineers

- Help desk personnel

 UNIX is both a computer operating system and a network operating system. UNIX certifications—including the Solaris Network Administrator, the SCO Server, and the Silicon Graphics IRIX Network Administrator certifications—are covered in Chapter 4.

Banyan Certifications

Banyan Vines is a networking operating system designed by Banyan for use in large corporate networks, typically operating on UNIX-based servers. The current version—Vines 8.0—incorporates NT, Novell, and mainframe-based resources into directory services through Banyan's proprietary protocol, StreetTalk.

The Banyan Technical Certification Program offers two levels of certification on Vines: the Certified Banyan Specialist (CBS) and the Certified Banyan Expert (CBE). In addition, Banyan has just added a special designation entitled CBS/NT for professionals who will be implementing and administering StreetTalk for Windows NT. Banyan also intends to add a CBE/NT designation sometime in 1998; see Appendix C for information on how to access the Certification Update Web site and receive updated information on the CBE/NT credential.

Recertification or Maintenance Requirements Annual recertification is required to maintain the CBS or the CBE certification. Recertification involves taking one or more courses from a pool of approved recertification courses; contact Banyan for details and a current list of eligible courses.

Benefits of Certification As a Certified Banyan Specialist or Expert, you will receive:

- A plaque and letter of congratulations

- The current copy of the Banyan Knowledge Base CD-ROM

- Three free incident calls to the Banyan Response Center

Certified Banyan Specialist (CBS)

While the Certified Banyan Specialist is the first level of certification with the Banyan Vines network operating system, it is a significant certification on its own. The three required tests and one required five-day course focus on administering and maintaining Vines-based networks.

Who Needs It If your company uses Vines, this certification is an excellent way to move up in responsibility and pay in your current position; it can also help you to get a new position at a company that depends on Vines for networking.

Requirements for Certification The certification process requires the following steps:

1. Pass the Vines Administration test (Sylvan ID: 020-110).

2. Pass the Advanced Vines Administration test (Sylvan ID: 020-210).

3. Attend and complete the Problem Solving for Vines Networks course (Banyan ID: EDU 310).

4. Pass the Problem Solving for Vines Networks test (Sylvan ID: 020-310).

Administrator Tests are administered by Sylvan Prometric; call (800) 736-3926 to register for Banyan tests (see Chapter 15 for additional information on Sylvan Prometric). Required courses are offered through Banyan Certified Education Centers (see the Resources section that follows for more information).

Fee $120 per test. The required problem-solving course costs $1800.

Format These multiple-choice tests last 60 to 120 minutes; the time and number of questions depends on the test. Passing score is 65 percent.

Certified Banyan Specialist (CBS): Windows NT

The CBS Windows NT certification concentrates on the integration of Banyan's proprietary protocol, StreetTalk, into NT-based servers. The candidate must take two required courses and pass two Banyan tests. In addition, as part of this certification, the candidate must demonstrate the ability to administer NT servers by becoming a Microsoft Certified Professional (see Chapter 4 for details on this Microsoft certification).

Who Needs It This certification is an excellent way for network administrators to demonstrate to current or potential employers their knowledge and ability related to the successful integration and management of Vines and NT hybrid networks. It can also be of value to network planners and designers who must accommodate a variety of network operating systems in their organization.

Requirements for Certification The certification process requires the following steps:

1. Pass one of the four tests listed below. Meeting this requirement will also qualify you as a Microsoft Certified Professional (see Chapter 4 for more information on the MCP certification program).

Sylvan ID	Exam
70-73	Implementing and Supporting Microsoft Windows NT Workstation 4.0
70-42	Implementing and Supporting Microsoft Windows NT Workstation 3.51
70-67	Implementing and Supporting Microsoft Windows NT Server 4.0
70-43	Implementing and Supporting Microsoft Windows NT Server 3.5

2. Attend and complete the five-day StreetTalk for Windows NT Administration course (Banyan ID: EDU 1200).

3. Pass the StreetTalk for Windows NT Administration test (Sylvan ID: 020-123).

4. Attend and complete the three-day StreetTalk for Windows NT Internals and Performance Analysis course (Banyan ID: EDU 1250).

5. Pass the StreetTalk for Windows NT Internals and Performance Analysis test (Sylvan ID: 020-125).

Administrator Tests are administered by Sylvan Prometric; call (800) 736-3926 to register for Banyan tests (see Chapter 15 for additional information on Sylvan Prometric). Required courses are offered through Banyan Certified Education Centers (see the Resources section that follows for more information).

Fee $120 per test. The StreetTalk for Windows NT Administration course costs $1800 and the StreetTalk for Windows NT Internals and Performance Analysis course costs $1500.

Format These multiple-choice tests last 60 to 120 minutes; the time and number of questions depends on the test. Passing score is 65 percent.

Certified Banyan Engineer (CBE)

The Certified Banyan Engineer credential is the premium Banyan certification. It builds on the Certified Banyan Specialist title and requires extensive training and testing on Vines networking and troubleshooting. The candidate must complete two required courses and pass two exams.

Who Needs It Becoming a Certified Banyan Engineer is an excellent way to achieve a high level of responsibility for network administration in a company that uses Vines.

Requirements for Certification The certification process requires the following steps:

1. Attain the Banyan CBS Certification described above.

2. Attend and complete the five-day Supporting Network Services course (Banyan ID: EDU 620).

3. Pass the Supporting Network Services test (Sylvan ID: 020-620).

4. Attend and complete the five-day Network Communications course (Banyan ID: EDU 630).

5. Pass the Network Communications test (Sylvan ID: 020-630).

Administrator Tests are administered by Sylvan Prometric; call (800) 736-3926 to register for Banyan tests (see Chapter 15 for additional information on Sylvan Prometric). Required courses are offered through Banyan Certified Education Centers (see the Resources section that follows for more information).

Fee $120 per test. Each of the two required courses costs $2250.

Format These multiple-choice tests last 60 to 120 minutes; the time and number of questions depends on the test. Passing score is 65 percent.

Resources

The Banyan Web site offers study guides that detail the objectives of each exam. Banyan's Web site also offers a listing of Certified Education Centers and Banyan Certified Instructors. For more information on this organization's certifications and courses, contact Banyan at:

Web	http://www.banyan.com/support/techcert.htm
E-mail	jbernstein@banyan.com
Mail	Banyan Systems Incorporated
	Educational Services Department
	120 Flanders Road
	Westboro, MA 01581
Phone	(508) 898-1795
Fax	(508) 836-0225

IBM Certifications

During the 1980s, IBM and Microsoft worked together to develop the OS/2 operating system as a graphical interface for the PC. After a much-publicized breakup of the partnership, IBM continued to develop OS/2 while Microsoft took off in its own direction with Windows.

IBM also developed a PC-based server system for its OS/2 product line, which is called the OS/Warp Server. IBM offers two certifications on its OS/2 Warp Server network operating system: the IBM Certified Specialist OS/2 Warp Server Administration and the IBM Certified Systems Expert OS/2 Warp Server. In addition, IBM offers two certifications on its OS/2 LAN server product: the IBM Certified Specialist OS2/LAN Server 4.0 Administration and the IBM Certified Systems Expert OS/2 LAN Server 4.0.

Recertification or Maintenance Requirements The IBM OS/2 certifications apply to specific version numbers of this operating system, so there is no requirement for recertification on a particular version. Since your certification is tied to a certain version of a product, however, you will want become certified on the newest versions when they become available if you want to continue to have the most current credential in this area.

Benefits of Certification IBM Certified OS/2 Engineers receive these benefits:

- Logo for use in advertisements and business literature

- A certificate of completion, an ID card, and a lapel pin

- IBM will include your name in their directories of certified personnel

- Subscriptions to technical newsletters and magazines, other technical literature, and other special offers

- IBM-sponsored technical support

For information on other IBM certification programs, see Chapters 3, 4, and 9.

IBM Certified Specialist: OS/2 Warp Server Administration

Attaining this certification involves passing one required test. The exam covers basic OS/2 Warp Server features and operation, including handling file systems, installation, running applications, and printing. IBM recommends that those who seek this certification have basic knowledge of DOS and OS/2 Warp, as well as hands-on experience with OS/2 Warp Server, before attempting the exam.

Who Needs It The IBM Certified Specialist: OS/2 Warp Server Administration designation is a great credential for getting your first position in OS/2 Warp Server administration.

Requirements for Certification The certification process requires only one step:

1. Pass the IBM OS/2 Warp Server Administration test (Sylvan ID: 000-134).

Administrator Call Sylvan Prometric at (800) 959-3926 to register for an IBM exam. (See Chapter 15 for detailed information on taking tests from Sylvan.)

Fee Fees for IBM tests vary based on test length and format; call Sylvan Prometric at (800) 959-3926 for pricing.

Format Computer-based, multiple-choice test. Call Sylvan Prometric at (800) 959-3926 for current information on the number of questions, time limit, and passing score.

IBM Certified Systems Expert: OS/2 Warp Server

Attaining this certification involves passing three exams. The candidate has the option of taking either the OS/2 Warp or the OS/2 Warp 4 Fundamentals test; both cover the fundamentals of the OS/Warp operating system. The Warp Server Administration test covers basic OS/2 Warp Server operation, including handling file systems, installation, running applications, and printing. The Warp Server test covers basic concepts of planning, installation, customization, usage, and problem resolution with the OS/2 Warp Server platform.

IBM recommends that those who seek this certification have a basic knowledge of DOS and hands-on experience with OS/2 Warp 4 before attempting the exams.

Who Needs It The IBM Certified Systems Expert: OS/2 Warp Server designation is a excellent way to prove your expertise with OS/2 Warp Server networking. Whether you want to advance in your current company, or obtain a higher paying position elsewhere, this credential can help you meet your goals.

Requirements for Certification The certification process requires the following steps:

1. Pass one of the following tests:

   • IBM OS/2 Warp test (Sylvan ID: 000-133)

   • IBM OS/2 Warp 4 Fundamentals test (Sylvan ID: 000-200)

2. Pass the IBM OS/2 Warp Server Administration test (Sylvan ID: 000-134).

3. Pass the IBM OS/2 Warp Server test (Sylvan ID: 000-132).

It is recommended—but not required—that the tests be taken in this order.

Administrator Call Sylvan Prometric at (800) 959-3926 to register for an IBM exam. (See Chapter 15 for detailed information on taking tests from Sylvan.)

Fee Fees for IBM tests vary based on test length and format; call Sylvan Prometric at (800) 959-3926 for pricing.

Format Computer-based, multiple-choice test. Call Sylvan Prometric at (800) 959-3926 for current information on the number of questions, time limit, and passing score.

IBM Certified Specialist: OS/2 LAN Server 4.0 Administration

Attaining this certification involves passing one required exam. The test covers basic OS/2 LAN Server features and operation, file systems, installing and running applications, printing, and customizing. IBM recommends that those who seek this certification have a basic knowledge of DOS and OS/2 Warp, as well as hands-on experience with OS/2 LAN Server 4.0, before attempting the exam.

Who Needs It The IBM Certified Specialist: OS/2 LAN Server 4.0 Administration designation is a great credential for getting your first position in OS/2 LAN Server administration.

Requirements for Certification The certification process requires only one step:

1. Pass the IBM OS/2 LAN Server Administration test (Sylvan ID: 000-103).

Administrator Call Sylvan Prometric at (800) 959-3926 to register for an IBM exam. (See Chapter 15 for detailed information on taking tests from Sylvan.)

Fee Fees for IBM tests vary based on test length and format; call Sylvan Prometric at (800) 959-3926 for pricing.

Format Computer-based, multiple-choice test. Call Sylvan Prometric at (800) 959-3926 for current information on the number of questions, time limit, and passing score.

IBM Certified Systems Expert: OS/2 LAN Server 4.0

Attaining this certification involves passing a series of six exams covering the installation and operation of OS/2 and OS/2 LAN Server. IBM recommends that those who seek this certification have a basic knowledge of DOS and hands-on experience with OS/2 LAN Server 4.0 before taking the exams.

Who Needs It Completing the challenging Certified Systems Expert: OS/2 LAN Server program makes you stand out as an expert in LAN Server management. It can be the ticket to job offers, promotions, and salary increases in companies and government agencies that use OS/2 LAN Server.

Requirements for Certification The certification process requires the following steps:

1. Pass the Installing OS/2 test (Sylvan ID: 000-109).

2. Pass the OS/2 LAN Server Administration I test (Sylvan ID: 000-103).

3. Pass the OS/2 LAN Server Administration II test (Sylvan ID: 000-104).

4. Pass the OS/2 LAN Server Workstation Planning and Installation test (Sylvan ID: 000-106).

5. Pass the OS/2 LAN Server Performance test (Sylvan ID: 000-107).

6. Pass one of the following elective tests:

    • REXX for OS/2 test (Sylvan ID: 000-015)

    • IBM TCP/IP for Workstations test (Sylvan ID: 000-018)

    • OS/2 Warp Connection test (Sylvan ID: 000-126)

It is recommended—but not required—that the tests be taken in this order.

Administrator Call Sylvan Prometric at (800) 959-3926 to register for an IBM exam. (See Chapter 15 for detailed information on taking tests from Sylvan.)

Fee Fees for IBM tests vary based on test length and format; call Sylvan Prometric at (800) 959-3926 for pricing.

Format Computer-based, multiple choice test. Call Sylvan Prometric at (800) 959-3926 for current information on the number of questions, time limit, and passing score.

Resources

IBM's Web site offers a number of excellent resources for certification candidates, including test objectives, study guides, and sample tests. Several computer-based training courses and instructor-led training courses are also offered. Another excellent resource, the *OS/2 Warp 4 Certification Handbook*, is available for $59.95 from either Sylvan Prometric ((800) 959-3926) or Indelible Blue ((800) 776-8284). For more information on these courses and certification programs, contact IBM at:

Web	http://www.ibm.com/certify/
E-mail	ialine@us.ibm.com
Mail	IBM North America 1133 Westchester Avenue White Plains, NY 10604
Phone	(800) IBM-4YOU
Fax	(404) 238-6628
Faxback	(800) 426-4329

Microsoft Certification

The Microsoft Certified Systems Engineer (MCSE) is one of Microsoft's premium credentials. Attaining this certification requires passing six exams. The exams focus on using Microsoft Windows NT Server and related products.

MCSEs are in high demand. There are approximately 40,000 MCSEs in the world today, and that number is climbing steadily. Microsoft Solution Providers—companies authorized by Microsoft to provide integrated business solutions using Microsoft products—must maintain Microsoft-certified professionals on staff. In fact, Microsoft Solution Providers have approximately 40,000 unfilled positions for Microsoft Certified Systems Engineers worldwide (approximately 17,000 in North America).

Contributing to Microsoft Certified Professional Exams

Microsoft relies heavily on input from current MCSEs and other Microsoft-certified professionals to develop and maintain their certification exams. To get this valuable input from practicing professionals, Microsoft invites interested individuals to become technical contributors or contract writers for their exams.

Being a technical contributor involves offering your technical expertise to the exam-development process. A contract writer is a person who concentrates on the writing of exam questions.

Continued on next page

Contributing to Microsoft Certified Professional Exams (continued)

If you are interested in contributing to the exams for Microsoft's certification program, see `http://www.microsoft.com/mcp/examinfo/certsd.htm` for more information.

Recertification or Maintenance Requirements MCSEs must take action to maintain their certifications. As Microsoft introduces new products and new versions of its operating systems, it retires the tests for previous versions. If you hold a certification that is based on a test that Microsoft is retiring, you will be informed by certified mail of the need to take a current test to maintain your certification. You will have at least six months to complete this new test or your status as an MCSE will no longer be valid.

Benefits of Certification Microsoft Certified Systems Engineers receive the following benefits:

- An MCSE certificate

- Access to technical information through a secure MCSE-only Web site

- Use of MCSE logos on stationery and business cards

- Invitations to Microsoft-sponsored conferences and technical briefings

- A free subscription to *Microsoft Certified Professional* magazine

- A one-year subscription to the Microsoft TechNet Technical Information Network, which provides an informative CD each month

- A one-year subscription to the Microsoft Beta Evaluation program. Microsoft will send you free CDs each month containing beta versions of their newest software.

Microsoft Certified Systems Engineer (MCSE)

Attaining the Microsoft Certified Engineer certification requires passing four core exams and two elective exams. The core exams cover the basic concepts and skills involved with installing, using, and troubleshooting a Windows NT Server and a client operating system such as NT Workstation or Windows 95. One of the core exams is the Networking Essentials exam, which covers basic network technologies and troubleshooting. The two elective exams focus on other Microsoft server topics and advanced networking topics. Microsoft's Web site provides exam guidelines, sample tests, and links to authorized training providers (see the Resources section that follows for more information).

 The Windows NT 3.5.1 track will be retired shortly when the Windows NT 5.0 exams become available. For more information, visit http://www.microsoft.com/mcp/articles/winnt5.htm

Who Needs It The MCSE certification is one of the most widely recognized networking credentials. It is valuable as an entry point for technical professionals just getting into network and system administration of Microsoft operating systems, or for practicing networking professionals who seek a salary increase or promotion.

Requirements for Certification The certification process requires the following steps:

1. Pass the four core exams for one of the two tracks outlined in Table 7.1 (Windows NT 3.51 or Windows NT 4.0).

TABLE 7.1: Windows NT Tracks

Windows NT 3.51 Track	Windows NT 4.0 Track
Implementing and Supporting Microsoft Windows NT Server 3.51 (Sylvan ID: 70-043)	Implementing and Supporting Microsoft Windows NT Server 4.0 (Sylvan ID: 70-067)
Implementing and Supporting Microsoft Windows NT Workstation 3.51 (Sylvan ID: 70-042)	Implementing and Supporting Microsoft® Windows NT Server 4.0 in the Enterprise (Sylvan ID: 70-068)
Implementing and Supporting Microsoft Windows 95 (Sylvan ID: 70-064)	Implementing and Supporting Microsoft Windows NT Workstation 4.0 (Sylvan ID: 70-073) **OR** Implementing and Supporting Microsoft Windows 95 (Sylvan ID: 70-064)
Networking Essentials (Sylvan ID: 70-058)	Networking Essentials (Sylvan ID: 70-058)

If you are already certified as a Novell CNE, Master CNE, or CNI, or a Sun Certified Network Administrator for Solaris 2.5 or 2.5, Banyan CBS or CBE, Microsoft will waive the requirement for the Networking Essentials exam.

2. Pass two elective exams, selecting exams from two different categories listed in Table 7.2. Two additional exams will be available in beta during 1998; see the Certification Update Web site for the latest information. If you pass two exams within the same category, only one will qualify as an MCSE elective.

TABLE 7.2: MCSE Elective Exams

Category	Exam(s)
SNA Server	Implementing and Supporting Microsoft SNA Server 3.0 (Sylvan ID: 70-013) **OR** Implementing and Supporting Microsoft SNA Server 4.0 (Sylvan ID: 70-085)
SMS Server	Implementing and Supporting Microsoft Systems Management Server 1.2 (Sylvan ID: 70-018)
SQL Databases	Microsoft SQL Server 4.2 Database Implementation (Sylvan ID: 70-021) **OR** Implementing a Database Design on Microsoft SQL Server 6.5 (Sylvan ID: 70-027)
SQL Server	Microsoft® SQL Server 4.2 Database Administration for Microsoft Windows NT (Sylvan ID: 70-022) **OR** System Administration for Microsoft SQL Server 6.5 (Sylvan ID: 70-026)
Microsoft Mail	Microsoft Mail for PC Networks 3.2-Enterprise (Sylvan ID: 70-037)
TCP/IP	Internetworking Microsoft TCP/IP on Microsoft® Windows NT (3.5-3.51) (Sylvan ID: 70-053) **OR** Internetworking with Microsoft® TCP/IP on Microsoft Windows NT 4.0 (Sylvan ID: 70-059)
Exchange Server	Implementing and Supporting Microsoft Exchange Server 5 (Sylvan ID: 70-076) **OR** Implementing and Supporting Microsoft Exchange Server 5.5 (Sylvan ID: 70-081)

TABLE 7.2 (CONTINUED): MCSE Elective Exams

Category	Exam(s)
Internet Information Server	Implementing and Supporting Microsoft Internet Information Server 3.0 and Microsoft Index Server 1.1 (Sylvan ID: 70-077) **OR** Implementing and Supporting Microsoft Internet Information Server 4.0 (Sylvan ID: 70-087)
Proxy Server	Implementing and Supporting Microsoft Proxy Server 1.0 (Sylvan ID: 70-078) **OR** Implementing and Supporting Microsoft Proxy Server 2.0 (Sylvan ID: 70-088)
Internet Explorer	Implementing and Supporting Microsoft Internet Explorer 4.0 by Using the Internet Explorer Administration Kit (Sylvan ID: 70-079)

Administrator Tests are administered by Sylvan Prometric; call (800) 755-3926 to register for Microsoft tests (see Chapter 15 for additional information on Sylvan Prometric).

Fee $100 per test

Format Multiple-choice, closed-book tests. The number of questions and time limit depend on the test selected.

Microsoft recently created an extension to the MCSE credential— the MCSE + Internet certification. This credential is valuable for the numerous Microsoft professionals who use their expertise to maintain their company's Internet connectivity and presence. (See Chapter 9 for more information on the MSCE + Internet certification.)

Resources

The Microsoft Web site offers practice tests as well as study guides that details the objectives of each exam. Microsoft's Web site also offers a listing of Microsoft Authorized Education Centers. For more information on this organization's certification programs, contact Microsoft at:

Web	`http://www.microsoft.com/mcp/`
E-mail	`mcp@msprograms.com`
Mail	Microsoft Corporation One Microsoft Way Redmond, WA 98052-6399
Phone	(800) 636-7544
Fax	(206) 936-7329

CNE or MCSE? By Patrick Tracey

By far and away the most commonly asked question these days among would-be computer networkers is whether to train oneself as a Certified Novell Engineer (CNE) or as a Microsoft Certified Systems Engineer (MCSE).

To be an MCSE or CNE, the choice is not an easy one, according to Ray Sandwick, senior vice president of Rockville, MD–based Delta Microsystem's Computer Education Division, whose job is to offer guidance to ensure that all of Delta's students are trained in the latest technologies.

In an industry dominated, until very recently, by Novell, there was never any choice. But, Sandwick counsels,

Continued on next page

CNE or MCSE? (continued)
By Patrick Tracey

Microsoft is now complicating choices by coming on strong with Windows NT. So strong, in fact, that the number of MCSEs has grown by as much as 170 percent within the last year. "Considering that Microsoft happens to be the 600-pound gorilla," says Sandwick, "most new networks that are being sold are Windows NT. But of the networks in place right now in the marketplace, most are Novell."

For most, the decision comes down to calculating which businesses offer the most jobs. In this respect, Novell has had the distinct advantage of having put the majority of the networks in place, prior to the arrival of Windows NT. But in the fast-changing computer industry, everyone expects Windows to overtake Novell very soon.

Based on the number of networks that currently exist in the marketplace, there are only about 80,000 CNEs available to work on 170,000 networks, compared with about 20,000 MCSEs available for 100,000 networks. "Essentially there's more jobs for Novell engineers, but more new jobs for MCSEs," says Sandwick.

Delta's solution, like that of most certified trainers, is a two-track approach. "We teach both," says Sandwick, "and that's what we strongly advise people who want to change careers and become a true network professional. We tell them they can get away with one or the other for a while, but eventually they will have to know both."

The good news for network career seekers, at least, is that there are only two platforms to master. "95% of all client-server PC networks are either Novell NetWare or Windows NT," Sandwick points out. "Nobody else is playing that game."

Continued on next page

CNE or MCSE? (continued)
By Patrick Tracey

Better yet, the greatest barrier to filling job openings is the lack of qualified applicants. Both Novell and Windows NT jobs are opening up faster than the pool of qualified network engineers. This shortfall, known in the industry as the skills gap, is widening noticeably every month. "There's a crying need," says Sandwick. "And either way, it's a very powerful certification. I've seen waiters and gas station attendants. Some of them aren't even finished [being certified] and they're getting $55,000 a year."

Perhaps the best barometer of job demand is to compare salaries for MCSEs with CNEs. While there are more jobs out there for the CNE, the MCSE is already commanding higher salaries for his skills. According to Sandwick, most MCSEs can immediately land jobs in the range of $45,000 to $55,000 a year, whereas newly minted CNEs tend to make $35,000 to $45,000. Part of the reason is that Microsoft certification is considered a bit more difficult than Novell certification, with a harder series of tests required for full certification.

That Microsoft will soon eclipse Novell as the network of choice is generally without doubt in industry circles. It's only a question of when, according to observers, many of whom caution that the transition is expected to be patchy from area to area. In the Washington metropolitan area, for instance, Novell will be indispensable for the foreseeable future, if only because the federal government has weighed in heavily on the side of Novell. [Novell] certification is usually cheaper, in the $4,000 to $5,000 range, as opposed to $5,000 to $6,000 for Microsoft. "For the college student working his or her way through school or the

Continued on next page

Novell Certifications

In 1983, Novell began producing one of the first network operating systems using PC-based servers. At the time, many people were skeptical that PC-based servers could perform well enough to handle business applications. But as Novell kept improving their product— and as PCs became more powerful—people began to see the benefits of this cost-effective solution to file and printer sharing. While the popularity of Windows NT is growing, the majority of networks currently in place use Novell products. Novell has also developed a number of other applications and programs—such as the GroupWise product for e-mail and collaboration—that are very popular.

In 1987, Novell was the first company to offer a certification—the Certified Novell Engineer (CNE)—that validated individuals' expertise in using the Novell network operating system. Novell has since worked hard to develop and promote this certification. As a result, there are currently over 100,000 certified Novell professionals, including over 75,000 CNEs. Novell's certification program is one of the most diverse available today; it allows the candidate to specialize in a wide range of products at each level of certification. Some of Novell's tests are adaptive exams. See Chapter 15 for discussion of adaptive testing.

Novell offers three basic levels of certification: Certified Novell Administrator (CNA), Certified Novell Engineer (CNE), and Master Certified Novell Engineer (Master CNE). Within each of these levels, a candidate can specialize in one or more Novell products, such as NetWare, IntranetWare, or GroupWise. In the case of the Master Certified Novell Engineer, specialization can be obtained in one of four general categories (Management, Connectivity, Messaging, or Internet/Intranet Solutions) or one of three client categories (AS/400 Integration, UNIX Integration, or Windows NT Integration).

 Novell also offers a number of Internet certification tracks (see Chapter 9 for details).

Every professional certified by Novell must submit a signed Novell Certification Agreement, which states the conditions for use of the Novell name and the terms under which certification can be revoked.

Recertification or Maintenance Requirements Both CNEs and Master CNEs are required to meet continuing certification requirements as specified by Novell. Because recertification requirements vary, contact Novell for current details (see the Resources section that follows for contact information).

Benefits of Certification As a Certified Novell Administrator, you will receive these benefits:

- Access to the password-protected CNA Web site

- Use of CNA logos

- Up-to-date Novell product information

- Online access to key publications and programs

As a Certified Novell Engineer, you will receive these benefits:

- Access to the password-protected CNE Net Web site, which offers exclusive benefits for CNEs

- CNE certificate and logo

- Beta products and early releases

- Quick access to patches, fixes, and press releases

- 50 percent discount on charges for technical support calls

- Free subscription to the *NetWare Connection* magazine

- Free and discounted technical seminars and programs

- Demonstration versions of the latest products from Novell for a nominal fee

- Novell Support Connection advanced technical training videos at a substantial discount

- Novell Power Partner CD containing technical sales information and demonstration software

- Discounts on Novell Applications Notes, Novell Support Connection CD, NCS Tool Kit and Novell Press books

As a Master Certified Novell Engineer, you will receive the CNE benefits plus the following additional benefits:

- Master CNE certificate and logo

- Access to a special Master CNE section on the CNE Net Web site

Certified Novell Administrator (CNA): NetWare 3

NetWare is one of Novell's PC-based server products that allows users to share files and printers on a local area network. The one test required for this certification program covers basic knowledge of installation and troubleshooting, but concentrates mainly on daily administrative tasks, e.g., adding users and groups, and managing printers. Novell offers a preparatory course for this exam (see the Resources section that follows for more information).

Who Needs It The CNA designation is a great credential for getting your first job in the field of computer networking. Employers know that CNAs have the ability to perform a wide variety of basic networking tasks. This Certified Novell Administrator (CNA) certification is for technical professionals who work with basic administration of NetWare 3 networks on a day-to-day basis.

Requirements for Certification The certification process requires the following steps:

1. Pass the NetWare 3.1*x* Administration exam (Sylvan ID: 050-130).

2. Sign and submit the Novell Certification Agreement (available at http://education.novell.com/certinfo/certagrm.htm).

Administrator Tests are administered by Sylvan Prometric; call (800) RED-EXAM to register for Novell tests (see Chapter 15 for additional information on Sylvan Prometric).

Fee $85 per test

Format This is a computer-based adaptive test that consists of 15 to 25 questions and must be completed in 30 minutes. See Chapter 15 for information on adaptive testing.

Certified Novell Administrator (CNA): IntranetWare

IntranetWare is Novell's latest release of their PC-based server product for local area networks. IntranetWare goes beyond NetWare 3 to allow seamless integration of multiple servers across LANs and WANs (through Novell's Directory Services). The one test required for this certification program concentrates on basic knowledge of the routine administrative tasks associated with IntranetWare. Novell offers a preparatory course for this exam (see the Resources section that follows for more information).

Who Needs It The CNA designation is a great credential for getting your first job in the field of computer networking. Employers know that CNAs have the ability to perform a wide variety of basic networking tasks. This Certified Novell Administrator (CNA) certification is designed for technical professionals who work with the administration of IntranetWare networks on a day-to-day basis.

Requirements for Certification The certification process requires the following steps:

1. Pass the IntranetWare: NetWare 4.11 Administration exam (Sylvan ID: 050-613).

2. Sign and submit the Novell Certification Agreement (available at http://education.novell.com/certinfo/certagrm.htm).

Administrator Tests are administered by Sylvan Prometric; call (800) RED-EXAM to register for Novell tests (see Chapter 15 for additional information on Sylvan Prometric).

Fee $85 per test

Format This is a computer-based adaptive test that consists of 15 to 25 questions and must be completed in 30 minutes. See Chapter 15 for more information on adaptive testing.

Certified Novell Administrator (CNA): GroupWise 4

GroupWise is Novell's group collaboration and mail system. The one test required for this certification program covers basic knowledge of installation and troubleshooting with GroupWise version 4, but concentrates mainly on basic daily administrative tasks. Novell offers a preparatory course for this exam (see the Resources section that follows for more information).

Who Needs It The CNA designation is a great credential for getting your first job in the field of computer networking. Employers know that CNAs have the ability to perform a wide variety of basic networking tasks. This Certified Novell Administrator (CNA) certification is designed for professionals who work with basic administration of GroupWise version 4 on a day-to-day basis.

Requirements for Certification The certification process requires the following steps:

1. Pass the GroupWise 4 Administration exam (Sylvan ID: 050-154).

2. Sign and submit the Novell Certification Agreement (available at
http://education.novell.com/certinfo/certagrm.htm).

Administrator Tests are administered by Sylvan Prometric; call
(800) RED-EXAM to register for Novell tests (see Chapter 15 for
additional information on Sylvan Prometric).

Fee $85 per test

Format This is a computer-based exam that consists of 65 questions
and must be completed in 90 minutes.

Certified Novell Administrator (CNA): GroupWise 5

GroupWise is Novell's group collaboration and mail system. The one
test required for this certification program covers basic knowledge of
installation and troubleshooting with Groupwise version 5, but concentrates mainly on daily administrative tasks. Novell offers a preparatory course for this exam (see the Resources section that follows
for more information).

Who Needs It The CNA designation is a great credential for getting
your first job in the field of computer networking. Employers know
that CNAs have the ability to perform a wide variety of basic networking tasks. This Certified Novell Administrator (CNA) designation is for professionals who work with basic administration of
GroupWise version 5 on a day-to-day basis.

Requirements for Certification The certification process
requires the following steps:

1. Pass the GroupWise 5 Administration exam (Sylvan ID:
050-618).

2. Sign and submit the Novell Certification Agreement (available at `http://education.novell.com/certinfo/certagrm.htm`).

Administrator Tests are administered by Sylvan Prometric; call (800) RED-EXAM to register for Novell tests (see Chapter 15 for additional information on Sylvan Prometric).

Fee $85 per test

Format This is a computer-based exam that consists of 64 questions and must be completed in 75 minutes.

Certified Novell Engineer (CNE): NetWare 3

The Certified Novell Engineer (CNE) program builds on the CNA program described above, but requires considerably more effort. Attaining the CNE requires the accumulation of 19 "credits"—by passing a combination of core CNE exams, "target" exams on NetWare 3, and elective exams—as described in the following sections. These CNE exams test the candidate's ability to provide high-end, solutions-based technical support for Novell networks using NetWare 3. Novell offers a preparatory course for each of these exams (see the Resources section that follows for more information).

Who Needs It The CNE designation—one of the most widely recognized networking credentials—is an excellent way to prove your expertise with Novell networking. Whether you want to advance in your current company, or obtain a higher paying position elsewhere, the CNE can help you meet your goals.

Requirements for Certification The certification process requires the following steps:

1. Accumulate 8 credits by passing the following two core CNE tests:

Sylvan ID	Credits	Exam
050-147	3	Networking Technologies
050-626	5	Service and Support

2. Accumulate 9 credits by passing the following NetWare 3 Target Requirements tests:

Sylvan ID	Credits	Exam
050-130	3	NetWare 3.1x Administration
050-131	2	NetWare 3.1x Advanced Administration
050-132	2	NetWare 3 Installation and Configuration
050-615	2	IntranetWare: NetWare to NetWare 4.11 Update

3. Accumulate 2 additional credits by passing an exam from the following list of CNE elective tests:

Sylvan ID	Credits	Exam
050-606	2	Fundamentals of Network Management
050-622	2	Printing in an Integrated NetWare Environment
050-605	3	NetWare for SAA: Installation and Troubleshooting
050-145	2	NetWare TCP/IP Transport

Sylvan ID	Credits	Exam
050-160	2	NetWare NFS Services: Management, File Sharing, and Printing

4. Sign and submit the Novell Certification Agreement (available at `http://education.novell.com/certinfo/certagrm.htm`).

Administrator Tests are administered by Sylvan Prometric; call (800) RED-EXAM to register for Novell tests (see Chapter 15 for additional information on Sylvan Prometric).

Fee Test fees vary based on length and format; call Sylvan Prometric at (800) RED-EXAM for pricing.

Format CNE tests include both adaptive and traditional format exams. They vary from 30 to 120 minutes in length. For detailed information on the number of questions, length and format of each test see Novell's education Web site (`http://education.novell.com/testinfo/testdata.htm`).

Certified Novell Engineer (CNE): IntranetWare

The Certified Novell Engineer (CNE) program builds on the CNA program described above, but requires considerably more effort. Attaining the CNE requires the accumulation of 19 "credits"—by passing a combination of core CNE exams and "target" exams on IntranetWare—as described below. These CNE exams test the candidate's ability to provide high-end, solutions-based technical support for Novell networks using IntranetWare. Novell offers a preparatory course for each of these exams (see the Resources section that follows for more information).

Who Needs It The CNE designation—one of the most widely recognized networking credentials—is an excellent way to prove your expertise with Novell networking. Whether you want to advance in your current company, or obtain a higher paying position elsewhere, the CNE can help you meet your goals.

Requirements for Certification The certification process requires the following steps:

1. Accumulate 8 credits by passing the following two core CNE tests:

Sylvan ID	Credits	Exam
050-147	3	Networking Technologies
050-626	5	Service and Support

2. Accumulate 11 credits by passing the following IntranetWare Target Requirements tests:

Sylvan ID	Credits	Exam
050-613	3	IntranetWare: NetWare 4.11 Administration
050-614	2	IntranetWare: NetWare 4.11 Advanced Administration
050-617	2	IntranetWare: NetWare 4.11 Installation and Configuration
050-601	2	IntranetWare: NetWare 4.11 Design and Implementation
050-627	2	Building Intranets with IntranetWare

3. Sign and submit the Novell Certification Agreement (available at http://education.novell.com/certinfo/certagrm.htm).

Administrator Tests are administered by Sylvan Prometric; call (800) RED-EXAM to register for Novell tests (see Chapter 15 for additional information on Sylvan Prometric).

Fee Test fees vary based on length and format; call Sylvan Prometric at (800) RED-EXAM for pricing.

Format CNE tests include both adaptive and traditional format exams. They vary from 30 to 120 minutes in length. For detailed information on the number of questions, length, and format of each test, see Novell's education Web site (`http://education.novell` `.com/testinfo/testdata.htm`).

Certified Novell Engineer (CNE): GroupWise 4

The Certified Novell Engineer (CNE) program builds on the CNA program described previously, but requires considerably more effort. Attaining the CNE requires the accumulation of 19 "credits"—by passing a combination of core CNE exams, "target" exams on Group-Wise Version 4, and elective exams—as described below. These CNE exams test the candidate's ability to provide high-end, solutions-based technical support for Novell networks using GroupWise 4. Novell offers a preparatory course for each of these exams (see the Resources section that follows for more information).

Who Needs It The CNE designation—one of the most widely recognized networking credentials—is an excellent way to prove your expertise with Novell networking. Whether you want to advance in your current company, or obtain a higher paying position elsewhere, the CNE can help you meet your goals.

Requirements for Certification The certification process requires the following steps:

1. Accumulate 8 credits by passing the following two core CNE tests:

Sylvan ID	Credits	Exam
050-147	3	Networking Technologies
050-626	5	Service and Support

2. Accumulate 9 credits by passing the following GroupWise 4 Target Requirements tests:

Sylvan ID	Credits	Exam
050-613	3	IntranetWare: NetWare 4.11 Administration
050-154	3	GroupWise 4 Administration
050-612	1	GroupWise 4 Async Gateway & GroupWise Remote
050-604	2	GroupWise 4 Advanced Administration

3. Accumulate 2 additional credits by passing an exam from the following list of CNE elective tests:

Sylvan ID	Credits	Exam
050-606	2	Fundamentals of Network Management
050-622	2	Printing in an Integrated NetWare Environment
050-605	3	NetWare for SAA: Installation and Troubleshooting
050-145	2	NetWare TCP/IP Transport

Sylvan ID	Credits	Exam
050-160	2	NetWare NFS Services: Management, File Sharing, and Printing

4. Sign and submit the Novell Certification Agreement (available at `http://education.novell.com/certinfo/certagrm.htm`).

Administrator Tests are administered by Sylvan Prometric; call (800) RED-EXAM to register for Novell tests (see Chapter 15 for additional information on Sylvan Prometric).

Fee Test fees vary based on length and format; call Sylvan Prometric at (800) RED-EXAM for pricing.

Format CNE tests include both adaptive and traditional format exams. They vary from 30 to 120 minutes in length. For detailed information on the number of questions, length, and format of each test, see Novell's education Web site (`http://education.novell.com/testinfo/testdata.htm`).

Certified Novell Engineer (CNE): GroupWise 5

The Certified Novell Engineer (CNE) program builds on the CNA program described previously, but requires considerably more effort. Attaining the CNE requires the accumulation of 19 "credits"—by passing a combination of core CNE exams, "target" exams on Group-Wise 5, and elective exams—as described below. These CNE exams test the candidate's ability to provide high-end, solutions-based technical support for Novell networks using GroupWise 5. Novell offers a preparatory course for each of these exams (see the Resources section that follows for more information).

Who Needs It The CNE designation—one of the most widely recognized networking credentials—is an excellent way to prove your expertise with Novell networking. Whether you want to advance in your current company, or obtain a higher-paying position elsewhere, the CNE can help you meet your goals.

Requirements for Certification The certification process requires the following steps:

1. Accumulate 8 credits by passing the following two core CNE tests:

Sylvan ID	Credits	Exam
050-147	3	Networking Technologies
050-626	5	Service and Support

2. Accumulate 9 credits by passing the following GroupWise 5 Target Requirement tests:

Sylvan ID	Credits	Exam
050-613	3	IntranetWare: NetWare 4.11 Administration
050-618	3	GroupWise 5 Administration
050-619	2	GroupWise 5 Advanced Administration
TBD	1	GroupWise 5 Connectivity

3. Accumulate 2 additional credits by passing an exam from the following list of CNE elective tests:

Sylvan ID	Credits	Exam
050-606	2	Fundamentals of Network Management
050-622	2	Printing in an Integrated NetWare Environment
050-605	3	NetWare for SAA: Installation and Troubleshooting

Sylvan ID	Credits	Exam
050-145	2	NetWare TCP/IP Transport
050-160	2	NetWare NFS Services: Management, File Sharing, and Printing

4. Sign and submit the Novell Certification Agreement (available at http://education.novell.com/certinfo/certagrm.htm).

Administrator Tests are administered by Sylvan Prometric; call (800) RED-EXAM to register for Novell tests (see Chapter 15 for additional information on Sylvan Prometric).

Fee Test fees vary based on length and format; call Sylvan Prometric at (800) RED-EXAM for pricing.

Format CNE tests include both adaptive and traditional format exams. They vary from 30 to 120 minutes in length. For detailed information on the number of questions, length, and format of each test, see Novell's education Web site (http://education.novell.com/testinfo/testdata.htm).

Master Certified Novell Engineer (MCNE): Management

The Master CNE, Novell's top-of-the-line certification, designates an individual as an expert in Novell networking. This certification builds on the Certified Novell Engineer (CNE) program described previously. Attaining the Master CNE in management requires completion of a CNE certification plus the accumulation of 10 additional "credits"—by passing a combination of required Master CNE core exams, "target" exams on management, and elective exams—as described below. Novell offers a preparatory course for each of these exams (see the Resources section that follows for more information).

Who Needs It Completing this highly challenging Master CNE program makes you stand out as an expert in managing multiple Novell servers and networks. It can be the ticket to job offers, promotions, and salary increases in companies and government agencies that use Novell.

Requirements for Certification The certification process requires the following steps:

1. Obtain certification as a Certified Novell Engineer in any specialization (see CNE sections above).

2. Accumulate 4 credits by passing the following two Master CNE core tests:

Sylvan ID	Credits	Exam
050-611	2	Fundamentals of Internetworking
050-601	2	IntranetWare: Design and Implementation

3. Accumulate 2 credits by passing the following Management Target Requirement test:

Sylvan ID	Credits	Exam
050-613	2	Network management Using ManageWise 2.1

4. Accumulate 4 additional credits from by taking exams from the following list of CNE elective tests:

Sylvan ID	Credits	Exam
050-606	2	Fundamentals of Network Management
050-622	2	Printing in an Integrated NetWare Environment

Sylvan ID	Credits	Exam
050-627	2	Building Intranets with IntranetWare
050-629	2	Securing Intranets with BorderManager
050-142	2	Internetworking with NetWare MultiProtocol Router
050-605	3	NetWare for SAA: Installation and Troubleshooting
050-145	2	NetWare TCP/IP Transport
050-160	2	NetWare NFS Services: Management, File Sharing, and Printing

Administrator Tests are administered by Sylvan Prometric; call (800) RED-EXAM to register for Novell tests (see Chapter 15 for additional information on Sylvan Prometric).

Fee Test fees vary based on length and format; call Sylvan Prometric at (800) RED-EXAM for pricing.

Format CNE tests include both adaptive and traditional format exams. They vary from 30 to 120 minutes in length. For detailed information on the number of questions, length, and format of each test, see Novell's education Web site (`http://education.novell.com/testinfo/testdata.htm`).

Master Certified Novell Engineer (MCNE): Connectivity

The Master CNE, Novell's top-of-the-line certification, designates an individual as an expert in Novell networking. This certification builds on the Certified Novell Engineer (CNE) program described previously. Attaining the Master CNE in connectivity requires completion of a CNE certification plus the accumulation of 10 additional "credits"— by passing a combination of required Master CNE core exams, "target" exams on connectivity, and elective exams—as described below. Novell offers a preparatory course for each of these exams (see the Resources section that follows for more information).

Who Needs It Completing this highly challenging Master CNE program makes you stand out as an expert in interconnecting multiple Novell servers and managing wide area networks. It can be the ticket to job offers, promotions, and salary increases in companies and government agencies that use Novell.

Requirements for Certification The certification process requires the following steps:

1. Obtain certification as a Certified Novell Engineer in any specialization (see CNE sections above).

2. Accumulate 4 credits by passing the following two Master CNE core tests:

Sylvan ID	Credits	Exam
050-611	2	Fundamentals of Internetworking
050-601	2	NIntranetWare: Design and Implementation

3. Accumulate 2 credits by passing one of the following Connectivity Target Requirements tests:

Sylvan ID	Credits	Exam
050-142	2	Internetworking with NetWare MultiProtocol Router
050-629	2	Securing Intranets with BorderManager

4. Accumulate 4 additional credits by taking exams from the following list of CNE elective tests:

Sylvan ID	Credits	Exam
050-606	2	Fundamentals of Network Management
050-622	2	Printing in an Integrated NetWare Environment
050-627	2	Building Intranets with IntranetWare
050-613	2	Network management Using ManageWise 2.1
050-629	2	Securing Intranets with BorderManager
050-142	2	Internetworking with NetWare MultiProtocol Router
050-605	3	NetWare for SAA: Installation and Troubleshooting
050-145	2	NetWare TCP/IP Transport
050-160	2	NetWare NFS Services: Management, File Sharing, and Printing

Administrator Tests are administered by Sylvan Prometric; call (800) RED-EXAM to register for Novell tests (see Chapter 15 for additional information on Sylvan Prometric).

Fee Test fees vary based on length and format; call Sylvan Prometric at (800) RED-EXAM for pricing.

Format CNE tests include both adaptive and traditional format exams. They vary from 30 to 120 minutes in length. For detailed

information on the number of questions, length, and format of each
test, see Novell's education Web site (`http://education.novell`
`.com/testinfo/testdata.htm`).

Master Certified Novell Engineer (MCNE): Messaging

The Master CNE, Novell's top-of-the-line certification, designates an
individual as an expert in Novell networking. This certification builds
on the Certified Novell Engineer (CNE) program described previously.
Attaining the Master CNE in messaging requires completion of a CNE
certification, plus the accumulation of 10 additional "credits"—by
passing a combination of required Master CNE core exams, "target"
exams on messaging, and elective exams—as described below. Novell
offers a preparatory course for each of these exams (see the Resources
section that follows for more information).

Who Needs It Completing this highly challenging Master CNE program makes you stand out as an expert in setting up and troubleshooting enterprise-wide Novell messaging and database
applications. It can be the ticket to job offers, promotions, and salary
increases in companies and government agencies that use Novell.

Requirements for Certification The certification process
requires the following steps:

1. Obtain certification as a Certified Novell Engineer in any specialization (see CNE sections above).

2. Accumulate 4 credits by passing the following two Master
   CNE core tests:

Sylvan ID	Credits	Exam
050-611	2	Fundamentals of Internetworking

Sylvan ID	Credits	Exam
050-601	2	IntranetWare: Design and Implementation

3. Accumulate 2 credits by passing one of the following Messaging Target Requirements tests:

Sylvan ID	Credits	Exam
050-619	2	GroupWise 5 Advanced Administration
050-623	2	GroupWise 4.1 to 5 Differences

4. Accumulate 4 additional credits by taking exams from the following list of CNE elective tests:

Sylvan ID	Credits	Exam
050-606	2	Fundamentals of Network Management
050-622	2	Printing in an Integrated NetWare Environment
050-627	2	Building Intranets with IntranetWare
050-613	2	Network management Using ManageWise 2.1
050-629	2	Securing Intranets with BorderManager
050-142	2	nternetworking with NetWare MultiProtocol Router
050-605	3	NetWare for SAA: Installation and Troubleshooting
050-145	2	NetWare TCP/IP Transport
050-160	2	NetWare NFS Services: Management, File Sharing, and Printing

Administrator Tests are administered by Sylvan Prometric; call (800) RED-EXAM to register for Novell tests (see Chapter 15 for additional information on Sylvan Prometric).

Fee Test fees vary based on length and format; call Sylvan Prometric at (800) RED-EXAM for pricing.

Format CNE tests include both adaptive and traditional format exams. They vary from 30 to 120 minutes in length. For detailed information on the number of questions, length, and format of each test, see Novell's education Web site (`http://education.novell.com/testinfo/testdata.htm`).

Master Certified Novell Engineer (MCNE): Internet/Intranet Solutions

The Master CNE, Novell's top-of-the-line certification, designates an individual as an expert in Novell networking. This certification builds on the Certified Novell Engineer (CNE) program described previously. Attaining the Master CNE in Internet/intranet solutions requires completion of a CNE certification, plus the accumulation of 10 additional "credits"—by passing a combination of required Master CNE core exams, "target" exams on Internet/intranet solutions, and elective exams—as described below. Novell offers a preparatory course for each of these exams (see the Resources section that follows for more information).

Who Needs It Completing this highly challenging Master CNE program makes you stand out as an expert in building and managing Internet/intranet infrastructure for your organization. It can be the ticket to job offers, promotions, and salary increases in companies and government agencies that use Novell.

Requirements for Certification The certification process requires the following steps:

1. Obtain certification as a Certified Novell Engineer in any specialization (see CNE sections above).

2. Accumulate 6 credits by passing the following two Master CNE core tests:

Sylvan ID	Credits	Exam
050-611	2	Fundamentals of Internetworking
050-601	2	IntranetWare: Design and Implementation
050-145	2	NetWare TCP/IP Transport

3. Accumulate 2 credits from the Internet/Intranet Target Requirements by passing the following tests:

Sylvan ID	Credits	Exam
050-710	1	Web Server Management
050-625	1	DNS and FTP Server Installation and Configuration

4. Accumulate 2 additional credits by taking exams from the following list of CNE elective tests:

Sylvan ID	Credits	Exam
050-606	2	Fundamentals of Network Management
050-622	2	Printing in an Integrated NetWare Environment
050-627	2	Building Intranets with IntranetWare

Sylvan ID	Credits	Exam
050-613	2	Network management Using ManageWise 2.1
050-629	2	Securing Intranets with BorderManager
050-142	2	Internetworking with NetWare MultiProtocol Router
050-605	3	NetWare for SAA: Installation and Troubleshooting
050-160	2	NetWare NFS Services: Management, File Sharing, and Printing

Administrator Tests are administered by Sylvan Prometric; call (800) RED-EXAM to register for Novell tests (see Chapter 15 for additional information on Sylvan Prometric).

Fee Test fees vary based on length and format; call Sylvan Prometric at (800) RED-EXAM for pricing.

Format CNE tests include both adaptive and traditional format exams. They vary from 30 to 120 minutes in length. For detailed information on the number of questions, length, and format of each test, see Novell's education Web site (`http://education.novell.com/testinto/testdata.htm`).

Master Certified Novell Engineer (MCNE): AS/400 Integration

The Master CNE, Novell's top-of-the-line certification, designates an individual as an expert in Novell networking. This certification builds on the Certified Novell Engineer (CNE) program described previously.

Attaining the Master CNE in AS/400 Integration requires completion of a CNE certification, plus the accumulation of nine additional "credits"—by passing a combination of required Master CNE exams and a "target" exam on AS/400 integration—as described below. Novell offers a preparatory course for each of their exams (see the Resources section that follows for more information).

Who Needs It   Completing this highly challenging Master CNE program makes you stand out as an expert in integrating Novell and AS/400 applications and networks. It can be the ticket to job offers, promotions, and salary increases in companies and government agencies that use Novell.

Requirements for Certification   The certification process requires the following steps:

1.   Obtain certification as a Certified Novell Engineer in any specialization (see CNE sections above).

2.   Accumulate 6 credits by passing the following three Master CNE core tests:

Sylvan ID	Credits	Exam
050-611	2	Fundamentals of Internetworking
050-601	2	IntranetWare: Design and Implementation
050-605	3	NetWare for SAA: Installation and Troubleshooting

3.   Accumulate 3 credits by passing the AS/400 Integration Target Requirements test, which is offered by IBM. See Chapter 4 for details on this test: IntranetWare and AS/400 Integration exam (Sylvan ID: 000-051).

Administrator Tests are administered by Sylvan Prometric; call (800) RED-EXAM to register for Novell tests (see Chapter 15 for additional information on Sylvan Prometric).

Fee Test fees vary based on length and format; call Sylvan Prometric at (800) RED-EXAM for pricing.

Format CNE tests include both adaptive and traditional format exams. They vary from 30 to 120 minutes in length. For detailed information on the number of questions, length, and format of each test, see Novell's education Web site (`http://education.novell` `.com/testinfo/testdata.htm`).

Master Certified Novell Engineer (MCNE): UNIX Integration

The Master CNE, Novell's top-of-the-line certification, designates an individual as an expert in Novell networking. This certification builds on the Certified Novell Engineer (CNE) program described previously. Attaining the Master CNE in UNIX Integration requires completion of a CNE certification, plus the accumulation of 10 additional "credits"—by passing a combination of required Master CNE exams, "target" exams on management, and elective exams—as described below. Novell offers a preparatory course for each of these exams (see the Resources section that follows for more information).

Who Needs It Completing this highly challenging Master CNE program makes you stand out as an expert in integrating Novell and UNIX applications and networks. It can be the ticket to job offers, promotions, and salary increases in companies and government agencies that use Novell.

Requirements for Certification The certification process requires the following steps:

1. Obtain certification as a Certified Novell Engineer in any specialization (see CNE sections above).

2. Accumulate 4 credits by passing the following two Master CNE core tests:

Sylvan ID	Credits	Exam
050-611	2	Fundamentals of Internetworking
050-601	2	IntranetWare: Design and Implementation

3. Accumulate 2 credits by passing one of the following three tests offered by Novell or SCO (see Chapter 4 for details on SCO exams):

Sylvan ID	Credits	Exam
050-145	2	NetWare TCP/IP Transport
090-005	2	SCO TCP/IP
090-054	2	SCO OpenServer Network Administration

3. Accumulate 4 credits from the UNIX Integration Target Requirements by passing one of the following tests from SCO (see Chapter 4 for details on these tests):

Sylvan ID	Credits	Exam
095-153	4	SCO OpenServer Release 5
095-154	4	SCO OpenServer Network Administration

Administrator Tests are administered by Sylvan Prometric; call (800) RED-EXAM to register for Novell tests (see Chapter 15 for additional information on Sylvan Prometric).

Fee Test fees vary based on length and format; call Sylvan Prometric at (800) RED-EXAM for pricing.

Format CNE tests include both adaptive and traditional format exams. They vary from 30 to 120 minutes in length. For detailed information on the number of questions, length, and format of each test, see Novell's education Web site (`http://education.novell.com/testinfo/testdata.htm`).

Master Certified Novell Engineer (MCNE): Windows NT Integration

The Master CNE, Novell's top-of-the-line certification, designates an individual as an expert in Novell networking. This certification builds on the Certified Novell Engineer (CNE) program described previously. Attaining the Master CNE in Windows NT Integration requires completion of a CNE certification, plus the accumulation of 10 additional "credits"—by passing a combination of required Master CNE exams, "target" exams on Windows NT Integration, and elective exams—as described below. Novell offers a preparatory course for each of these exams (see the Resources section that follows for more information).

Who Needs It This highly respected Master CNE certification is a good way to make yourself stand out as an expert in integrating Novell and Windows NT networks. It can be the ticket to job offers, promotions, and salary increases in companies and government agencies that use Novell and Windows NT.

Requirements for Certification The certification process requires the following steps:

1. Obtain certification as a Certified Novell Engineer in any specialization (see CNE sections above).

2. Accumulate 6 credits by passing the following three Master CNE core tests:

Sylvan ID	Credits	Exam
050-611	2	Fundamentals of Internetworking
050-601	2	IntranetWare: Design and Implementation
050-145	2	NetWare TCP/IP Transport

3. Accumulate 2 credits by passing the Management Target Requirements test: Novell 555 IntranetWare: Integrating Windows NT exam (Sylvan ID: 050-624).

4. Accumulate 2 additional credits from by passing one of the following CNE elective tests:

Sylvan ID	Credits	Exam
050-606	2	Fundamentals of Network Management
050-622	2	Printing in an Integrated NetWare Environment
050-627	2	Building Intranets with IntranetWare
050-629	2	Securing Intranets with BorderManager
050-142	2	Internetworking with NetWare MultiProtocol Router

Sylvan ID	Credits	Exam
050-605	3	NetWare for SAA: Installation and Troubleshooting
050-160	2	NetWare NFS Services: Management, File Sharing, and Printing

Administrator Tests are administered by Sylvan Prometric; call (800) RED-EXAM to register for Novell tests (see Chapter 15 for additional information on Sylvan Prometric).

Fee Test fees vary based on length and format; call Sylvan Prometric at (800) RED-EXAM for pricing.

Format CNE tests include both adaptive and traditional format exams. They vary from 30 to 120 minutes in length. For detailed information on the number of questions, length, and format of each test, see Novell's education Web site (`http://education.novell .com/testinfo/testdata.htm`).

Resources

Novell offers an extensive set of classes for CNA, CNE, and Master CNE candidates. In fact, each of the exams listed above is tied directly to a related course and course number. For example, in order to prepare for the Novell 540: Building Intranets with IntranetWare exam, you could take the Novell 540: Building Intranets with IntranetWare course from a Novell Authorized Education Center.

The Novell Web site offers exam bulletins that detail each test's objectives. Novell's Web site also offers a listing of Novell Authorized Education Centers and Novell Education Academic Partners. For more information on this organization's certifications and courses, contact Novell at:

Web	http://education.novell.com/
E-mail	edcustomer@novell.com
Mail	Novell, Inc. 122 East 1700 South Provo, Utah 84606
Phone	(800) 233-EDUC
Fax	(801) 222-7875
Faxback	(800) 233-EDUC

8

Client/Server and Database System Certifications

FEATURING

- Borland Certification

- Centura Certifications

- Informix Certifications

- Oracle Certification

- Sybase Certifications

This chapter covers several highly specialized certification programs designed by vendors that make database and client/server products. Borland, Centura, Informix, Oracle, and Sybase all offer certifications on their database products. These certifications focus on the tasks involved in administering and managing large databases for a variety of purposes.

Professionals seeking these certifications might include:

- Database administrators

- Database programmers

- Network administrators

- Information systems managers

Borland Certification

Borland produces a number of different pieces of software. One of Borland's best-known products is Delphi, which is one of the most popular client/server development systems. Borland offers a certification program on its latest version of Delphi, version 3. Borland also offers a certification program for trainers (see Chapter 10 for more information).

Recertification or Maintenance Requirements Borland requires its certified professionals to become recertified within 60 days of the release of each new version of the Delphi Client/Server Suite.

The recertification requirements vary from one release to the next; they may include passing another certification exam, additional fees, or attendance at a Borland authorized training course.

Benefits of Certification   Delphi 3 Certified Developers receive these benefits:

- Certificate of recognition

- Use of the Borland Delphi Certified Developer logo

- Partners in the Borland solutions Program will be listed on Borland's Online Resource Locator, a database of Delphi Certified Developers that companies can use to find qualified individuals for consulting or contract work (see `http://www.borland .com/programs/bsp/` for more information).

Delphi 3 Certified Developer

Attaining this certification involves passing one exam which covers the tasks involved in administering and managing the Delphi 3 Client/Server Suite. Candidates may attempt the exam twice. If both attempts are unsuccessful, the candidate is expected to attend a Delphi C/S training course taught by a certified instructor before making a third attempt to pass the exam. After successful completion of the exam, you will receive a certification agreement which you must sign and return to Borland.

Who Needs It   Certification as a Delphi 3 Developer can be valuable to independent consultants and contractors who want to validate their abilities for potential clients. Certification can also be helpful in obtaining a job that involves developing client/server applications at a company that uses Delphi.

Requirements for Certification The certification process requires the following steps:

1. Pass the Delphi 3 Client/Server Foundation Exam (Sylvan ID: 9J0-002).

2. Sign and return the Delphi 3 Developer Agreement.

Administrator Call Sylvan Prometric at (800) 430-EXAM to register for a Borland test. (See Chapter 15 for more information on Sylvan.)

Fee $150

Format This test consists of 100 multiple-choice questions and must be completed in 120 minutes. A score of 80 percent or better is required to pass.

Resources

The Borland Web site offers a list of test objectives and sample questions. For more information on this organization's certifications and courses, contact Borland at:

Web   `http://www.borland.com/`

E-mail   `kalderman@corp.borland.com`

Mail   Manager of Training and Certification
          103 Eagleview Ct.
          Henderson, NV 89014

Phone   (408) 431-1277

Centura Certifications

Centura Software makes a number of database products, but their core product line is the scalable SQLBase 7 database product. Centura offers two certifications on SQLBase and related products: the Centura Database Developer (DBD) and the Centura Database Administrator (DBA). The Developer certification is based on in-depth knowledge of client technology, object-oriented programming, and application design. The DBA certification is based on in-depth knowledge of server technology, including SQLBase advanced features, performance tuning, and database design.

Recertification or Maintenance Requirements   The SQLBase certifications apply to specific version numbers of the database product, so there is no requirement for recertification on a particular version. Since your certification is tied to a certain version of a product, however, you will want become certified on the newest versions when they become available, if you want to continue to have the most current credential.

Benefits of Certification   Centura Database Developers and Administrators receive these benefits:

- A listing in Centura's Web-based referral service

- Logo for use on business cards and stationery

- Access to Centura technical e-mail lists and newsgroups

Centura Database Developer

Attaining this certification involves passing one exam. The Database Developer test focuses on the following topics: knowledge of basic Centura Team Developer (formerly SQLWindows); SQL fundamentals; object-oriented programming; MDI Windows; building a database application; table windows; and generating reports.

Who Needs It   Certification as a Centura Database Developer can be very valuable to independent consultants and contractors who want to document their abilities for potential clients. This certification can also be helpful to individuals seeking a job as a developer of client/server applications.

Requirements for Certification   The certification process requires only one step:

1.   Pass the Centura Developer exam.

Administrator   Call Sylvan Prometric at (800) 387-3926 to register for a Centura test. (See Chapter 15 for more information on Sylvan.)

Fee $120

Format   Multiple-choice exam consisting of approximately 82 questions. Call Sylvan Prometric at (800) 387-3926 for current information on exam length and passing score.

Centura Database Administrator

Attaining certification as a Centura Database Administrator involves passing only one exam. The DBA certification exam tests the candidate's in-depth knowledge of server technology, including SQLBase advanced features, performance tuning, and database design.

Who Needs It Certification as a Centura Database Developer can be very valuable to independent consultants and contractors who want to document their abilities for potential clients. This certification can also be helpful to individuals seeking a job developing client/server applications.

Requirements for Certification The certification process requires only one step:

1. Pass the Centura Database Administrator exam.

Administrator Call Sylvan Prometric at (800) 387-3926 to register for a Centura test. (See Chapter 15 for more information on Sylvan.)

Fee $120

Format Multiple-choice exam consisting of approximately 42 questions. Call Sylvan Prometric at (800) 387-3926 for current information on the exam length and passing score.

Resources

The Centura Web site offers a listing of exam objectives and sample questions for each exam. In addition, Centura can provide you with a listing of Centura Certified Training Partners—organizations that offer training courses on Centura products. For more information on this organization's certifications and courses, contact Centura at:

Web	`http://www.centurasoft.com/`
E-mail	`centuraps@centurasoft.com`
Mail	Centura Software 975 Island Drive Redwood Shores, CA 94065
Phone	(650) 596-3400 or (800) 444-8782

Informix Certifications

Informix produces a popular database program (also called Informix) for UNIX-based computers. Informix offers several certifications on its products: the Database Specialist: Informix Dynamic Server, the System Administrator: Informix Dynamic Server, and the INFORMIX-4GL Certified Professional.

Recertification or Maintenance Requirements   All certifications offered in the Informix Certified Professional Program are based on specific versions of Informix products. As products and respective certifications become available, certifications should be updated accordingly. Certified Professionals may only represent themselves as being certified for the specific version of the product that is listed on their certificate.

Benefits of Certification   Informix Certified Professionals receive:

- Certificate of achievement

- Use of the Informix Certified Professional logo

- Informix Certified Professionals who are employed by a company that has a valid Informix support contract will also receive a personalized account with the InformixLink TechInfo Center. (The TechInfo Center is a private, 24-hour support section of the Informix Web site, which includes product defect reports, porting schedules, product alerts, and technical publications.)

- Subscription to TechNotes, a quarterly Technical Support journal

- Subscription to CS Times, a quarterly Customer Services newsletter

Database Specialist: Informix Dynamic Server

The Database Specialist certification is designed for individuals who implement and manage Informix Dynamic Server databases. To attain this certification you must pass two exams, which will test your proficiency in the areas of database and data models, entity relationships, SQL constructs, data integrity, Informix data types, creating Informix databases, and the commands needed to maintain and manage Informix databases.

Informix recommends that candidates take the following courses as preparation for the required tests:

- Relational Database Design

- Structured Query Language

- Managing and Optimizing Informix Dynamic Server Databases

Who Needs It Informix Database Specialist certification is valuable if you want to get a job developing client/server applications or administering databases at a company that uses Informix. It can also be a valuable title for independent consultants and contractors who want to document their abilities for potential clients.

Requirements for Certification The certification process requires the following steps:

1. Pass the Database Fundamentals exam (Sylvan ID: 660-111).

2. Pass the Managing and Optimizing Informix Dynamic Server Databases exam (Sylvan ID: 660-112).

Administrator Call Sylvan Prometric at (800) 977-3926 to register for an Informix test. (See Chapter 15 for more information on Sylvan.)

Fee $150 per exam

Format The Database Fundamentals multiple-choice exam consists of 68 questions that must be completed in 90 minutes. A score of 82 percent is required to pass. The Managing and Optimizing Informix Dynamic Server Databases multiple-choice exam consists of 70 questions that must be completed in 90 minutes. A score of 80 percent is required to pass.

System Administrator: Informix Dynamic Server

The System Administrator certification is designed for individuals who configure, maintain, and tune Informix Dynamic Server databases. Attaining this certification involves passing two exams, which test your database proficiency regarding knowledge of the components of a Dynamic Server system, configuring and monitoring Dynamic Server, UNIX utilities for Dynamic Server processing, managing logs and archives of databases, and performance management of the Dynamic Server system.

Informix recommends that candidates take the following courses to prepare for the required tests:

- System Administration: Informix Dynamic Server

- Performance Tuning: Informix Dynamic Server

Who Needs It   The System Administrator—Informix Dynamic Server certification is valuable if you are looking for a job administrating mission-critical client/server applications at a company that uses Informix. It can also be a valuable title for independent consultants and contractors who want to document their abilities for potential clients.

Requirements for Certification   The certification process requires the following steps:

1. Pass the Informix Dynamic Server System Administration exam (Sylvan ID: 660-211).

2. Pass Informix Dynamic Server Performance Tuning exam (Sylvan ID: 660-212).

Administrator   Call Sylvan Prometric at (800) 977-3926 to register for an Informix test. (See Chapter 15 for more information on Sylvan.)

Fee $150 per exam

Format   The Informix Dynamic Server System Administration multiple-choice exam consists of 71 questions that must be completed in 90 minutes. A score of 74 percent is required to pass. The Informix Dynamic Server Performance Tuning multiple-choice exam consists of 44 questions that must be answered in 60 minutes. A score of 84 percent is required to pass.

INFORMIX-4GL Certified Professional

To become an INFORMIX-4GL Certified Professional, you must be proficient in using INFORMIX-4GL to write custom database applications. The two required exams for this certification cover the following topics: databases and data models; entity relationships; SQL constructs; data integrity; Informix data types; creating menus; handling concurrent users; managing screen interaction; managing forms and windows; using program variables; selecting, inserting, updating, and deleting data; managing cursors; handling program and user errors; managing transactions; handling query-by-example logic; and writing reports.

Informix recommends that candidates take the following courses to prepare for the required tests:

- Relational Database Design

- Structured Query Language

- Developing Applications Using INFORMIX-4GL

Who Needs It   The INFORMIX-4GL Certified Professional credential is valuable if you are looking for a job creating custom database applications at a company that uses Informix. It can also be a valuable title for independent consultants and contractors who want to document their abilities for potential clients.

Requirements for Certification   The certification process requires the following steps:

1.   Pass the Database Fundamentals exam (Sylvan ID: 660-111).

2.   Pass the INFORMIX-4GL Development exam (Sylvan ID: 660-301).

Administrator Call Sylvan Prometric at (800) 977-3926 to register for an Informix test. (See Chapter 15 for more information on Sylvan.)

Fee $150 per exam

Format The Database Fundamentals multiple-choice exam consists of 68 questions that must be completed in 90 minutes. A score of 82 percent is required to pass. The INFORMIX-4GL Development multiple-choice exam consists of 90 questions that must be completed in 90 minutes. A score of 78 percent is required to pass.

Resources

The Informix Web site offers additional information and sample tests for each exam, as well as information on taking the recommended courses. For more information on this organization's certifications and courses, contact Informix at:

Web	`http://www.informix.com/`
E-mail	`certification@informix.com`
Mail	Informix Software 4100 Bohannon Drive Menlo Park, CA 94025
Phone	(800) 331-1763
Fax	(913) 599-8542

Oracle Certifications

Certified Professional

Oracle produces a number of different software programs, but the company is best known for its Oracle database system. Oracle offers two certification programs: the Oracle Certified Professional and the Oracle Masters of Technology program. The Oracle Certified Professional program offers two certification paths: the Certified Database Administrator and the Certified Application Developer for Developer/2000. (See the Oracle Web site at http://www.oracle .com/ for information on the Oracle Masters of Technology program, which is not included here because it does not involve an evaluation component.)

Recertification or Maintenance Requirements   Oracle announces requirements for recertification based on the release of new products and upgrades. Previously obtained certifications are valid for six months following an announcement of recertification requirements.

Benefits of Certification   Oracle Certified Professionals receive:

- Use of Oracle Certified Professional logo
- Certificate

Certified Database Administrator

To become an Oracle Certified Database Administrator, you must pass four tests. These exams cover knowledge of the essential aspects of the SQL language, Oracle 7 administration, backup and recovery, and performance tuning of the system.

Who Needs It The Certified Database Administrator credential demonstrates your skill and expertise in administering Oracle database systems. If you are already using Oracle 7 at your company, it may be a great way to move up to a position of higher responsibility and pay.

Requirements for Certification The certification process requires the following steps:

1. Pass the Introduction to Oracle: SQL and PL/SQL exam.

2. Pass the Oracle 7 Database Administration exam.

3. Pass the Oracle 7 Backup and Recovery exam.

4. Pass the Oracle 7 Performance and Tuning exam.

If you fail a test, you must wait at least 30 days before you re-take that exam. You may attempt a particular test up to three times in a twelve-month period. Requests for exemption from this requirement must be made in writing to Robert Pedigo, Manager, Oracle Certified Professional Program, Oracle Corporation, 500 Oracle Parkway-M/S SB-4, Redwood Shores, CA 94065.

Administrator Call Sylvan Prometric at (800) 891-3926 to register for an Oracle test. (See Chapter 15 for more information on Sylvan.)

Fee $125 per exam

Format The exams are multiple-choice tests consisting of 60 to 70 questions that must be completed in 90 minutes.

Certified Application Developer for Developer/2000

To become an Oracle Certified Application Developer for Developer/ 2000, you must pass five tests. These exams cover knowledge of the essential aspects of the SQL language, creating procedures using Oracle Procedure Builder, using Developer/2000, and managing the user interface.

Who Needs It   The Certified Application Developer for Developer/ 2000 credential demonstrates your skill and expertise in developing Oracle database systems. If you are already using Oracle 7 at your company, it can be a great way to move up to a position of higher responsibility and pay.

Requirements for Certification   The certification process requires the following steps:

1. Pass the Introduction to Oracle: SQL and PL/SQL exam.

2. Pass the Developer PL/SQL and PL/SQL.

3. Pass the Developer/2000 Forms 4.5 I.

4. Pass the Developer/2000 Forms 4.5 II.

5. Pass the Developer/2000 Reports 2.5.

If fail a test, you must wait at least 30 days before you retake that exam. You may attempt a particular test up to three times in a twelve-month period.

Administrator   Call Sylvan Prometric at (800) 891-3926 to register for an Oracle test (see Chapter 15 for more information on Sylvan).

Fee $125 for each exam

Format The exams are multiple-choice tests consisting of 60 to 70 questions that must be completed in 90 minutes.

Resources

The Oracle Web site offers a program guide that details the objectives for each exam. For more information on this organization's certifications and courses, contact Oracle at:

Web	`http://www.oracle.com/`
Mail	Oracle Corporation 500 Oracle Parkway Redwood Shores, CA 94065
Phone	(650) 506-7000
Fax	(650) 506-7200

Sybase Certifications

Sybase produces the PowerBuilder database application development tool, as well as the Sybase SQL server database system. The Certified PowerBuilder Developer (CPD) program for PowerBuilder 5.0 offers the Certified PowerBuilder Developer Associate and the Certified PowerBuilder Developer Professional designations. The Certified Sybase Professional (CSP) track—based on the Sybase SQL Server database system—includes the Certified Database Administrator, and Certified Performance & Tuning Specialist.

Sybase plans to release new certification exams for PowerBuilder 6.0 and Adaptive Server Enterprise 11.5 by May, 1998. At that time, the names of the four certifications will change as well. The new names are noted below in the sections on each certification program. A fifth certification—the Certified Sybase Open Interfaces Developer—has recently been discontinued. For more information, check the Certification Update Web site (see Appendix C for information on how to access this site).

Recertification or Maintenance Requirements   To ensure that skills are kept current, all Sybase-certified professionals are required to take a migration test with each major new release of PowerBuilder. All certifications offered in the Sybase program are based upon specific product versions. Certified professionals may only represent themselves as certified for the specific product and product version listed on their certificate.

Benefits of Certification   Certified PowerBuilder Developers receive the following benefits:

- CPD certificate and ID card

- Use of the CPD logo

- Listing in the CPD Directory, a listing of client/server developers that employers can consult to locate qualified technical professionals

- A discount on technical support

Certified Sybase Professionals receive the following benefits:

- CSP certificate and ID card

- Use of the CSP logo

- A CSP logo-branded gift

- Newsletters and other publications from Sybase

Certified PowerBuilder Developer Associate

The Certified PowerBuilder Developer Associate certification is designed to validate the abilities of experienced PowerBuilder developers whose knowledge covers the spectrum of PowerBuilder client/ server development topics. To obtain this certification, candidates must pass two exams. These tests assess a candidate's knowledge of the PowerBuilder environment's underlying technologies, including client/server architecture, object-oriented programming, event-driven programming, graphical user interfaces, relational databases, SQL, and the PowerScript language. With the release of certification exams for PowerBuilder 6.0, anticipated in May, 1998, the name of this certification will change to the Sybase Certified Associate: PowerBuilder Developer.

Who Needs It The Certified PowerBuilder Developer Associate credential is valuable if you want to get a job creating client-server applications. It can also be a valuable title for independent consultants and contractors who want to document their abilities for potential clients.

Requirements for Certification The certification process requires the following steps:

1. Pass the PowerBuilder 5.0 Fundamentals exam (Sylvan ID: 360-201).

2. Pass the PowerBuilder 5.0 Advanced Concepts exam (Sylvan ID: 360-202).

Administrator Call Sylvan Prometric at (800) 407-3926 or Virtual University Enterprises (VUE) at (800) 243-7184 to register for a Sybase test. (See Chapter 15 for more information on Sylvan and VUE.)

Fee Fees for Sybase tests can vary; call Sylvan Prometric at (800) 407-3926 or VUE at (800) 243-7184 for pricing.

Format Both tests are multiple-choice tests that must be completed in one hour. Contact Sylvan at (800) 407-3926 or VUE at (800) 243-7184 for the latest information on the number of questions and passing score.

Certified PowerBuilder Developer Professional (CPD)

The Certified PowerBuilder Developer Professional certification program builds on the Certified PowerBuilder Developer Associate credential. This certification, which recognizes technical mastery of the PowerBuilder database application development tool, is a popular database certification; there are currently over 3,000 Certified Power-Builder Developer Professionals.

Passing the one required performance-based exam necessitates an in-depth understanding of PowerBuilder as a client/server application development tool and experience building real-world PowerBuilder applications. Exam results are evaluated in terms of the extent to which instructions are correctly implemented, the extent to which an optimum approach was used, and demonstration of good application development practice—including the ability to implement appropriate error handling, use comments in code, and adhere to naming conventions. With the release of new certification exams for PowerBuilder 6.0, anticipated in May, 1998, the name of this certification will change to Sybase Certified Professional: PowerBuilder Developer.

Who Needs It The Certified PowerBuilder Developer Professional credential is valuable if you want to get a high-level job creating client/server applications. It can also be a valuable title for independent consultants and contractors who want to document their abilities for potential clients.

Requirements for Certification The certification process requires the following steps:

1. Achieve Certified PowerBuilder Developer Associate status, as described above.

2. Pass the Certified PowerBuilder Developer Application exam (ID: 360-203).

Administrator The Professional application exam is offered at selected Sylvan authorized Prometric Testing Centers (over 40 in North America). Call Sylvan Prometric at (800) 407-3926 to register for the exam.

Fee Fees for Sybase tests can vary; call Sylvan Prometric at (800) 407-3926 for pricing.

Format This performance-based exam consists of building an application using PowerBuilder. Exams are evaluated by Sybase professionals and test score reports are provided within 6-8 weeks.

Certified Database Administrator

Attaining this certification requires the candidate to pass two exams within a designated time period. The tests for the Sybase Certified Database Administrator (DBA) credential assess a candidate's skill in designing, administering, and supporting Sybase databases.

With the release of new certification exams for Adaptive Server Enterprise 11.5, anticipated in May, 1998, the name of this certification will change to Sybase Certified Associate: Adaptive Server Administrator.

Who Needs It The Certified Database Administrator credential is valuable if you are seeking a job administrating Sybase SQL Server. It can also be a valuable title for independent consultants and contractors who want to document their abilities for potential clients.

Requirements for Certification   The certification process requires the following steps:

1. Pass the SQL Server System 11: FastTrack exam (Sylvan: 510-007).

2. Pass the SQL Server System Administration 11: Server Administration exam (Sylvan ID: 510-008).

Exam requirements must be completed within one year of passing the first exam.

Administrator   Call Sylvan Prometric at (800) 407-3926 or Virtual University Enterprises (VUE) at (800) 243-7184 to register for a Sybase test. (See Chapter 15 for more information on Sylvan and VUE.)

Fee   Fees for Sybase tests can vary; call Sylvan Prometric at (800) 407-3926 or VUE at (800) 243-7184 for pricing.

Format   Both exams are multiple-choice tests that must be completed in 60 minutes. Contact Sylvan at (800) 407-3926 or VUE at (800) 243-7184, for the latest information on the number of test questions and passing score.

Certified Performance and Tuning Specialist

This certification builds on the Certified Database Administrator certification described above. The one additional exam required for the Certified Performance and Tuning Specialist designation tests the candidate's proficiency across a range of database administration, performance, and tuning concepts.

With the release of certification exams for Adaptive Enterprise 11.5, anticipated in May, 1998, the name of this certification will change to Sybase Certified Professional: Adaptive Server Administrator.

Who Needs It The Certified Performance and Tuning Specialist credential is valuable if you are seeking a high-level job administrating Sybase SQL Server. It can also be a valuable title for independent consultants and contractors who want to validate their abilities for potential clients.

Requirements for Certification The certification process requires the following steps:

1. Achieve Certified Database Administrator status, as described above.

2. Pass the SQL Server 11: Performance and Tuning exam (Sylvan ID: 510-009).

Administrator Call Sylvan Prometric at (800) 407-3926 or Virtual University Enterprises (VUE) at (800) 243-7184 to register for a Sybase test. (See Chapter 15 for more information on Sylvan.)

Fee Fees for Sybase tests can vary; call Sylvan Prometric at (800) 407-3926 or VUE at (800) 243-7184 for pricing.

Format This exam is a multiple-choice test that must be completed in one hour. Contact Sylvan at (800) 407-3926 or VUE at (800) 243-7184, for the latest information on the number of questions and passing score.

Resources

The Sybase Web site offers study guides that detail the objectives of each exam. Sybase also offers a number of self-study and instructor-led courses through Sybase Authorized Education Partners. For more information on this organization's certifications and courses, contact Sybase at:

Web	http://slc.sybase.com/
Mail	SYBASE, Inc. Corporate Headquarters 6475 Christie Avenue Emeryville, CA 94608-1050
Phone	(800) 8-SYBASE
Faxback	(888) 792-7329

CHAPTER

9

Internet Certifications

FEATURING

- IBM Certifications

- Learning Tree International Certification

- Microsoft Certifications

- Novell Certifications

- Prosoft/Net Guru Technologies Certifications

- USWeb Learning Certifications

T he list of certification programs related to the Internet is growing and changing rapidly. Within the past year, Microsoft has renamed and redesigned their Internet certification; Novell has created, scrapped, and then re-created their Internet certification program; and new vendor-based certification programs have emerged almost every month. As yet, however, no single Internet certification has become known as the one best certification to get. We have tried to include in this chapter the most interesting and reputable offerings that were available at the time we went to press. Be sure to check the Certification Update Web site for the latest information; several new Internet certification programs are currently under development (see Appendix C for details on how to access the Web site).

Most of the growth and change in Internet certifications has paralleled the burgeoning growth in the use of the Internet by business and industry. More and more companies desperately want to hire professionals who can design, implement, and maintain their Internet presence. Many individuals have found that it was well worthwhile to spend $5,000 to $10,000 on training and certification in order to snag a high-paying job with such a company.

Professionals seeking an Internet certification might include:

- Webmasters

- Web page designers

- Internet service provider staff

- Java, Perl, or ActiveX programmers

- Internet and intranet managers

- Network administrators

To promote quality in existing and emerging Internet certification programs, the Association of Internet Professionals—which recently merged with a related organization, the Webmasters Guild—has formed a certification council. This council will design standards—in the form of a "common core" of skills—to provide benchmarks that all Internet certifications should test. They are trying to make sure that this "core" is applied across the board to academic, organization-based, and vendor-based certification programs. This will help certification candidates to distinguish which programs meet basic quality standards by looking for the Association of Internet Professionals endorsement (see `http://www.isip.org/` for more information on this topic).

This chapter covers both vendor-specific and vendor-independent certification programs that address Internet strategies, procedures, and protocols. IBM offers two Internet certifications: the IBM Certified Solutions Expert: Net.Commerce certification addresses security for financial transactions on the Internet, while the Certified Solution Expert: Firewall certification targets technical professionals who install secure links between company networks and the Internet. The vendor-independent Learning Tree International certification program covers TCP/IP protocols for setting up and administering intranets and Internet connections. The two Microsoft certifications covered in this chapter—Microsoft Certified Professional + Internet and Microsoft Certified Systems Engineer + Internet—are new certifications focused on the implementation of intranet and Internet solutions using Microsoft products. Prosoft/Net Guru Technologies offers certification programs in all aspects of the Internet, from Web site design and business strategies to server administration and TCP/IP security. Novell offers a number of brand new certifications for Internet professionals. USWeb Learning offers two vendor-neutral certifications that focus on broadly-applicable fundamentals and principles of Web development.

IBM Certifications

IBM currently offers two Internet certification programs: the Certified Solutions Expert: Firewall and the Certified Solutions Expert: Net.Commerce. These two certifications are based on IBM's Firewall and Net.Commerce products. The Net.Commerce product facilitates secure financial transactions on the Internet, and the Firewall product facilitates security for links between the Internet and private company intranets.

Recertification or Maintenance Requirements IBM Internet certifications apply to specific version numbers of the Firewall and Net.Commerce products, so there is no requirement for recertification on a particular version. Since your certification is tied to a specific version of a product, however, you will want become certified on the newest versions, when they become available, if you want to continue to have the most current credential in this area.

Benefits of Certification IBM Certified Solutions Experts receive these benefits:

- IBM certification logo for use in advertisements and business literature

- A certificate of completion, an ID card, and a lapel pin

- Your name included in IBM's directories of certified personnel

- Subscriptions to technical newsletters and magazines, other technical literature, and other special offers

- IBM technical support

Certified Solutions Expert: Net.Commerce

To attain certification as a Certified Solutions Expert in Net.Commerce, a candidate must pass one exam. The exam for this certification covers planning, configuring, and implementing Net.Commerce to meet customer needs for secure financial transactions over the Internet. IBM recommends that the candidate have hands-on experience with the Net.Commerce System, Windows NT, and AIX (IBM's version of UNIX) prior to taking the exam.

Who Needs It This certification is an excellent credential for those responsible for Internet "store fronts" and other financial transactions over the Internet. It can also be valuable to consultants who design and implement Internet stores for clients.

Requirements for Certification The certification process requires only one step:

1. Pass the Planning, Implementing and Supporting IBM Net.Commerce Product exam (Sylvan ID: 000-558).

Administrator Tests are administered by Sylvan Prometric; call (800) 959-3926 to register for IBM tests. (See Chapter 15 for additional information on Sylvan Prometric.)

Fee Fees for IBM tests vary based on test length and format; call Sylvan Prometric at (800) 959-3926 for pricing.

Format Computer-based, multiple-choice test. Call Sylvan Prometric at (800) 959-3926 for current information on the number of questions, time limit, and passing score.

Certified Solutions Expert: Firewall

To attain certification as an IBM Certified Solutions Expert: Firewall, a candidate must pass one exam. This exam tests the candidate's knowledge of designing and installing a firewall using IBM's AIX Firewall product (AIX is IBM's version of UNIX). IBM recommends that the certification candidate have hands-on experience with TCP/IP and AIX Firewall (see Chapter 4 for more information on IBM's AIX certifications).

Who Needs It The IBM Certified Solutions Expert: Firewall certification identifies you as being qualified to hold a high level of responsibility for company Internet and intranet security. This certification is also valuable to freelance security consultants.

Requirements for Certification The certification process requires only one step:

1. Pass the IBM Certified Solution Expert Firewall exam (Sylvan ID: 000-558).

Administrator Tests are administered by Sylvan Prometric; call (800) 959-3926 to register for IBM tests. (See Chapter 15 for additional information on Sylvan Prometric.)

Fee Fees for IBM tests vary based on test length and format; call Sylvan Prometric at (800) 959-3926 for pricing.

Format Computer-based, multiple-choice test. Call Sylvan Prometric at (800) 959-3926 for current information on the number of questions, time limit, and passing score.

Resources

IBM's Web site offers a number of excellent resources for certification candidates, including test objectives, study guides, and sample tests. For more information on these courses and certification programs, contact IBM at:

Web	`http://www.ibm.com/certify/`
E-mail	`ialine@us.ibm.com`
Mail	IBM North America 1133 Westchester Avenue White Plains, NY 10604
Phone	(800) IBM-4YOU
Fax	(404) 238-6628
Faxback	(800) 426-4329

Learning Tree International Certification

Learning Tree International is a worldwide training organization that currently offers over 150 computer and networking courses in the United States, Europe, and Asia. As part of their curriculum in information technology, Learning Tree International offers 27 different vendor-independent professional certification programs, one of which is oriented toward Internet and intranet experts. (For information on additional Learning Tree International certification programs, see Chapter 3, 4, and 6.)

The Learning Tree PC Internet/Intranet Certified Professional certification is based on the mastery of a comprehensive set of internetworking service and support courses. This credential may be useful to Webmasters, network support staff, Internet service providers, network engineers, and anyone else involved with the maintenance and support of intranets and Internet connections.

Recertification or Maintenance Requirements There is no recertification requirement for any of Learning Tree International's certification programs.

It is possible to obtain college credit for Learning Tree International certifications or courses. The American Council of Education (ACE) in Washington, D.C. has worked in cooperation with Learning Tree International to determine college course equivalencies for these courses and certifications. Approximately 1,500 colleges and universities in the United States will accept ACE recommendations for college credit. As a general rule, ACE will recommend two college credit hours for each four-day course. Learning Tree International will pay to have your Learning Tree International credentials registered with ACE and you can then request that your transcript be sent from ACE to any college or university. (Check with your college or university registrar to make sure that your institution accepts ACE recommendations for credit.)

Benefits of Certification Learning Tree International PC Service and Support Certified Professionals receive the following benefits:

- Framed diploma of Professional Certification
- An official record of the courses that you have completed
- Option of obtaining college credit

Learning Tree International Internet/Intranet Certified Professional

This certification program consists of taking four core courses and one elective course, and passing the tests given at the end of each course. The courses and exams are designed to teach and test the candidate's ability to choose and implement various Internet connection options; install, configure, and maintain an Internet or intranet server; develop a Web site using HTML and CGI; use all major TCP/IP application services including FTP, Gopher, and Web browsers; analyze security threats from the Internet; and develop a comprehensive security policy to protect an organization's systems and data.

Who Needs It   The Learning Tree International Internet/Intranet Certified Professional credential is a respected vendor-independent certification for those who want to develop Web site strategies for businesses, design and implement intranets, or connect internal networks to the Internet. Since the certification program requires comprehensive training classes, Learning Tree International certifications offer a means for those just beginning their networking careers to gain hands-on experience and training that may not currently be available on the job.

Requirements for Certification   The certification process requires the following steps:

1. Complete the four core courses listed below, and pass the test given at the end of each course:

Course Number	Length	Course
Course 469	four days	Hands-On Internet/Intranet for Business
Course 470	four days	Internet/Intranet Web Site Development

Course Number	Length	Course
Course 475	four days	Building an Intranet: A Hands-on Workshop
Course 468	four days	Internet and System Security: Attacks and Countermeasures

2. Complete one of the elective courses from the following list and pass the test given at the end of the course:

Course Number	Length	Course
Course 471	five days	Java Programming
Course 163	four days	Microsoft Internet Information Server
Course 485	four days	Netscape Suitespot Servers for Intranet/Internet
Course 179	four days	Lotus Notes R4.5 Introduction
Course 374	four days	ISDN for Data Communication
Course 308	four days	Building Office 97 Intranet Applications
Course 238	four days	Integrating Web Sites with Oracle7
Course 455	four days	Windows NT 4.0
Course 488	four days	Deploying Internet and Intranet Firewalls
Course 431	four days	Perl Programming
Course 367	four days	Introduction to TCP/IP

Administrator Learning Tree International (Call (800) THE-TREE)

Fee At this writing, the prices for Learning Tree International courses are $1295 for a two-day course, $1745 for a three-day course, $2195 for a four-day course, and $2495 for a five-day course. Learning Tree offers some significant discounts for those taking more than one course and for government employees. There is no additional charge for the tests.

Format   Each exam consists of 40 to 60 questions based on the course material. If you fail to pass on the first try, Learning Tree International will arrange for you to take a proctored exam at your place of work.

Resources

For more information this organization's courses and certification programs, contact Learning Tree at:

Web	http://www.learningtree.com/
E-mail	uscourses@learningtree.com
Mail	Learning Tree International 1805 Library Street Reston, VA 20190-5630
Phone	(800) THE-TREE
Fax	(800) 709-6405

Microsoft Certifications

In 1997, Microsoft created two new Internet-specific certifications as extensions to their well-known Microsoft Certified Professional (MCP) and Microsoft Certified Systems Engineer (MCSE) programs (see Chapters 4 and 7, respectively, for more information on the MCP and MCSE certification programs). These certifications are titled the Microsoft Certified Professional + Internet and Microsoft Certified Systems Engineer + Internet.

By the end of 1997, 5,600 people had already earned the MCP + Internet certification. The MCP + Internet credential affirms an individual's ability to install, maintain, enhance, and troubleshoot an Internet server using Microsoft products. The MSCE + Internet credential, in addition to certifying the basic MCSE competencies, indicates an individual's ability to customize, deploy, and support Microsoft Internet Explorer 4.0; host a Web server; implement, administer, and troubleshoot systems that use Microsoft's implementation of TCP/IP; develop and publish Web sites; and set up facilities for online commerce while maintaining a high degree of security.

Recertification or Maintenance Requirements As Microsoft introduces new products and new versions of its operating systems, it retires the tests for previous versions. If you hold a certification that is based on a test that Microsoft is retiring, you will be informed by certified mail of the need to take a current test to maintain your certification. You will have at least six months to complete this new test or your status as an MCP + Internet or MCSE + Internet will no longer be valid.

Benefits of Certification As an MCP + Internet or MCSE + Internet, you will receive the following benefits:

- A certificate

- Access to technical information through a secured Web site

- Logo for use on stationery and business cards

- Invitations to Microsoft-sponsored conferences and technical briefings

- A free subscription to *Microsoft Certified Professional* magazine

As an MCSE + Internet, you will also become eligible for MCSE benefits if you have not already received them (see Chapter 7 for more on the MCSE certification program).

Microsoft Certified Professional + Internet

Attaining the Microsoft Certified Professional + Internet certification requires passing three exams. If you are not already an MCP, passing the first test toward this certification will make you a Microsoft Certified Professional (see Chapter 4 for more information on this certification). The two additional required exams for this certification can also be applied toward achieving higher-level Microsoft certifications. The MCP + Internet is a good stepping stone on the path to one of Microsoft's premium certifications, such as the Microsoft Certified Systems

Engineer (MCSE) or the Microsoft Certified Systems Engineer + Internet (MCSE + Internet). See Chapter 7 for more information on the MCSE certification; the MCSE + Internet is described in this chapter.

Who Needs It   The MCP + Internet certification is a good entry point for technical professionals interested in network and system administration of Internet Web sites using Microsoft products. This certification can also be valuable to support and help desk personnel.

Requirements for Certification   The certification process requires the following steps:

1. Pass the Implementing and Supporting Microsoft Windows NT Server 4.0 exam (Sylvan ID: 070-067).

2. Pass the Implementing and Supporting Internet Information Server 3.0 and Microsoft Index Server 1.1 exam (Sylvan ID: 070-077) or the Implementing and Supporting Microsoft Internet Information Server 4.0 exam (Sylvan ID: 070-087).

3. Pass the Internetworking Microsoft TCP/IP on Microsoft Windows NT 4.0 exam (Sylvan ID: 070-059).

Administrator   Tests are administered by Sylvan Prometric; call (800) 755-3926 to register for Microsoft tests. (See Chapter 15 for additional information on Sylvan Prometric.)

Fee $100 per test

Format   Multiple-choice, closed-book tests. The number of questions and time limit depend on the test selected.

Microsoft Certified Systems Engineer + Internet

Attaining this certification requires passing seven core exams and two elective exams. Many of these exams, however, are the same tests required for other Microsoft certifications. If one attains the MCP + Internet certification discussed previously, all three of those exams will apply toward this certification. Likewise, if one has already attained an MCSE, some of those courses may apply; specifically, the MCSE tests on the Windows NT 4.0 track and the optional exams related to the Internet can be applied toward this certification.

The core exams for this certification cover the basic concepts and skills involved with installing, using, and troubleshooting a Windows NT Server and a client operating system such as Windows NT Workstation or Windows 95. Also required are the networking essentials exam, which covers basic network technologies and troubleshooting, and the TCP/IP exam, which covers TCP/IP networking and troubleshooting. The other required exams focus on setting up a Web site using Microsoft Internet Information Server and installing client Web software. The two elective exams focus on other Microsoft server topics and advanced networking topics. Microsoft's Web site provides exam guidelines, sample tests, etc., and links to authorized training providers. (See the Resources section that follows for more information.)

Who Needs It The MCSE certification is one of the most widely recognized networking credentials. The MCSE + Internet is ideal for those who want to distinguish themselves as having an expert level of technical knowledge and skills relating to the Internet; it can be a great way to get a salary increase or promotion.

Requirements for Certification The certification process requires the following steps:

1. Pass the Implementing and Supporting Microsoft Windows NT Server 4.0 exam (Sylvan ID: 070-067).

2. Pass the Implementing and Supporting Microsoft Internet Information Server 3.0 and Microsoft Index Server 1.1 exam (Sylvan ID: 070-077) or the Implementing and Supporting Microsoft Internet Information Server 4.0 exam (Sylvan ID: 070-087).

3. Pass the Internetworking with Microsoft TCP/IP on Microsoft Windows NT 4.0 exam (Sylvan ID: 070-059).

4. Pass the Networking Essentials exam (Sylvan ID: 070-058).

5. Pass the Implementing and Supporting Microsoft Windows 95 (Sylvan ID: 070-064) or the Implementing and Supporting Microsoft Windows NT Workstation 4.0 exam (Sylvan ID: 070-073).

6. Pass the Implementing and Supporting Microsoft Windows NT Server 4.0 in the Enterprise exam (Sylvan ID: 070-068).

7. Pass the Implementing and Supporting Microsoft Internet Explorer 4.0 by Using the Internet Explorer Administration Kit exam (Sylvan ID: 070-079).

8. Pass two elective exams, selecting exams from different categories listed in Table 9.1. (If you pass two exams within the same category, only one will qualify as an MCSE + Internet elective.)

TABLE 9.1: Microsoft Elective Exams

Category	Sylvan ID	Exam(s)
SQL Server	070-026	System Administration for Microsoft SQL Server 6.5
Database Design	070-027	Implementing a Database Design on Microsoft SQL Server 6.5
Exchange Server	070-076	Implementing and Supporting Microsoft Exchange Server 5
		OR
	070-081	Implementing and Supporting Microsoft Exchange Server 5.5
SNA Server	070-085	Implementing and Supporting Microsoft SNA Server 4.0
Proxy Server	070-078	Implementing and Supporting Microsoft Proxy Server 1.0
		OR
	070-088	Implementing and Supporting Microsoft Proxy Server 2.0

If you are already certified as a Novell CNE, Master CNE, or CNI, a Banyan CBS or CBE, or a Sun Certified Network Administrator for Solaris 2.5 or 2.6, Microsoft will waive the requirement for the networking essentials exam (Sylvan ID: 70-058).

Administrator Tests are administered by Sylvan Prometric; call (800) 755-3926 to register for Microsoft tests. (See Chapter 15 for additional information on Sylvan Prometric.)

Fee $100 per test

Format Multiple-choice, closed-book tests. The number of questions and time limit depend on the test selected.

Resources

The Microsoft Web site offers practice exams as well as study guides that detail the objectives of each exam. Microsoft's Web site also offers a listing of Microsoft Authorized Education Centers. For more information on this organization's certification programs, contact Microsoft at:

Web	`http://www.microsoft.com/mcp/`
E-mail	`mcp@msprograms.com`
Mail	Microsoft Corporation One Microsoft Way Redmond, WA 98052-6399
Phone	(800) 636-7544
Fax	(206) 936-7329

Novell Certifications

The Novell Certified Internet Professional (CIP) program was developed in 1997 to certify Internet professionals who maintain and support Internet connections and sites. The program currently includes four tracks relating to key job categories for Internet professionals: Internet Business Strategist, Web Designer, Intranet Manager, and Internet Architect. Novell also will be finalizing a Web Developer certification in early 1998; check the Certification Update Web site for details (see Appendix C for details on how to access the Web site).

Recertification or Maintenance Requirements Certified Internet Professionals are required to meet continuing certification requirements as specified by Novell. Because recertification requirements can vary from year to year, contact Novell for current details (see the Resources section that follows for more information).

Benefits of Certification All Novell Certified Internet Professionals receive the following benefits:

- Access to the Certified Internet Professionals Web site

- A free two-user (demonstration) version of IntranetWare

- Discount on Corel's Web Graphics Suite

- Discounts on Novell Press books

- Discounts and free passes to industry conferences and events

Internet Business Strategist

The Internet Business Strategist certification is designed for those who plan how a company can best use the Internet to meet its business goals. The certification program includes topics such as how to develop a business plan for the deployment of a Web site; how to contract for and manage Web development; how to design an online marketing strategy; and how to increase company productivity using Internet technology.

Only one test is required for this certification. Novell recommends the following two courses for preparation for this test:

- Novell 650: Mastering the Net with Netscape Navigator

- Novell 600: Internet Business Strategies

Who Needs It   The CIP Internet Business Strategist certification is a great way to demonstrate your expertise in leveraging the Internet to meet your company's goals. It can also be a valuable credential for freelance Internet business consultants who want to validate their skills for potential clients.

Requirements for Certification   The certification process requires only one step:

1.   Pass the Internet Business Strategies Test (Sylvan ID: 050-701).

Administrator   Tests are administered by Sylvan Prometric; call (800) 733-3926 to register for Novell tests. (See Chapter 15 for additional information on Sylvan Prometric.)

Fee   Test fees vary based on length and format; call Sylvan Prometric at (800) 733-3926 for pricing.

Format   Novell tests include both adaptive and traditional format exams. Call Sylvan Prometric at (800) 733-3926 for current test information.

Web Designer

Novell's CIP Web Designer credential targets computer professionals who design and publish intranet and Internet Web pages. This certification is valuable to graphic artists, writers, editors, and anyone else who is actively involved in the production of Web pages. The certification program covers the following topics: designing effective user interfaces; designing Web pages to be viewed by a variety of Web clients; how to product fast-loading Web pages; and how to effectively use multimedia and animation in Web pages.

The certification process involves passing four tests. Novell recommends taking the following courses as preparation for the tests:

- Novell 600: Internet Business Strategies
- Novell 650: Mastering the Net with Netscape Navigator
- Novell 654: Web Authoring and Publishing
- Novell 655: Advanced Web Authoring
- Novell 660: Designing an Effective Web Site

Who Needs It The CIP Web Designer certification is a great way to demonstrate your expertise in creating and publishing effective Web sites for your company. It can also be a valuable credential for free-lance Web designers who want to validate their skills for potential clients.

Requirements for Certification The certification process requires the following steps:

1. Pass the Internet Business Strategies exam (Sylvan ID: 050-701).

2. Pass the Web Authoring and Publishing exam (Sylvan ID: 050-700).

3. Pass the Advanced Web Authoring exam (Sylvan ID: 050-705).

4. Pass the Designing an Effective Web Site exam (Sylvan ID: 050-703).

Administrator Tests are administered by Sylvan Prometric; call (800) 733-3926 to register for Novell tests. (See Chapter 15 for additional information on Sylvan Prometric.)

Fee   Test fees vary based on length and format; call Sylvan Prometric at (800) 733-3926 for pricing.

Format   Novell tests include both adaptive and traditional format exams. Call Sylvan Prometric at (800) 733-3926 for current test information.

Intranet Manager

The Novell CIP Intranet Manager program targets already-certified Certified Novell Administrators (CNAs) and Certified Novell Engineers (CNEs) who need to deploy and manage intranets (see Chapter 7 for more information about the CNA and CNE certification programs). CNA or CNE certification is not a prerequisite for this program; if you are not already a CNA, however, you will become one during the completion of the Intranet Manager certification program.

Five tests are required for this certification. These tests cover topics including Web authoring and publishing using HTML; developing CGI and Perl scripts; and managing a Web server. Novell recommends the following courses for preparation for these tests:

- Novell 600: Internet Business Strategies

- Novell 650: Mastering the Net with Netscape Communicator

- Novell 654: Web Authoring and Publishing

- Novell 655: Advanced Web Authoring

- Novell 656: Web Server Management

- Novell 520: IntranetWare: NetWare 4.11 Administration

Who Needs It   Jobs are plentiful for those who can create and manage intranet and Internet Web sites and connections. This certification allows you to demonstrate to potential employers that you have advanced knowledge and skill in this area. The Novell CIP Intranet Manager certification can also be a valuable credential for freelance Internet consultants.

Requirements for Certification The certification process requires the following steps:

1. Pass the Novell 654 Web Authoring and Publishing exam (Sylvan ID: 050-700).

2. Pass the Novell 655 Advanced Web Authoring exam (Sylvan ID: 050-705).

3. Pass the Novell 520 IntranetWare: NetWare 4.11 Administration exam (Sylvan ID: 050-613).

4. Pass the Novell 605 NetWare TCP/IP Transport exam (Sylvan ID: 050-145).

5. Pass the Novell 656 Web Server Management exam (Sylvan ID: 050-656).

Administrator Tests are administered by Sylvan Prometric; call (800) 733-3926 to register for Novell tests. (See Chapter 15 for additional information on Sylvan Prometric.)

Fee Test fees vary based on length and format; call Sylvan Prometric at (800) 733-3926 for pricing.

Format Novell tests include both adaptive and traditional format exams. Call Sylvan Prometric at (800) 733-3926 for current test information.

Internet Architect

The Novell CIP Internet Architect certification is designed for network administrators who are responsible for providing their organization with a secure and efficient connection to the Internet.

Five tests are required for this certification. These tests cover the following topics: configuring and installing TCP/IP; planning TCP/IP addressing; installing and configuring DNS and FTP services; installing and configuring a proxy server; planning and configuring an internetwork; and installing and managing a Web server. Novell recommends the following courses for preparation for these tests:

- Novell 216: Fundamentals of Internetworking
- Novell 605: NetWare TCP/IP Transport
- Novell 658: DNS and FTP Server Installation and Configuration
- Novell 770: Securing Intranets with BorderManager
- Novell 656: Web Server Management

Who Needs It This certification is an excellent way to demonstrate your expertise in TCP/IP networking and Internet services. It can be the ticket to employment with an Internet service provider or Web-hosting service.

Requirements for Certification The certification process requires the following steps:

1. Pass the Fundamentals of Internetworking exam (Sylvan ID: 050-611).

2. Pass the NetWare TCP/IP Transport exam (Sylvan ID: 050-145).

3. Pass the Web Server Management exam (Sylvan ID: 050-710).

4. Pass the DNS & FTP Server Installation and Configuration exam (Sylvan ID: 050-625).

5. Pass the Securing Intranets with BorderManager exam (Sylvan ID: 050-629).

Administrator Tests are administered by Sylvan Prometric; call (800) 733-3926 to register for Novell tests. (See Chapter 15 for additional information on Sylvan Prometric.)

Fee Test fees vary based on length and format; call Sylvan Prometric at (800) 733-3926 for pricing.

Format Novell tests include both adaptive and traditional format exams. Call Sylvan Prometric at (800) 733-3926 for current test information.

Resources

The Novell Web site offers practice exams as well as study guides that detail the objectives of each exam. The Novell Web site also provides a listing of Novell Authorized Education Centers. For more information on this organization's certification programs, contact Novell at:

Web   `http://education.novell.com/`

E-mail   `edcustomer@novell.com`

Mail   Novell, Inc.
          122 East 1700 South
          Provo, Utah 84606

Phone   (800) 233-EDUC

Fax   (801) 222-7875

Prosoft/Net Guru Technologies Certifications

Through its Certified Internet Webmaster (CIW) program, Prosoft/Net Guru Technologies (NGT) has developed a comprehensive set of vendor-neutral certifications for Internet professionals. These certifications can be useful to a broad range of computer and networking professionals, from hardcore TCP/IP and UNIX networkers to Web page designers. The company offers training at their main office in Chicago and at locations throughout the US and Europe. All Prosoft/NGT certification programs involve hands-on courses.

The CIW program offers several levels of certification. The CIW Designer certification, referred to as a "level one" credential, is the entry point in the CIW program. At the next level, candidates choose between the Administrator and Developer tracks. Professionals that choose the Developer track can work toward certification as a Developer I and then a Developer II. Those choosing the Administrator track can pursue the Administrator certification or the Network Professional designation. The most advanced administrator certification is the Security Professional, which builds on the Network Professional program. A certification is also offered in E-Commerce.

The Prosoft/NGT CIW programs are recognized by the Association of Internet Professionals (AIP), the National Association of Webmasters (NAW), the Institute for Certification of Computing Professionals (ICCP), and the Internet Certification Institute International (ICII).

Recertification or Maintenance Requirements Prosoft/NGT
Certified Internet Webmaster certifications must be renewed every year.

Benefits of Certification All Prosoft/NGT Certified Internet
Webmasters receive logos to use on business cards and stationery.

Certified Internet Webmaster Designer

The Certified Internet Webmaster Designer credential is an introductory level certification designed to introduce end users and managers
to Web basics and the development of Web pages. Attaining this certification involves passing one exam. The exam covers Internet termi-
nology, standards, architecture, utilities, and Internet addressing;
using Web browsers and searching the Internet; and developing Web
applications based on HTML. The candidate is expected to have some
prior experience using either Windows 95, UNIX, Novell, Macintosh,
or the Windows NT operating system and to have familiarity with
operating system concepts.

A three-day training program is recommended as preparation for the
exam. The program includes the Prosoft/NGT Internet Basics course (one
day); the Prosoft/NGT Planning & Building a Web Site course (one day);
and the Prosoft/NGT Web Development Using HTML course (one day).

Who Needs It This certification is a great way to learn the fundamentals of creating and maintaining Web pages. It can help you get
your foot in the door with a company that wants to have an Internet
presence. It can also be a valuable first credential for becoming a freelance Web site designer.

Requirements for Certification The certification process
requires only one step:

1. Pass the CIW Designer exam.

Administrator Tests are administered by Sylvan Prometric; call (800) 380-3926 to register for Prosoft/NGT tests. (See Chapter 15 for additional information on Sylvan Prometric.)

Fee The test costs $150, but if you take the three days of course-work, the cost of the courses ($995) includes a voucher that lets you take the Sylvan test once for free.

Format Multiple-choice, closed-book test with a minimum score of 75 percent overall and 70 percent in each module.

Certified Internet Webmaster Developer I

The Certified Internet Webmaster Developer track is for professionals interested in client-side Web applications using languages such as HTML, XML, and JavaScript. The Developer I credential is designed for computer professionals who want to create and maintain Web pages that require scripting languages. Attaining this certification involves passing one exam. The exam covers HTML, and JavaScript programming, with emphasis on Java class libraries, objects, applets, and the Java Development Kit. The candidate should have prior appli-cation development experience with languages such as C, C++, For-tran, or Pascal or equivalent knowledge.

A five-day training program is recommended as preparation for this exam. The program includes the Prosoft/NGT Advanced HTML course (one day), the Prosoft/NGT Web Development Using JavaScript course (three days), and a course on Web scripting (one day).

Who Needs It This certification is a great way to get a job creating and maintaining Web pages for a company that wants to have an Internet presence. It is also a valuable credential for a freelance Web site designer.

Requirements for Certification The certification process requires the following steps:

1. Attain CIW Designer certification (described previously).

2. Pass the CIW Developer I exam.

Administrator Tests are administered by Sylvan Prometric; call (800) 380-3926 to register for Prosoft/NGT tests. (See Chapter 15 for additional information on Sylvan Prometric.)

Fee The test costs $150, but if you take the five days of coursework, the cost of the courses ($2275) includes a voucher that lets you take the Sylvan test once for free.

Format Multiple-choice, closed-book test with a minimum score of 75 percent overall and 70 percent in each module.

Certified Internet Webmaster Developer II

The Certified Internet Webmaster Developer II credential is designed for professionals who create and develop server-side Web applications. The technology focus is on SQL, DBMS, CGI, Perl, and Active Server Pages. Attaining this certification involves passing one exam. The exam covers advanced Web development concepts and practices, including CGI and Perl scripting, ODBC queries, and development of Active Server Pages. The candidate is expected to have prior experience with database concepts.

A five-day training program is recommended as preparation for this exam. The program includes the Prosoft/NGT SQL and DBMS Concepts course (one day), the Prosoft/NGT CGI and Perl Web Scripting course (two days), and the Prosoft/NGT Active Server Pages course (two days).

Who Needs It This certification is a great way to get a job creating and developing advanced interactive Web applications. It is also a valuable credential for a freelance Web site designer.

Requirements for Certification The certification process requires the following steps:

1. Attain CIW Developer I certification.

2. Pass the CIW Developer II exam.

Administrator Tests are administered by Sylvan Prometric; call (800) 380-3926 to register for Prosoft/NGT tests. (See Chapter 15 for additional information on Sylvan Prometric.)

Fee The test costs $150, but if you take the five days of coursework, the cost of the courses ($2275) includes a voucher that lets you take the Sylvan test once for free.

Format Multiple-choice, closed-book test with a minimum score of 75 percent overall and 70 percent in each module.

Certified Internet Webmaster Administrator

The Certified Internet Webmaster Administrator credential is designed for professionals who support, manage, and configure Internet and Web systems and software. Attaining this certification involves passing one exam. The exam covers network fundamentals, Internet service providers, Internet connections, TCP/IP architecture, TCP/IP network security, and how to plan an Internet environment using FTP, DNS, and Web server systems. Emphasis is also placed on Web server performance and security. The candidate is expected to have prior UNIX, Novell, or Windows NT experience or equivalent knowledge.

Two courses are recommended as preparation for the exam. The recommended courses are the Prosoft/NGT Internet & Web Infrastructure & Security course (two days), and the Prosoft/NGT Internet & Web System Administration course (three days).

Who Needs It   This certification is an excellent credential for technical professionals who want to get a job installing and administering Web servers for Internet service providers or Web hosting services.

Requirements for Certification   The certification process requires the following steps:

1.   Attain the CIW Designer certification.

2.   Pass the CIW Administrator exam.

Administrator   Tests are administered by Sylvan Prometric; call (800) 380-3926 to register for Prosoft/NGT tests. (See Chapter 15 for additional information on Sylvan Prometric.)

Fee   The test costs $150, but if you take the five days of coursework, the cost of the courses ($2275) includes a voucher that lets you take the Sylvan test once for free.

Format   Multiple-choice, closed-book test with a minimum score of 75 percent overall and 70 percent in each module.

Certified Internet Webmaster Network Professional

The Certified Internet Webmaster Network Professional credential is designed for professionals who define, manage, and troubleshoot a corporate network infrastructure. Attaining this certification involves passing one exam. The exam covers TCP/IP architecture; layers and dominant protocols; Ethernet, ARP and RARP; core protocols such as IP, TCP, and UDP; BOOTP and DHCP; routing; DNS architecture; managing TCP/IP networks, SNMP and MIBs; and TCP/IP's trouble-shooting protocol, ICMP. The candidate is expected to have prior experience with UNIX, Novell, or Windows NT system and network administration.

Two courses are recommended as preparation for the exam. The recommended courses are the Prosoft/NGT TCP/IP Internetworking course (two days), and the Prosoft/NGT Advanced TCP/IP Concepts and Practices course (three days).

Who Needs It   This certification is an excellent way to demonstrate your expertise in dealing with UNIX, Windows NT, and TCP/IP net-working. It can help you get a job designing and managing networks, for example, with an Internet service provider or a Web-hosting service.

Requirements for Certification   The certification process requires the following steps:

1.   Attain CIW Designer certification.

2.   Pass the CIW Network Professional exam.

Administrator   Tests are administered by Sylvan Prometric; call (800) 380-3926 to register for Prosoft/NGT tests. (See Chapter 15 for additional information on Sylvan Prometric.)

Fee   The test costs $150, but if you take the five days of coursework, the cost of the courses ($2275) includes a voucher that lets you take the Sylvan test once for free.

Format   Multiple-choice, closed-book test with a minimum score of 75 percent overall and 70 percent in each module.

Certified Internet Webmaster Security Professional

The Certified Internet Webmaster Security Professional credential, designed to be a follow-up to the CIW Network Professional certification, targets technical professionals who work with firewalls and maintain Internet and intranet security. Attaining this certification involves passing one exam. The exam covers network (TCP/IP), operating system (UNIX and Windows NT), and security concepts, including UNIX and NT authentication, UNIX and NT access control, TCP/IP architecture and protocols, security protocols, security organizations, security standards, encryption standards, and firewall systems.

A ten-day training program is recommended as preparation for this exam; two of the courses in the program are courses that are recommended for the CIW Network Professional track (described above). The recommended courses include either the Windows NT System & Network Administration course (three days) or the Unix System & Network Administration course (three days); the TCP/IP Internetworking course (two days); the Advanced TCP/IP Concepts and Practices course (three days); and the Internet Security & Firewall Systems course (two days).

These courses focus on Internet, intranet, TCP/IP, and operating system security concepts and practices, with the objective of securing access to key systems and intellectual information. The courses cover basic system and network administration concepts, security policy, encryption products/technology, authentication and access control mechanisms supported by operating systems such as UNIX or Windows NT, and firewall systems.

Who Needs It This certification is an excellent credential for technical professionals who are responsible for developing and maintaining customized security for company Internet connections and intranets, Internet service providers, or Web-hosting services. This is also a valuable certification for freelance Internet security consultants.

Requirements for Certification The certification process requires the following steps:

1. Attain the CIW Designer certification.

2. Pass the CIW Security Professional exam.

Administrator Tests are administered by Sylvan Prometric; call (800) 380-3926 to register for Prosoft/NGT tests. (See Chapter 15 for additional information on Sylvan Prometric.)

Fee The test costs $150, but if you take the ten days of coursework, the cost of the courses ($4400) includes a voucher that lets you take the Sylvan test once for free.

Format Multiple-choice, closed-book test with a minimum score of 75 percent overall and 70 percent in each module.

Certified Internet Webmaster ECommerce Professional

The CIW ECommerce Professional credential is designed for technical professionals who implement and support electronic commerce. Attaining this certification involves passing one exam. The exam covers ECommerce models; the Secure Electronic Transactions (SET) standard; the relationship between the cardholder, issuer, merchant, acquirer, payment gateway, and third parties; cryptography standards and protocols; certificate authorities and digital signatures; vendor products, such as those from VeriSign and CyberCash; and payment infrastructure. The candidate is expected to have prior experience with UNIX, Novell, or Windows NT system and network administration.

The Prosoft/NGT ECommerce Professional course (three days) is recommended as preparation for this exam.

Who Needs It This certification demonstrates that you can implement, support, and secure electronic commerce for a company. It can be a hot ticket to help you secure a position with a company that is (or wants to be) active in Internet commerce. This is also a valuable certification for independent consultants who design Internet transaction systems.

Requirements for Certification The certification process requires the following steps:

1. Attain the CIW Designer certification.

2. Pass the CIW ECommerce Professional exam.

Administrator Tests are administered by Sylvan Prometric; call (800) 380-3926 to register for Prosoft/NGT tests. (See Chapter 15 for additional information on Sylvan Prometric.)

Fee The test costs $150, but if you take the three days of coursework, the cost of the courses ($1445) includes a voucher that lets you take the Sylvan test once for free.

Format Multiple-choice, closed-book test with a minimum score of 75 percent overall and 70 percent in each module.

Resources

The Prosoft/NGT Web site offers up-to-date course location information and details about registration. For more information on this organization's certification programs, contact Prosoft/NGT at:

Web   http://www.prosofttraining.com/

E-mail   pabrai@prosofttraining.com

Mail	Prosoft/NGT
	2625 Butterfield Road, Suite 312E
	Oak Brook, IL 60523
Phone	(630) 574-4878 or (800) KNOWNET
Fax	(630) 990-9635

USWeb Learning Certifications

USWeb Learning's vendor-neutral certification programs provide candidates with Web development knowledge and skills by providing a foundation in broadly-applicable Internet concepts. USWeb Learning's courses incorporate the company's well-developed conceptual framework for using Internet technology in business. They emphasize the use of cross-functional Internet development teams that possess technical, creative, and management skills. Their hands-on training focuses on addressing real-world business problems and building a comprehensive set of Internet business skills.

These certification programs are not focused on the products of any one vendor. As a result, they provide a grounding in the fundamentals and principles of Web development that should have broad job applicability. USWeb Learning is involved in the current effort to develop standards for the set of key skills that all Internet certifications should test.

USWeb Learning currently offers only instructor-led training, but plans to offer self-study materials and Internet-based training by late 1998.

Recertification or Maintenance Requirements Because of the changing nature of vendor products and certification, USWeb Learning may require annual recertification in the vendor-specific components of the certification. Check with USWeb Learning for current recertification information.

Benefits of Certification US Web Learning Specialists and Architects receive the use of the certification logo on business cards and stationery.

USWeb Learning Certified Specialist

USWeb Learning's Certified Specialist credential is designed for those who will be producing and deploying Web sites. The program emphasizes fundamental Web skills and knowledge, development principles, and in-depth mastery of specific Web products and tools.

The certification process has three components. First, the Foundations Component involves passing a USWeb Learning exam. USWeb Learning recommends the Web Development and Web Sites Logistics course as preparation for the foundations exam. The second component, the Skills-Based Principles Component, allows a choice of four areas of specialization; the candidate must pass an elective USWeb Learning exam in their area of specialization. Finally, the Technology Specialization Component builds on the Skills-Based Component by providing vendor-specific skills in the same elective area. Meeting this requirement involves passing a vendor-based exam.

Who Needs It This certification provides evidence that you have a foundation in the technical issues and principles of Internet technology implementation and can apply those skills in a cross-platform environment.

Requirements for Certification The certification process requires the following steps:

1. Pass the Foundations exam.

The Foundations exam may soon be replaced by two new exams. Contact USWeb Learning, or check the Certification Update Web site for more information.

2. Complete the Skills-Based Principles Component by taking one of these elective USWeb Learning exams:

- Programming & Database Principles

- Networking and Security Administration Principles

- Web Design Principles

- Web Administration Principles

3. Complete a Technology Specialization in the area that corresponds to the elective chosen in Step 2. You must complete a vendor-specific exam in one of the broad categories listed below (contact USWeb Learning for a current list of approved exams in each category):

- Programming & Development (elective exams in programming database tools)

- Networking and Security Administration (elective exams in firewall and security systems)

- Web Design & Multimedia (elective exams in graphic design and multimedia tools)

- Web Administration (elective exams in Web server and Web application administration)

Administrator USWeb Learning exams are administered by Sylvan Prometric, call (800) 798-3926 to register for a USWeb Learning exam.

Fee Test fees vary based on test length and format; call Sylvan Prometric at (800) 798-3926 for pricing.

Format Call Sylvan Prometric at (800) 798-3926 for current test information.

USWeb Learning Certified Architect

USWeb Learning's Certified Architect credential is designed for Internet architects and project managers who will be defining and administering Web development. The program involves taking a required course and passing three exams.

The certification process has three components. The Foundations Component involves taking one exam. USWeb Learning recommends the Web Development and Web Sites Logistics course as preparation for the Foundations exam. The Skills-Based Principles Component involves passing a Web Project Management exam and one elective exam. Finally, the Business-Related Skills Component involves passing one exam and taking one of two courses on conducting electronic business.

Who Needs It The USWeb Learning Certified Architect credential demonstrates that you have a broad understanding of Web development, including skills in project management, graphic design, programming, electronic commerce, legacy application integration, Web administration, networking and security.

Requirements for Certification The certification process requires the following steps:

1. Pass the Foundations exam.

NOTE   The Foundations exam may soon be replaced by two exams. Contact USWeb Learning, or check the Certification Update Web site for more information.

2.   Pass the Web Project Management exam.

3.   Complete the Skills-Based Principles Component by taking one of these elective USWeb Learning exams:

- Programming & Database Principles

- Networking and Security Administration Principles

- Web Design Principles

- Web Administration Principles

4.   Pass the Re-Engineering Legacy Applications for the Internet exam.

5.   Complete the Business-Related Skills Component by taking one of these two elective courses::

- Applying Internet Technologies to Business Processes

- E-business Workshop

Administrator   USWeb Learning exams are administered by Sylvan Prometric, call (800) 798-3926 to register for a USWeb Learning exam.

Fee   Test fees vary based on test length and format; call Sylvan Prometric at (800) 798-3926 for pricing.

Format   Call Sylvan Prometric at (800) 798-3926 for current test information.

Resources

The USWeb Learning Web site offers practice exams as well as study guides that detail the objectives of each exam. For more information on this organization's certification programs and their related preparation courses, contact USWeb Learning at:

Web   `http://www.usweb.com/`

Mail   USWeb Learning Corporation
2880 Lakeside Drive, Suite 350
Santa Clara, CA 95054

Phone   (800) 99USWEB

CHAPTER

10

Instructor and
Trainer Certifications

FEATURING

- Adobe Certification

- Banyan Certifications

- Borland Certification

- Chauncey Group Certification

- Corel Certifications

- IBM Certifications

- Lotus Certifications

- Microsoft Certification

- Novell Certifications

- Prosoft/Net Guru Technologies Certifications

Several of the vendors and organizations that offer the certification programs described in this book also offer related training, either at their own corporate facilities or through authorized training centers. These training programs and courses are taught by instructors that the vendor or the training center recognizes as qualified to teach an "official" course. When courses are offered directly by a vendor, the course instructors are usually selected and qualified through an internal training program. However, many of the vendors that partner with training centers have designed instructor certification programs that are open to anyone who wants to become an instructor or trainer.

Becoming a certified instructor can lead to lots of great career opportunities. Companies and individuals spend millions of dollars each year to take training programs. As a result, trainers are in high demand and are often well paid, with salaries that can range from $50,000 to over $100,000 per year. In fact, in her third annual salary survey of Microsoft professionals, Linda Briggs indicates that salaries for Microsoft Certified Trainers are up by $12,000 in the last year alone, to an average of $77,000 nationwide (*Microsoft Certified Professional* magazine, February, 1998). See the "Microsoft Certification" section that follows for more data on the costs and benefits of being an MCT.

Individuals seeking training certifications include computer and networking professionals who want to be able to deliver training either within their current organization or as an employee or contractor for a training organization. (See Chapter 13 for information on different types of training organizations.)

Certification programs for instructors or trainers tend to involve three educational components. To become certified as an instructor by a particular company, an individual will typically need to:

- Demonstrate technical competence with one or more of the company's products

- Provide evidence of competence in instructional techniques

- Complete training on the specific course content and sequence associated with the company's education curriculum

This chapter covers certification programs for instructors and trainers who want to provide authorized training for specific vendors, including Adobe, Banyan, Borland, Corel, IBM, Lotus, Microsoft, Novell, and Prosoft/Net Guru Technologies. The vendor-independent Certified Technical Trainer credential, offered by the Chauncey Group, is also covered. This widely respected certification program is a required component of several of the vendor-based training certifications.

Adobe Certification

Adobe produces a number of excellent page layout and imaging programs used in desktop publishing and for producing Web pages, and it offers a number of related product-specific certifications through the Adobe Certified Expert program (see Chapter 5 for details). In addition, Adobe endorses courses taught by Adobe Certified Instructors that are offered through Adobe Authorized Learning Providers training centers. Becoming an Adobe Certified Instructor allows you to teach the official Adobe curriculum for the product(s) for which you are certified as an Adobe Certified Expert. Candidates can obtain certification to teach one or more of the following products: Illustrator 7.0, Acrobat 3.0, After Effects 3.1, FrameMaker 5.5, PageMaker 6.5, PageMill 2.0, and PhotoShop 4.0.

Recertification or Maintenance Requirements To maintain certification as an Adobe Certified Instructor, an individual must maintain current Adobe Certified Expert certification as described in Chapter 5.

Benefits of Certification   Adobe maintains lists of qualified instructors and makes those lists available to Adobe customers who are looking for an expert trainer. As soon as you are qualified as an Adobe Certified Instructor, your name will be listed on the Adobe Web site for referrals. Adobe Certified Instructors also receive the following benefits:

- Certificate

- Subscription to the monthly *Adobe Authorized Learning Provider* newsletter

- Promotion of your services to Adobe software users on the Web

- Direct link from the Adobe Authorized Learning Provider site to your Web site

- Discounts on Adobe Press books purchased from Macmillan Computer Publishing

Adobe Certified Instructor

Adobe Certified Instructors are highly qualified technical trainers, proficient both in using Adobe software and in teaching others how to use it. To this end, certification candidates must pass an Adobe Product Proficiency exam to demonstrate skill in using a particular product, and must also fulfill the requirements involved in becoming a Chauncey Group Certified Technical Trainer.

Who Needs It   This certification allows you to train people within your company or at an outside training facility using the official Adobe curriculum. This can be an excellent way to increase your worth to your company or to get started on a lucrative career as a professional trainer.

Requirements for Certification The certification process requires the following steps:

1. Pass an Adobe Product Proficiency exam. (See Chapter 5 for details on the numerous proficiency exams.)

2. Obtain the Certified Technical Trainer credential (see the "Chauncey Group Certification" section in this chapter).

3. Submit proof of your completion of these requirements to Adobe.

Resources

The Adobe Web site offers exam bulletins that detail the objectives of each proficiency test. Adobe's Web site also offers a listing of Adobe Authorized Learning Providers and Adobe Certified Instructors. For more information on this organization's certifications and courses, contact Adobe at:

Web	`http://www.adobe.com/supportservice/training/acipinfo.html`
E-mail	`adobe.train@adobe.com`
Mail	Certification Coordinator Adobe Systems, Inc. M/S WT7-120 345 Park Avenue San Jose, CA 95110-2704
Phone	(800) 685-4172
Fax	(408) 537-4033

Banyan Certifications

Banyan Vines is a networking operating system designed by Banyan for use in large corporate networks, typically operating on UNIX-based servers. The current version—Vines 8.0—incorporates NT, Novell, and mainframe-based resources into directory services through Banyan's proprietary protocol, StreetTalk.

The Certified Banyan Instructor (CBI) credential is necessary for professional trainers who want to teach the Banyan education curriculum. The CBI is the most basic credential for teaching Banyan courses and workshops. CBIs are authorized to teach the VINES Administration and Advanced VINES Administration courses.

Additional training can allow CBIs to teach other Banyan courses. CBIs currently can receive an endorsement that allows them to teach the Problem Solving for Vines Networks course. The requirements for teaching other Banyan courses are still under development, but all will require completion of the CBI credential as a prerequisite.

Recertification or Maintenance Requirements Banyan Certified Instructors are not required to take any action to maintain their instructor credential per se, but they must maintain their Certified Banyan Expert (CBE) status. To maintain CBE certification you may be required to take a class or pass a test in order to teach a new course or to teach courses on newer software versions.

Benefits of Certification Banyan Certified Instructors will receive these benefits:

- A congratulatory letter and plaque
- A "Certified Banyan Instructor" black briefcase bag
- Subscription to the *CBInsider* quarterly newsletter

Certified Banyan Instructor (CBI)

The process of becoming a Certified Banyan Instructor has three steps. The CBI candidate must demonstrate instructional skills, prove technical competence, and attend an authorization session that covers a review of the content and the flow of Banyan courses. The first two steps must be completed prior to attending the CBI Authorization Session at Banyan. On completion of the basic CBI certification program, you will be authorized to teach the VINES Administration (EDU110) and Advanced VINES Administration (EDU210) courses.

Who Needs It The CBI certification is necessary for those who want to teach any Banyan courses or workshops. This credential can be an excellent way to increase your worth to your company. It can also be a useful credential for acquiring an instructor position with a training organization.

Requirements for Certification The certification process requires the following steps:

1. Provide proof of instructional skills by one of the following methods:

    • Obtain certification as a Certified Technical Trainer (see "Chauncey Group Certification" below).

    • Become certified as an instructor for another vendor (Lotus, Microsoft, or Novell).

    • Attend one of the following instructional skills courses approved by Banyan:

        • Instructional Techniques course from Friesen, Kaye and Associates (see www.fka.com or call (800) FKA-5585 for details)

- Effective Classroom Instruction from Practical Management, Inc. (call (800) 444-9101 for details)

2. Prove your technical competence by obtaining a Certified Banyan Expert (CBE) credential (see Chapter 7 for information on the CBS certification). Note that as a Certified Banyan Instructor candidate you must pass the CBE exams with an overall score of 85 percent on each test, and you may not score less than 75 percent on more than one section of any test.

3. Attend a Banyan Instructor Authorization Session (Course ID: AUT400-7). These sessions are offered only twice each year at Banyan's Westboro Education Center, in Massachusetts.

Administrator   The Banyan authorization session is scheduled directly with Banyan (see the Resources section below for information). The Certified Banyan Expert exams are scheduled through Sylvan Prometric (see Chapter 7 for information on Certified Banyan Expert tests).

Fee   The fees for the authorization tests can vary; call Banyan at (508) 898-1795 for current pricing.

Format   The authorization session consists of a three-day course taught by an authorized instructor.

Certified Banyan Instructor (CBI): Problem Solving for VINES Networks Authorization

CBIs who want to teach the hands-on Problem Solving for VINES Networks (EDU310) course must meet one additional requirement beyond the CBI certification. They will need to participate in an additional Banyan authorization session specific to this course. In this session, candidates will receive the instructor guide for the course and assist a Banyan instructor with the lab set-up and classroom activities for a Problem Solving for VINES Networks course.

Who Needs It This credential is necessary for technical trainers who want to teach the Banyan Problem Solving for VINES Networks course.

Requirements for Certification The certification process requires the following steps:

1. Obtain certification as a CBI (see "Certified Banyan Instructor (CBI)" above).

2. Attend the Problem Solving for VINES Networks Authorization session at Banyan's Westboro Education Center in Massachusetts.

Administrator The Banyan authorization session is scheduled directly with Banyan (see the Resources section).

Fee The fees for the authorization tests can vary; call Banyan at (508) 898-1795 for current pricing.

Format The authorization session for the troubleshooting course consists of co-teaching a three-day course taught with an authorized instructor.

Resources

For more information on this organization's certifications and courses, contact Banyan at:

Web   http://www.banyan.com/support/techcert.htm

E-mail   jbernstein@banyan.com

Mail	Judi Bernstein
	Program Coordinator/Certification Programs
	Banyan Systems Incorporated
	Educational Services Department
	120 Flanders Road
	Westboro, MA 01581
Phone	(508) 898-1795
Fax	(508) 836-0225

Borland Certification

Borland offers a number of product-specific certifications (see Chapter 8). Certification as a Delphi 3 Trainer makes you eligible to teach Borland's Delphi 3 courseware and to deliver training courses as part of Delphi 3 product and service bundles. Certified Trainers must be employed by a Borland Premier Authorized Education Center or be a member of the Borland Business Solutions Program prior to seeking certification as a trainer; see http://www.borland.com/programs/bsp/ for more information.

Recertification or Maintenance Requirements   Annual recertification is not required. However, since your certification is tied to this version of Delphi, you will want to take an update test when a new version comes out in order to maintain the most current Delphi certification.

Benefits of Certification Borland Delphi 3 Certified Trainers receive these benefits:

- Certificate of recognition

- Use of the Borland Delphi Certified Trainer logo

- A listing on Borland's Online Resource Locator

Borland Delphi 3 Certified Trainer

Borland Delphi 3 Trainers must demonstrate a high level of product knowledge and an understanding of the proper use of Delphi courseware. Successful candidates will be authorized to teach the Delphi 3 Foundations, Delphi 3 Component Design, and the Delphi 2 C/S/ Techniques courses. Borland expects certification candidates to have:

- A working knowledge of Windows

- A working knowledge of another Windows database programming platform (e.g., Paradox for Windows, dBase for Windows, Visual Basic, PowerBuilder)

- Experience with at least one of the following SQL database servers: InterBase 3.3/4.0, Microsoft SQL Server, Sybase, Oracle, Informix, or another ODBC-supported server

Who Needs It This certification allows you to teach courses within your company or at an outside training facility using official Borland courseware. This can be an excellent way to increase your worth to your present employer or to begin a career as a professional trainer.

Requirements for Certification The certification process requires the following steps:

1. Pass the Delphi 3 Client/Server certification exam with a score of at least 80 percent (see Chapter 8 for details).

2. Submit a signed Delphi 3 trainer agreement.

3. Attend a five-day train-the-trainer course at a Borland facility (contact Borland for a listing of locations and dates).

 If you are already certified as a Borland Delphi 2 Trainer, you may take a two-day update course instead.

Fee $1000 for the five-day course, a courseware manual, a student guide, and an instructor guide. The two-day update course costs $800, and includes one copy of both the student and instructor guides.

Resources

For more information on this organization's certifications and courses, contact Borland at:

Web `http://www.borland.com/`

E-mail `kalderman@corp.borland.com`

Mail Borland International Inc.
World Wide Headquarters
100 Borland Way
Scotts Valley, CA 95066

Phone (408) 431-1227

Faxback (206) 628-5737

Chauncey Group Certification

The Chauncey Group is a subsidiary of the Educational Testing Service (ETS), a private measurement and research organization that develops and administers academic tests, such as the GRE and SAT. The Chauncey Group has developed several certification programs, including the premier vendor-independent certification for technical trainers: the Certified Technical Trainer (CTT) program.

The CTT program, created in 1995, is based on a set of professional standards for instructor knowledge and classroom performance defined by the International Board of Standards for Training, Performance and Instruction (ibstpi). These widely recognized standards for technical training are described in the book *Instructor Competencies: The Standards, Volume I* (published by The Chauncey Group), and are also referred to as the ibstpi standards.

While the CTT program has been most widely acknowledged and used within the computer industry, the knowledge and skills it provides are also applicable to other types of technical training. The CTT credential will be valuable in a wide variety of settings.

Recertification or Maintenance Requirements   The CTT credential is good for five years. When five years have passed, trainers must repeat the certification process to retain their credential.

Benefits of Certification   Certified Technical Trainers receive these benefits:

- A certificate and a CTT lapel pin

- Copies of the CTT logo for use on business cards and stationery

- Listing in the CTT Certification Registry, which is available to employers and industry groups

Certified Technical Trainer (CTT)

The CTT Program was initially created to eliminate redundancies among instructor certification programs in the computer training and education business. The CTT certification process involves a computer-based exam and a videotaped performance assessment. The exam must be taken prior to the performance assessment.

The questions on the computer-based exam are designed to assess the trainer's understanding of the content and application of the ibstpi standards. Bring along a photograph of yourself when you take the test. The Sylvan testing center will mark the photo with a special stamp. When you later submit your performance video, you will also enclose the stamped photo so it can be compared with your likeness in the videotape.

The performance video is used to evaluate the trainer's ability to apply the ibstpi standards in a real training setting. You will need to make a videotape of yourself teaching a training class using a specified set of the competencies from the ibstpi standards. It will be graded and the results reported back within a few weeks. The videotape must be submitted within three months of passing the computer-based exam.

Who Needs It   This widely recognized certification can be the first important step toward a career in training in a variety of technical arenas. The CTT is an excellent way for computer professionals to prove their abilities to teach training courses, and is a key component in obtaining additional training certifications with a number of vendors.

Requirements for Certification   The certification process requires the following steps:

1. Pass the computer-based CTT exam. At the same time, get your photograph stamped, as described above.

2. Within three months of passing the test, submit the 20-minute performance assessment videotape.

Administrator The CTT exam is administered by Sylvan Prometric; call (800) 727-8490 to register for Chauncey Group tests. (See Chapter 15 for additional information on Sylvan Prometric.)

Fee $150 for the computer-based exam; $135 for evaluation of the performance video.

Format The computer-based exam consists of 105 multiple-choice questions and must be completed in 90 minutes.

Resources

The Chauncey Group Web site offers a summary of the ibstpi standards as well as hints on preparing for the written exam and creating your video submission. For more information on this organization's certifications and courses, contact The Chauncey Group at:

Web	http://www.chauncey.com/itt/cttp001.html
E-mail	cttp@chauncey.com
Mail	The Chauncey Group International P.O. Box 6541 Princeton, NJ 08541-6541
Phone	(800) 258-4914
Fax	(609) 720-6550

Corel Certifications

Corel Corporation, maker of several excellent word processing, spreadsheet, presentation, and drafting programs, offers a certification program for instructors who want to teach courses on these programs. Corel's certified instructors can teach these courses at numerous training companies that have been authorized as Corel Training Partners. Corel now offers two certifications for professional trainers: the Corel WordPerfect Suite Certified Instructor, for those who will teach courses on WordPerfect, Quattro Pro, or Presentations, and the Corel-Draw 5 Certified Instructor.

Recertification or Maintenance Requirements Corel Certified Instructor certifications are based on specific products and specific versions. As new products and versions become available, certification should be updated accordingly.

Benefits of Certification Corel Certified Instructors receive these benefits:

- Your name included in a listing of Corel Certified Instructors, which is available to employers and industry groups

- Discounts on single copies of Corel academic products

- Access to private Web site for Corel certified professionals

- Monthly newsletter from Corel's education division

- Free issue of *Corel* magazine, with discount on full subscription

- CCI Certificate

- CCI program logos for your advertising needs

Corel WordPerfect Suite 7 Certified Instructor

This certification program has two main components. First, the candidate must obtain qualification as a Corel Certified Expert on the three products in the Corel WordPerfect 7 Suite: WordPerfect, Quattro Pro, and Presentations. (The process for achieving certification as a Corel Certified Expert is covered in Chapter 5.) Second, the candidate must become a Certified Technical Trainer (see "Chauncey Group Certification" above), or achieve an equivalent certification as designated in the requirements listed below.

It is expected that a candidate will acquire a minimum of six months of experience working with computer applications—word processors, spreadsheets, and database applications—prior to applying for this certification, as well as a minimum of six months of teaching experience, tutoring, or hands-on consulting work.

Who Needs It This certification allows you to teach Corel courses for your company or at an outside training facility. This can be an excellent way to increase your worth to your present employer or to begin a career as a professional trainer.

Requirements for Certification The certification process requires the following steps:

1. Attain Corel Certified Expert certification on the three applications in the Corel WordPerfect Suite: WordPerfect, Quattro

Pro, and Presentations. (See Chapter 5 for information on these exams.)

2. Submit proof of successful completion of the Certified Technical Trainer program (see "Chauncey Group Certification" above) or an industry-recognized equivalent (Certified Novell Instructor, WordPerfect Certified Instructor, Lotus Notes Certified Instructor, or Microsoft Certified Trainer).

3. Submit a completed CCI application form, a signed trademark usage agreement, a detailed resume, and an application fee of $200.

Fee $200 application fee. This fee may be waived; contact Corel for details.

CorelDRAW 5 Certified Instructor

Attaining certification as a CorelDRAW 5 Certified Instructor is a simpler process than the WordPerfect Suite Certified Instructor Program described above. This certification is based on passing one computer-based exam that assesses the candidate's ability to provide efficient support and training to those who are learning to use CorelDRAW 5.

Who Needs It This certification allows you to teach CorelDRAW 5 for your company or at an outside training facility. Having a CorelDRAW Certified Instructor can be valuable to organizations that want to train graphic designers and technical artists.

Requirements for Certification The certification process requires the following step:

1. Pass the CorelDRAW 5 Certified Instructor exam.

Administrator The CorelDRAW 5 Certified Instructor exam is administered by Sylvan Prometric; call (800) 662-6735 to register for Corel tests. (See Chapter 15 for additional information on Sylvan Prometric.)

Fee $100

Format This test consists of 80 multiple-choice questions and must be completed in 90 minutes with a minimum score of 81 percent.

Resources

The Corel Web site offers exam bulletins that detail the objectives of each exam. For more information on this organization's certifications and courses, contact Corel at:

Web   `http://www.corel.com/learning/training/`

E-mail   `custserv2@corel.com`

Mail   Corel Corporation
1600 Carling Avenue
Ottawa, Ontario
K1Z 8R7
Canada

Phone   (800) 772-6735

Fax   (613) 761-9176

Faxback (613) 728-0826, ext. 3080

IBM Certifications

IBM offers a vast number of training courses. In fact, their catalog of courses is over an inch thick. Most of the trainers that teach these courses are certified within IBM's organization. But three IBM instructor certifications are readily available to other trainers: IBM Certified Instructor: OS/2 Warp, IBM Certified Instructor: OS/2 LAN Server, and IBM Certified Instructor: OS/2 Warp Server. IBM certifies these instructors to teach courses in their respective specialty, either at IBM sites or at other training facilities.

Recertification or Maintenance Requirements   The IBM Instructor certifications allow you to teach courses on specific versions of IBM operating systems, so there is no requirement for recertification on a particular version. Since your certification is tied to a certain version of a product, however, you will want become certified on the newest versions when they become available if you want to be able to teach the newest courses.

Benefits of Certification   IBM Certified Instructors receive these benefits:

- Logo for use in advertisements and business literature

- A certificate of completion, an ID card, and a lapel pin

- Subscriptions to technical newsletters and magazines, other technical literature, and other special offers

IBM Certified Instructor: OS/2 Warp

The candidate for this certification must first be certified as an IBM Certified Systems Expert on OS/2 Warp or OS/2 Warp Version 4. These certifications involve passing three to four tests that concentrate on the core skills involved in installing and administering these operating systems. IBM Certified Instructors on OS/2 Warp are qualified to teach a number of courses on OS/2 Warp (contact IBM for current course descriptions).

Who Needs It   This certification allows you to teach courses on OS/2 Warp—within your company or at an outside training facility—using official IBM courseware. This can be an excellent way to increase your worth to your present employer or to begin a career as a professional trainer.

Requirements for Certification   The certification process requires the following steps:

1. Obtain certification as a Certified Systems Expert: OS/2 Warp. (See Chapter 4 for details on this credential.)

2. Obtain proof of teaching experience or instructor training by means of one of the following:

   • Provide a list of all classes taught in the past 12 months

   • Provide proof of a degree in education or completion of an in-company or public instructional skills course

   • Provide evidence of certification as a Certified Banyan Instructor, a Microsoft Certified Trainer, or a Certified Novell Instructor

3. Complete an instructor application (obtained from IBM's faxback service at (800) IBM-4FAX) and submit it along with

the proof of instructor experience/training from step 2, a current resume, and two letters of recommendation to:

The Professional Certification Program from IBM
ATTN: Instructor Certification
11400 Burnet Road, Internal Zip 3013
Austin, Texas 78758

IBM Certified Instructor: OS/2 LAN Server

The candidate for this certification must first be certified as an IBM Certified Systems Expert on OS/2 LAN Server. This certification involves passing a total of six tests that assess the core skills involved in installing and administering OS/2 LAN Server. IBM Certified Instructors on OS/2 LAN Server are qualified to teach a number of courses related to LAN Server technology (contact IBM for current course descriptions).

Who Needs It   This certification allows you to teach courses on OS/2 LAN technology—within your company or at an outside training facility—using official IBM courseware. This can be an excellent way to increase your worth to your present employer or to begin a career as a professional trainer.

Requirements for Certification   The certification process requires the following steps:

1.   Obtain certification as a Certified Systems Expert: OS/2 LAN Server. (See Chapter 7 for details on this credential.)

2.   Obtain proof of teaching experience or instructor training by means of one of the following:

   • Provide a list of all classes taught in the past 12 months

- Provide proof of a degree in education or completion of an in-company or public instructional skills course

- Provide evidence of certification as a Certified Banyan Instructor, a Microsoft Certified Trainer, or a Certified Novell Instructor

3. Complete an instructor application (obtained from IBM's faxback service at (800) IBM-4FAX) and submit it along with the proof of instructor experience/training from step 2, a current resume and two letters of recommendation to:

> The Professional Certification Program from IBM
> ATTN: Instructor Certification
> 11400 Burnet Road, Internal Zip 3013
> Austin, Texas 78758

IBM Certified Instructor: OS/2 Warp Server

The candidate for this certification must first be certified as an IBM Certified Systems Expert on OS/2 Warp Server. This certification involves passing three tests that concentrate on the core skills involved in installing and administering OS/2 Warp Server. IBM Certified Instructors on OS/2 Warp Server are qualified to teach a number of courses on OS/2 Warp Server (contact IBM for current course descriptions).

Who Needs It This certification allows you to teach courses on OS/2 Warp Server—within your company or at an outside training facility—using official IBM courseware. This can be an excellent way to increase your worth to your present employer or to begin a career as a professional trainer.

Requirements for Certification The certification process requires the following steps:

1. Obtain certification as an IBM Certified Systems Expert: OS/2 Warp Server. (See Chapter 7 for details on this credential.)

2. Obtain proof of teaching experience or instructor training by means of one of the following:

   - Provide a list of all classes taught in the past 12 months

   - Provide proof of a degree in education or completion of an in-company or public instructional skills course

   - Provide evidence of certification as a Certified Banyan Instructor, a Microsoft Certified Trainer, or a Certified Novell Instructor

3. Complete an instructor application (obtained from IBM's faxback service at (800) IBM-4FAX) and submit it along with the proof of instructor experience/training from step 2, a current resume, and two letters of recommendation to:

   The Professional Certification Program from IBM
   ATTN: Instructor Certification
   11400 Burnet Road, Internal Zip 3013
   Austin, Texas 78758

Resources

For more information on this organization's certifications and courses, contact IBM at:

Web	http://www.ibm.com/certify
E-mail	ialine@us.ibm.com
Mail	IBM North America 1133 Westchester Avenue White Plains, NY 10604
Phone	(800) IBM-TEACH ((800) 426-8322)
Fax	(800) 426-9006
Faxback	(800) IBM-4FAX ((800) 426-4329)

Lotus Certifications

Lotus was launched in 1982 with the popular spreadsheet program, Lotus 1-2-3. Since then, Lotus has branched out into several other areas, including business collaboration software (Lotus Notes) and the software for the Internet (Lotus Domino). Lotus offers an instructor certification program for those who want to teach courses on Lotus products.

The Certified Lotus Instructor (CLI) program is designed for individuals who will be employed by Lotus Authorized Education Centers (LAECs) or plan to become Independent Certified Lotus Instructors—Lotus trainers not employed directly by an LAEC. The CLI program is open only to persons who are already experienced technical trainers, and requires Lotus product knowledge and familiarity with the Lotus curriculum.

Lotus offers several levels of instructor certification for those who want to teach courses on Lotus products. Level One Certified Lotus Instructors (CLIs) can teach Level One Lotus classes. Level Two CLIs can teach both Level One and Level Two Lotus classes. In most cases, the teaching of more advanced Lotus classes requires that—after completion of Level Two certification—the trainer attend the additional course he or she wants to teach, purchase the instructor kit for that course, and pass the certification exam for that course.

Recertification or Maintenance Requirements To maintain their certifications, CLIs are required to attend instructor update training courses on the courses they teach when the related Lotus products are upgraded.

Benefits of Certification Certified Lotus Instructors receive these benefits:

- Updates on product and courseware changes

- Access to the online discussion forum

- Access to to private Web site

Certified Lotus Instructor (CLI): Level One

Level One CLIs can teach Notes Application Development I and Notes System Administration I courses. Lotus recommends that CLI candidates allow a minimum of three months to achieve Level One certification. The following prerequisites are required for acceptance into the CLI program:

- At least one year of technical training experience in a networked environment

- At least one year of experience with networks, PC hardware, software installation, and maintenance on any platform

- A minimum of three months of experience with Lotus products

Those who seek CLI certification must actually attend each Lotus course they intend to teach. While technical professionals seeking software certifications as Certified Lotus Professionals (see Chapter 5 for more information) may use self-study and computer-based training to prepare for these same certification tests, those who seek CLI status must attend the required courses. Each course you attend must be taught by a Certified Lotus Instructor; a copy of your Course Completion Certificate will be required as proof of attendance.

Who Needs It   The CLI certification is necessary for individuals who will be employed by Lotus Authorized Education Centers or plan to become Independent Certified Lotus Instructors. Level One CLI certification allows the teaching of Level One courses.

Requirements for Certification   The certification process requires the following steps:

1. Meet the prerequisites described above.

2. Submit the following items to the CLI Program for approval:

    • Completed Certified Lotus Instructor application

    • Sample class evaluations

    • Current resume and references

3. If approved, attend the Level One Lotus classes listed below and pass the corresponding CLP certification exams (see Chapter 5 for more information on these tests):

    • Notes Application Development I

    • Notes System Administration I

4. Attain certification as a CLP Application Developer or CLP System Administrator (this requires passing one additional exam; see Chapter 5 for information on these certifications).

5. Pass the Lotus Level I Instructor Certification Evaluation (ICE) class. This is a three-day course that evaluates a candidate's ability to teach Level One Notes courses (i.e., Application Development I and System Administration I).

Administrator   The ICE course is conducted by CLIs in Lotus's education department. The ICE courses are available at Lotus headquarters and at Lotus Authorized Education Centers (LAECs).

Lotus exams can be taken from Sylvan Prometric (call (800) 745-6887 to register for a Lotus exam) or from CATGlobal (see their Web site at http://www.catglobal.com/ for registration information). Chapter 15 contains detailed information on taking tests from both Sylvan and CATGlobal.

Fee   The exams for the Level One Lotus classes are $90 each. The fees for Lotus Level One courses vary; contact your local LAEC for information. The Level One ICE class fee is $1500, which includes the cost of two instructor guide kits.

Independent CLIs must maintain membership in the Lotus Business Partners Program and pay any associated fees.

Format   The Level One Instructor Certification Evaluation (ICE) class incorporates an in-class performance evaluation. The format of the CLP exams is covered in Chapter 5.

Certified Lotus Instructor (CLI): Level Two

Level Two of the CLI program builds on the Level One certification above. Level Two CLIs can teach Notes Application Development II and Notes System Administration II in addition to the Level One Lotus courses.

Lotus recommends that CLI candidates allow up to a year for completion of the process for Level Two or higher instructor certification, depending upon their level of product knowledge and degree of flexibility when scheduling classes.

Those who seek CLI certification must actually attend each Lotus course they intend to teach. While technical professionals seeking software certifications as Certified Lotus Professionals (see Chapter 5 for more information) may use self-study and computer-based training to prepare for these same certification tests, those who seek CLI status must attend the required courses. Each course you attend must be taught by a Certified Lotus Instructor; a copy of your Course Completion Certificate will be required as proof of attendance.

Who Needs It   The CLI program is necessary for individuals who will be employed by Lotus Authorized Education Centers or plan to become Independent Certified Lotus Instructors. Level Two CLIs can teach Level One and Level Two Lotus courses.

Requirements for Certification   The certification process requires the following steps:

1. Attain Level One CLI certification.

2. Gain experience teaching Level One courses.

3. Attend the two Level Two Lotus classes listed below and pass the corresponding CLP certification exams (see the Certified Lotus Professional section in Chapter 5 for details on these tests):

    • Notes Application Development II

    • Notes System Administration II

4. Pass a separate two-day Lotus Instructor Certification Evaluation (ICE) class on each of the two courses.

Administrator   The ICE course is conducted by CLIs in Lotus's education department. The ICE courses are available at Lotus headquarters and at Lotus Authorized Education Centers (LAECs).

Lotus exams can be taken from Sylvan Prometric (call (800) 745-6887 to register for a Lotus exam) or from CATGlobal (see their Web site at http://www.catglobal.com/ for registration information). Chapter 15 contains detailed information on taking tests from both Sylvan and CATGlobal.

Fee   The exams for the Level Two Lotus classes are $90 each. The fees for Lotus Level Two courses vary; contact your local LAEC for information. Each of the two ICE classes is $1000, which includes the cost of the instructor guide kit.

Independent CLIs must maintain membership in the Lotus Business Partners Program and pay any associated fees.

Format The Level Two Instructor Certification Evaluation (ICE) class incorporates an in-class performance evaluation. The format of the CLP exams is covered in Chapter 5.

Certified Lotus Instructor (CLI): Advanced Courses

The teaching of the more advanced Lotus classes requires that—after the completion of the Level Two certification process and successful instruction of Level Two Lotus courses—the trainer attend the additional course he or she wants to teach. The candidate must then purchase the instructor guide kit and pass the certification exam (if one is available—contact Lotus to check) for that course. This process is necessary for those who want to teach Notes Application Development III or Lotus Script classes. Each course you attend must be taught by a Certified Lotus Instructor; a copy of your Course Completion Certificate will be required as proof of attendance.

Who Needs It The CLI program is necessary for individuals who will be employed by Lotus Authorized Education Centers or plan to become Independent Certified Lotus Instructors. Advanced-level certification is necessary for those who want to teach the most advanced Lotus courses.

Requirements for Certification The certification process requires the following steps:

1. Attain Level Two CLI certification.

2. Gain experience teaching Level Two courses.

3. Attend the course you want to teach and pass the corresponding certification exam (see the Certified Lotus Professional section in Chapter 5 for details on these tests). Options include:

- Notes Application Development III

- LotusScript in Notes

Administrator The ICE course is conducted by CLIs in Lotus's education department. The ICE courses are available at Lotus headquarters and at Lotus Authorized Education Centers (LAECs). Lotus exams can be taken from Sylvan Prometric (call (800) 745-6887 to register for a Lotus exam) or from CATGlobal (see their Web site at http://www.catglobal.com/ for registration information). Chapter 15 contains detailed information on taking tests from both Sylvan and CATGlobal.

Fee The exams for the Level Two Lotus classes are $90 each. The fees for Lotus Level Two courses vary; contact your local LAEC for information.

Independent CLIs must maintain membership in the Lotus Business Partners Program and pay any associated fees.

Format The format of the CLP exams is covered in Chapter 5.

Resources

For more information on this organization's certifications and courses, contact Lotus at:

Web http://www.lotus.com/

Mail Lotus Education Programs
55 Cambridge Parkway
Cambridge, MA 02142

Phone (800) 346-6409 or (617) 693-4436

Microsoft Certification

Microsoft courses are designed to educate computer professionals who use, support, and implement solutions that use Microsoft technology. Microsoft Certified Trainers (MCTs) are certified by Microsoft as technically and instructionally qualified to deliver Microsoft Official Curriculum instructor-led courses at Microsoft Authorized Technical Education Centers (ATECs).

In the February 1998 issue of *Microsoft Certified Professional* magazine, Linda Briggs provides survey data indicating a new MCT with less than six months of experience averages a starting salary of $47,500, while MCTs with over eight years of experience pull down average salaries of $85,600. Briggs notes that MCTs also tend to spend a lot of time and money on their *own* training in order to stay current, averaging over 200 hours per year at a cost of almost $7000. She also suggests that the hottest combination of training credentials to hold right now is the MCT with an MCP + Internet (see Chapter 9 for information on the MCP + Internet certification program); according to Briggs, trainers with these two credentials bill their time at an average of $159 per hour.

Recertification or Maintenance Requirements   Maintaining your status as a Microsoft Certified Trainer requires the following:

- Maintain high satisfaction ratings on student course evaluations

- Keep technical skills up-to-date and pass any additional required exams

- Meet any new continuing certification criteria developed by Microsoft

- Take part in activities sponsored by your local Microsoft field office

Benefits of Certification   Microsoft Certified Trainers receive these benefits:

- Logo for use on stationery and business cards

- Access to private MCT Web site, which provides the latest product and training information, access to newsgroups, and the *Microsoft Education Forum* newsletter

- Invitation to Microsoft training events

Microsoft Certified Trainer

In order to use Microsoft Official Curriculum for a training course, an instructor must be a Microsoft Certified Trainer, and must be authorized to teach that particular course.

The process of becoming an MCT requires that you submit for approval an application that substantiates your credentials as a technical trainer. Once your application is approved, you have 90 days to obtain your first course certification. You will go through an MCT course certification approval process for each course you want to teach. You will not be considered an MCT in full standing—eligible for MCT benefits—until you have completed the course certification requirements to teach at least one course. If you don't achieve your first course certification within 90 days, you must reapply.

If you are not already a Microsoft Certified Professional (MCP), you may become one during this process (if the course you want to teach requires an MCP exam). MCP exams (covered in Chapters 4 and 7) certify your ability to use and support Microsoft products.

Who Needs It   This certification allows you to teach courses— within your company or at an outside authorized training facility

(ATEC)—using official Microsoft courseware. This can be an excellent way to increase your worth to your present employer or to begin a career as a professional trainer.

Requirements for Certification The certification process requires the following steps:

1. Submit a completed Microsoft Certified Trainer Application, which requires proof of your instructional presentation skills as a technical trainer in one of the following ways:

   - Obtain the Certified Technical Trainer credential (see "Chauncey Group Certification" above).

   - Attend a Microsoft-approved instructional presentation skills course (see http://www.microsoft.com/ train_cert/mct/ for a list of approved courses).

   - Provide proof of certification as a trainer with another vendor—Novell, Lotus, Santa Cruz Operation, Banyan Vines, Cisco Systems, or Sun Microsystems.

2. If approved, complete your first course certification within 90 days. To attain MCT course certification approval for the first course you intend to teach:

   - Pass any prerequisite MCP exams.

   - Prepare to teach the course by studying the Microsoft trainer kit for that course (obtainable by approved MCT candidates by calling (800) 457-1766).

   - Attend the class at a Microsoft Authorized Technical Education Center—either a publicly taught course or a course designed specifically for trainer preparation (referred to as a T-prep course).

   - Complete a Microsoft course preparation checklist.

- Pass the MCP exam for the course; you also may be required to pass an MCT assessment exam (this information is found on a private Web site that is provided for MCTs).

- Apply for course certification.

3. To attain additional MCT course certifications, follow the steps outlined above, with one exception—you may either physically attend the course or learn the material through self-study.

4. If you are an independent MCT—not sponsored by an ATEC—you must submit an application fee.

Administrator Tests are administered by Sylvan Prometric; call (800) 755-3926 to register for Microsoft tests (see Chapter 15 for additional information on Sylvan Prometric). Courses are available from Microsoft Authorized Technical Education Centers (see Chapter 13 for contact information).

Fee Most of the exams cost $100 each, but cost may vary. The cost of attending each course will vary with location. For more information see the Microsoft sections of Chapters 4 and 7; consult Sylvan Prometric for exam information and Microsoft for course information.

The application fee for independent MCTs is $200.

Resources

The Microsoft Web site offers a detailed MCT application packet and other information about the certification program. For more information on this organization's certifications and courses, contact Microsoft at:

Web   `http://www.microsoft.com/train_cert/mct/`

E-mail   `mcp@msprograms.com`

Mail Microsoft Corporation
    One Microsoft Way
    Redmond, WA 98052-6399

Phone (800) 688-0496

Fax (801) 579-2815

Novell Certifications

Novell has offered a network operating systems certification—the Certified Novell Engineer (CNE)—since 1987, and has recently added new levels to this widely recognized technical certification. Likewise, the respected Certified Novell Instructor (CNI) credential has recently been revamped to provide three levels of instructor certification: Certified InfiLearning Instructor, Certified Novell Instructor (CNI), and Master Certified Novell Instructor (Master CNI).

Novell courses are taught only by Novell-certified instructors who are employed by or contract their services to Novell Authorized Education Centers (NAECs)—training organizations that are authorized to offer Novell courses, including Novell distributors, resellers, consultants, retail organizations, and independent training organizations—or Novell Education Academic Partners (NEAPs)—colleges and universities that teach Novell courses as part of their regular curriculum.

Instructors can teach only those Novell courses that they have acquired authorization to teach. (A list of Novell courses can be found on one of Sylvan Prometric's Web site at `http://www.1800training.com/`.) CNIs and Master CNIs can obtain authorization to teach any Novell course, while Certified InfiLearning Instructors can teach a large, but defined, set of courses and cannot become authorized to teach advanced Novell product topics.

Recertification or Maintenance Requirements Master CNIs must meet annual update requirements and keep their CNE status active and current in order to maintain their CNI status. Certification update requirements are flexible and can be selected from a list of options found on Novell's Education Web site at `http://education.novell.com/cni`.

Benefits of Certification Certified Novell Instructors, Master CNIs, and Certified InfiLearning Instructors receive these benefits:

- Quarterly Instructor Guide CDs ($200 per year)
- Certificate
- Access to the Novell Instructor Web site
- E-mail update via CNI Express
- Access to private NOVPRI instructor forum on Compuserve
- Discounts on Novell software and publications
- Name and course authorizations added to private list accessible to education centers
- Instructor conferences and events, including the BrainShare conference

Certified InfiLearning Instructor

The new Certified InfiLearning Instructor credential is the first level of Novell instruction certification. Certified Infilearning Instructors are not required to become CNE certified, and are limited as to which courses they can teach. They can teach the many new Novell courses that do not concentrate on Novell products, including:

325: GroupWise 4.1 Administration

350: GroupWise 5 Administration

508: NetWare 3.1*x* Administration

518: NetWare 3.1*x* Advanced Administration

802: NetWare 3.1*x* Installation and Configuration

520: IntranetWare: NetWare 4.11 Administration

600: Internet Business Strategies

650: Mastering the Net with Netscape Communicator

654: Web Authoring and Publishing

655: Advanced Web Authoring

660: Designing Effective Web Sites

Once a candidate completes an application and provides proof of instructional skills, he or she can begin accumulating authorizations to teach any of the above courses by meeting the attendance and testing requirements for that course.

Novell's requirement for demonstrated instructional skills can be met by providing evidence of Certified Technical Trainer (CTT) status (see "Chauncey Group Certification" above) or by passing a Novell Instructor Performance Evaluation (IPE). The IPE is a two-day evaluation given at a Novell corporate training facility. The IPE involves an orientation session and then the on-site preparation and delivery of a presentation on a course topic chosen by the evaluator.

Novell expects that instructors at all levels have in-depth knowledge of microcomputer concepts, including hardware and operating systems, at least one year of hands-on experience in the computing or networking industry, and at least one year of experience teaching adults in a classroom setting.

Who Needs It This certification allows you to teach Novell courses for your company or at an outside training facility. This can be an excellent way to increase your worth to your present employer or to boost your career as a professional trainer.

Requirements for Certification The certification process requires the following steps:

1. Submit an application and signed agreement. This can be done online at `http://education.novell.com/agreement .htm`, or when taking any Novell test at an authorized testing center.

2. Pass a Novell Instructor Performance Evaluation (IPE) or submit a Certified Technical Trainer (CTT) certificate (see "Chauncey Group Certification" above).

3. Acquire an initial, individual course instructor authorization by attending each course and passing the course exam at the instructor level.

4. Once certification is granted, additional course authorizations can be added by repeating step 3.

Administrator Tests are administered by Sylvan Prometric; call (800) RED-EXAM to register for Novell tests. (See Chapter 15 for additional information on Sylvan Prometric.)

Fee Test fees vary based on length and format; call Sylvan Prometric at (800) RED-EXAM for pricing. The required annual subscription to instructor guides on CD is $200.

Format All exams are closed-book, computer-based tests. Depending on the course, exams may be in traditional format (60-90 questions, 60-180 minute time limit, graded on a percentage), adaptive format

(30-minute exams that determine your level of proficiency using a minimum number of questions), or performance-based format (problem-solving scenarios and simulations).

Certified Novell Instructor

The Certified Novell Instructor (CNI) credential is for trainers that want to concentrate on teaching Novell products, including advanced topics. In addition to providing evidence of instructional skills, beginning on September 30, 1998, all new and current CNIs must also be certified as Certified Novell Engineers (CNEs).

Novell's requirement for demonstrated instructional skills can be met by providing evidence of Certified Technical Trainer (CTT) status (see "Chauncey Group Certification" above) or by passing a Novell Instructor Performance Evaluation (IPE). The IPE is a two-day evaluation given at a Novell corporate training facility. The IPE involves an orientation session and then the on-site preparation and delivery of a presentation on a course topic chosen by the evaluator.

Unlike Certified InfiLearning Instructors, CNIs are not restricted as to what Novell courses they can teach. Once certified, a CNI can become authorized to teach any instructor-led Novell course—including those in the CNA, CNE, Master CNE, and Certified Internet Professional tracks—by attending the course and passing the course exam at the instructor level (see Chapter 7 for more information on the several Novell networking certifications).

Novell expects that instructors at all levels have in-depth knowledge of microcomputer concepts, including hardware and operating systems, at least one year of hands-on experience in the computing or networking industry, and at least one year of experience teaching adults in a classroom setting.

Who Needs It   This certification allows you to teach Novell courses for your company or at an outside training facility. This can be an excellent way to increase your worth to your present employer or to boost your career as a professional trainer.

Requirements for Certification   The certification process requires the following steps:

1. Submit an application and signed agreement. This can be done online at http://education.novell.com/certinfo/ certagrm.htm, or when taking any Novell test at an authorized testing center.

2. Pass an IPE or submit a CTT certificate.

3. Obtain and maintain certification as a Certified Novell Engineer (see Chapter 7 for more information).

4. Acquire individual course instructor authorizations by attending each course and passing the course exam at the instructor level.

Administrator   Tests are administered by Sylvan Prometric; call (800) RED-EXAM to register for Novell tests. (See Chapter 15 for additional information on Sylvan Prometric.)

Fee   Test fees vary based on length and format; call Sylvan Prometric at (800) RED-EXAM for pricing.

Format   All exams are closed-book, computer-based tests. Depending on the course, exams may be in traditional format (60-90 questions, 60-180 minute time limit, graded on a percentage), adaptive format (30-minute exams that determine your level of proficiency using a minimum number of questions), or performance-based format (problem-solving scenarios and simulations).

Master Certified Novell Instructor

The Master Certified Novell Instructor (Master CNI) certification, initiated in November, 1997, is Novell's most prestigious credential for technical trainers. Master CNIs must have two years of teaching experience and be certified as Master Certified Novell Engineers (Master CNEs). In addition they must complete an Annual Update Requirement to keep their technical skills up to date.

Master CNIs can expand their course certifications for standard Novell Education courses simply by passing the course exams (regular CNIs must attend the courses). Master CNIs also may apply as speakers for Novell's annual BrainShare technical conference.

Who Needs It   The Master CNI certification offers CNIs a way to further their certification and improve their competitiveness in the job market.

Requirements for Certification   The certification process requires the following steps:

1.   Work as a CNI for two years.

2.   Earn and maintain certification as a Master CNE (see Chapter 7 for more information).

3.   Meet an Annual Update Requirement initially and annually thereafter.

4.   Obtain individual course instructor authorizations by passing the course exams at the instructor level.

Administrator   Tests are administered by Sylvan Prometric; call (800) RED-EXAM to register for Novell tests. (See Chapter 15 for additional information on Sylvan Prometric.)

Fee Test fees vary based on length and format; call Sylvan Prometric at (800) RED-EXAM for pricing.

Format All exams are closed-book, computer-based tests. Depending on the course, exams may be in traditional format (60-90 questions, 60-180 minute time limit, graded on a percentage), adaptive format (30-minute exams that determine your level of proficiency using a minimum number of questions), or performance-based format (problem-solving scenarios and simulations).

Resources

For more information on this organization's certifications and courses, contact Novell at:

Web	`http://education.novell.com/cni`
E-mail	`cniadmin@novell.com`
Mail	Novell Education Customer Solutions Team Novell, Inc. Mail Stop Orm-K25 1555 North Technology Way Orem, UT 84097
Phone	(800) 233-3383, Option 4 or (801) 222-7800
Fax	(801) 222-7875

Prosoft/Net Guru Technologies Certifications

Prosoft/Net Guru Technologies (Prosoft/NGT) specializes in certifying the skills of technical professionals in several areas, including the Internet, Internet security, TCP/IP, UNIX, Windows 95, and Windows NT (see Chapter 9 for details on their non-trainer certification programs). Prosoft/NGT courses—available at Net Guru locations and other training facilities—can be taught only by Prosoft/NGT Certified Instructors. Prosoft/NGT currently offers four Certified Instructor programs: Prosoft/NGT Certified Windows NT Instructor, Prosoft/NGT Certified Network Professional Instructor, Prosoft/NGT Certified Security Professional Instructor, and Prosoft/NGT Certified Web Developer Instructor.

Candidates for all four Prosoft/NGT Certified Instructor programs must meet training, testing, and evaluation criteria specific to the desired certification. Each program requires payment of a program fee at the beginning of the certification process. Candidates are required to complete all courses, tests, and the mentor evaluation within one year.

Benefits of Certification   As a certified Prosoft/NGT Instructor, you will receive:

- Prosoft/NGT certification logos for use on promotional materials
- E-mail technical support

Prosoft/NGT Certified Windows NT Instructor

Candidates for the Prosoft/NGT Certified Windows NT Instructor credential must provide proof of Microsoft Certified Professional status on Windows NT and attend five days of training at any of Prosoft/NGT's training centers in the United States and Europe. In addition, instructor candidates must spend one day co-teaching with an Prosoft/NGT mentor, where they will be evaluated on their subject matter knowledge and presentation skills.

Candidates are expected to have a working knowledge of Windows NT topics, such as domains, trusts, NT networks, users, groups, server/workstation, CD/network installation/configuration, and NT Performance Monitor. Payment of the program fee is required in advance of training.

Who Needs It   This certification is valuable if you want to conduct official Net Guru Windows NT courses in your area. This can be an excellent way to boost your career as a professional trainer.

Requirements for Certification   The certification process requires the following steps:

1.   Obtain Microsoft Certified Windows NT Professional status by passing a Windows NT certification test (see Chapter 4 for additional information).

2.   Audit the Prosoft/NGT Hands-on Windows NT System and Network Administration course (three days).

3.   Audit the Prosoft/NGT Hands-on Windows NT and TCP/IP Internetworking course (two days).

Administrator The Prosoft/NGT courses are offered at at any of Prosoft/NGT's training centers in the United States and Europe.

Fee The $3425 program fee is required in advance of training.

Prosoft/NGT Certified Network Professional Instructor

Candidates for the Prosoft/NGT Certified Network Professional Instructor credential must attend ten days of training at at any of Prosoft/NGT's training centers in the United States and Europe, and pass a Prosoft/NGT certification test (with an overall score of 90 percent and a minimum score of no less than 85 percent on any one section). In addition, instructor candidates must spend one day co-teaching with an Prosoft/NGT mentor, at which time they will be evaluated on their subject matter knowledge and presentation skills.

Candidates for this certification must have demonstrated hands-on experience and expertise in designing and managing TCP/IP networks. Areas of in-depth knowledge required include subnets, routing, and DNS. Payment of the program fee is required in advance of training.

Who Needs It This certification is valuable if you want to conduct official Net Guru courses in your area. This can be an excellent way to boost your career as a professional trainer.

Requirements for Certification The certification process requires the following steps:

1. Audit either the Prosoft/NGT Hands-on Windows NT System & Network Administration course (three days) or the Prosoft/ NGT Hands-on UNIX System & Network Administration course (three days).

2. Audit the Prosoft/NGT Hands-on TCP/IP Internetworking course (two days).

3. Audit the Prosoft/NGT Advanced TCP/IP Concepts & Practices course (three days).

4. Audit the Prosoft/NGT Hands-on Windows NT & TCP/IP Internetworking course (two days).

5. Pass the TCP/IP Network Professional Program exam.

Administrator The TCP/IP Network Professional Program exam is administered by Sylvan Prometric, call Sylvan at (800) 380-3926 (see Chapter 15 for contact information). The Prosoft/NGT courses are offered at at any of Prosoft/NGT's training centers in the United States and Europe.

Fee The $5700 program fee is required in advance of training. At the end of training you will receive an exam voucher. If you fail the exam and must repeat it, you will pay a fee of $150.

Format Computer-based, multiple-choice test. Call Sylvan Prometric at (800) 380-3926 for current information on the number of questions, time limit, and passing score.

Prosoft/NGT Certified Security Professional Instructor

Candidates for the Prosoft/NGT Certified Security Professional Instructor credential must attend fifteen days of training at at any of Prosoft/NGT's training centers in the United States and Europe, and pass three Prosoft/NGT certification tests (with an overall score of 90 percent on each test and a minimum score of no less than 85 percent on any one section). In addition, instructor candidates must spend one day co-teaching with an Prosoft/NGT mentor, at which time they will be evaluated on their subject matter knowledge and presentation skills.

Candidates for this certification must have demonstrated hands-on experience and expertise in TCP/IP networks, managing UNIX systems, security concepts, practices, and firewall systems. Payment of the program fee is required in advance of training.

Who Needs It   This certification is valuable if you want to conduct official Net Guru courses on network security. This can be an excellent way to boost your career as a professional trainer.

Requirements for Certification   The certification process requires the following steps:

1. Audit the Prosoft/NGT Hands-on UNIX System and Network Administration course (three days).

2. Audit the Prosoft/NGT Hands-on Internet Webmaster Administrator Program course (five days).

3. Audit the Prosoft/NGT Hands-on Certified Internet Webmaster Network Professional Program course (five days).

4. Audit the Prosoft/NGT Hands-on Internet Security & Firewall Systems course (two days).

5. Pass the Prosoft/NGT Webmaster Network Professional exam.

6. Pass the Prosoft/NGT Webmaster Administrator exam.

7. Pass the Prosoft/NGT Security Professional Programs exam.

Administrator   The Prosoft/NGT courses are offered at at any of Prosoft/NGT's training centers in the United States and Europe. The tests are administered by Sylvan Prometric (see Chapter 15 for contact information).

Fee The $7775 program fee is required in advance of training. At the end of training you will receive exam vouchers. If you fail any exam and must repeat it, you will pay a fee of $150.

Format Computer-based, multiple-choice tests. Call Sylvan Prometric at (800) 380-3926 for current information on the number of questions, time limit, and passing score.

Prosoft/NGT Certified Internet Web Developer Instructor

Candidates for the Prosoft/NGT Certified Internet Web Developer Instructor credential must attend thirteen days of training at at any of Prosoft/NGT's training centers in the United States and Europe, and pass three Prosoft/NGT certification tests (with an overall score of 90 percent on each test and a minimum score of no less that 85 percent on any one section). In addition, instructor candidates must spend one day co-teaching with an Prosoft/NGT mentor, at which time they will be evaluated on their subject matter knowledge and presentation skills.

Candidates for this certification must have demonstrated and proven hands-on experience and expertise in HTML, Perl, CGI, Java, JavaScript, and the development of Active Server Pages.

Who Needs It This certification is valuable if you want to conduct official Net Guru courses on Web development. This can be an excellent way to boost your career as a professional trainer.

Requirements for Certification The certification process requires the following steps:

1. Audit the Hands-on Internet Webmaster Designer Program course (three days).

   2. Audit the Hands-on Internet Webmaster Developer I Program
   course (five days).

   3. Audit the Hands-on Internet Webmaster Developer II Program
   course (five days).

   4. Pass the Internet Webmaster Designer test.

   5. Pass the Webmaster Developer I test.

   6. Pass the Webmaster Developer II test.

Administrator   The Prosoft/NGT courses are offered at at any of
Prosoft/NGT's training centers in the United States and Europe. The
tests are administered by Sylvan Prometric (see Chapter 15 for contact
information).

Fee   The $6645 program fee is required in advance of training. At
the end of training you will receive exam vouchers. If you fail any
exam and must repeat it, you will pay a fee of $150.

Format   Computer-based, multiple-choice tests. Call Sylvan Prometric at (800) 380-3926 for current information on the number of questions, time limit, and passing score.

Resources

For more information on this organization's certifications and courses,
contact Prosoft/Net Guru Technologies at:

Web   http://www.ngt.com/

E-mail   info@nirvana.ngt.com

Mail   Prosoft/Net Guru Technologies, Inc.
             2625 Butterfield Rd., Suite 312E
             Oak Brook, IL 60523

Phone	(630) 574-4878 or (800) KNOWNGT
Fax	(630) 990-9635

CHAPTER

11

Other Vendor-Based
Certifications

FEATURING

COMPUTER SECURITY

■ International Information Systems Security Certification Consortium Certification

■ Information Systems Audit and Control Association Certification

PROGRAMMING

■ Microsoft Certification

■ Sun Certifications

NETWORK MANAGEMENT

■ Computer Associates Certification

■ Hewlett-Packard Certifications

The certification programs covered in this chapter focus on aspects of computing and networking that did not fit neatly into the previous chapters, i.e., security, programming, and network management. The certifications included here are offered by individual vendors or by consortiums of industry and business interests.

Two certification programs concentrate on computer security: the Certified Information Systems Security Professional designation, offered by the International Information Systems Security Certification Consortium, and the Certified Information Systems Auditor credential, offered by Information Systems Audit and Control Association.

The next two certifications focus on programming. The Microsoft Certified Solution Developer certification program is designed for computer professionals who develop custom applications using Microsoft products and/or programming languages. The Sun Certified Java Programmer and Developer are two popular certifications offered by the inventors of the Java programming language.

The final two certifications covered in this chapter concentrate on network management software. This type of software is used for large-scale monitoring and troubleshooting of networks that are comprised of equipment and software from multiple vendors. The two network management certifications are Computer Associates' Certified Unicenter Engineer credential and Hewlett-Packard's OpenView Certified Consultant designation.

Professionals seeking these certifications might include:

- Help desk personnel
- Programmers
- Security specialists
- Consultants
- Network administrators

International Information Systems Security Certification Consortium Certification

The International Information Systems Security Certification Consortium, abbreviated as (ISC)^2, is a non-profit alliance formed by members of the SIG-CS of the Data Processing Management Association, the Computer Security Institute, the Information Systems Security Association, the Canadian Information Processing Society, the International Federation for Information Processing, several agencies of the United States and Canadian governments, and Idaho State University. In 1997, 501 professionals were certified, an increase of more than 75 percent when compared to 1996. These organizations have cooperated to formulate a standard certification program for computer security professionals—the Certified Information Systems Security Professional (CISSP) program.

There are currently more than 1500 CISSP certified professionals. (ISC)^2 estimates, however, that there may be as many as 20,000 individuals in the computer security field that could benefit from CISSP certification, and that number appears to be growing. According to an industry report, budgets for information security staffing are expected to rise 17.8 percent over the next year, and information security employment—as a percentage of total employment—has increased by nearly 100 percent over the last seven years. ("1997 Information Security Staffing Levels and the Standard of Due Care" Computer Security Institute and Charles Cresson Wood of Baseline Software; for more information see http://www.gocsi.com/prelease.htm.)

Recertification or Maintenance Requirements CISSP certified professionals must maintain their certification by one of the following two options:

- Earn 120 Continuing Professional Education (CPE) credits over each three-year recertification period. Two-thirds of the CPE credits must be earned in activities directly related to the information systems security profession while the other one-third may be earned in educational activities that enhance one's overall professional skills, knowledge, and competency.

- Retake and pass the certification exam every three years.

Benefits of Certification While this certification doesn't offer the incidental benefits provided with some other vendor-based certifications, it is likely to offer benefits with regard to career advancement. As a vendor-independent authentication of an individual's skill in information security, the CISSP certification is now specified as a preferred or required credential for a growing number of security-related positions.

Certified Information Systems Security Professional

(ISC)^2 requires that candidates for this certification have three years of hands-on experience in the computer security field before attempting the one required exam. The certification exam for each candidate is selected from a pool of 1700 multiple-choice questions that cover these ten topics: Access Control Systems & Methodology; Operations Security; Cryptography; Applications & Systems Development; Business Continuity & Disaster Planning; Telecommunications & Network Security; Security Architecture & Models; Physical Security; Security Management Practices; and Law, Investigation & Ethics.

The CISSP exam measures knowledge across the entire spectrum of topics in the Common Body of Knowledge (CBK) for the information systems security field. It is expected that most candidates will find the exam difficult unless they review the topics listed above. To help candidates prepare, (ISC)^2 has developed an information system security CBK Review Seminar to provide instruction in all ten of the test domains covered on the exam. This seminar consists of eight days of instruction, presented as two four-day modules.

Who Needs It The CISSP certification is an excellent way to prove your worth as a computer security expert, whether to your current employer or to potential employers. It can also be an excellent designation for independent consultants who want to showcase their computer security skills for potential clients.

Requirements for Certification The certification process requires the following steps:

1. Acquire the prerequisite three years of direct work experience in information systems security.

2. Agree to the (ISC)^2 Code of Ethics (contact (ISC)^2 for a copy).

3. Pass the CISSP exam.

Administrator (ISC)^2

Fee $395

Format The exam consists of 250 multiple-choice questions that must be completed in 6 hours. A scaled score of 700 out of 1000 is required for passing.

Resources

A draft Study Guide containing a description of the ten test domains, sample test questions, and a list of reference materials is available to candidates at cost (copying and shipping) upon request. To obtain a copy, send a large, self-addressed *shipping label* and $10 for Priority

Mail handling within the U.S. For Airmail delivery outside the U.S., the cost (including air mail) in U.S. dollars is: Canada - $10.42; Mexico - $13.46; other countries - $18.80. This study guide contains a description of the ten test domains, sample test questions, and a list of reference materials. For more information on this organization's certifications and courses, contact (ISC)^2 at:

Web	http://www.isc2.org/
E-mail	info@isc2.org
Mail	(ISC)^2 415 Boston Turnpike, Suite 105 Worcester, MA 01545
Phone	(508) 845-9200
Fax	(508) 845-2420

Information Systems Audit and Control Association (ISACA) Certification

The Information Systems Audit and Control Association (ISACA) is a professional organization of computer security professionals that has more than 17,000 members. ISACA sponsors a number of important conferences in the security field and they also offer one well-known certification—the Certified Information Systems Auditor—which has been offered since 1979.

Recertification or Maintenance Requirements To maintain certification, Certified Information Systems Auditors must pay maintenance fees and take a minimum of 20 contact hours of continuing education annually. In addition, a minimum of 120 contact hours of continuing education is required during each 3-year period. Contact hours—which refer to actual clock hours, not course credits—can be earned by attending conferences, courses, and other professional development opportunities in the field.

Benefits of Certification Certified Information Systems Auditors receive the following benefits:

- Logo for use on business cards and materials
- Wall certificate

Certified Information Systems Auditor (CISA)

Qualifying for the CISA designation requires the candidate to meet an experience prerequisite, adhere to a code of ethics, pass an examination, and maintain certification through substantive continuing education requirements (see ISACA section above for details). The CISA exam focuses on the following five topics:

- Information Systems Audit Standards and Practices and Information Systems Security and Control Practices
- Information Systems Organization and Management
- Information Systems Process
- Information Systems Integrity, Confidentiality, and Availability
- Information Systems Development, Acquisition, and Maintenance

Who Needs It The CISA certification is an excellent way to validate your skills as a computer security expert, whether for a current employer or for potential employers. It can also be an excellent designation for independent consultants who want to show potential clients proof of their abilities.

Requirements for Certification The certification process requires the following steps:

1. Have a minimum of five years of experience in information systems auditing, control, or security. (Contact ISACA about substitutions and waivers of the experience requirement. Experience is verified independently with employers.)

2. Pass the CISA exam.

3. Agree to abide by the Information Systems Audit and Control Foundation Code of Professional Ethics.

4. Submit an application for certification.

5. Meet the annual continuing education requirements.

A candidate may choose to take the CISA exam prior to meeting the experience requirement, although the CISA designation will not be awarded until all requirements are met. If this is done, the application for certification must be submitted within five years of passing the CISA exam.

Administrator ISACA administers all CISA exams.

Fee The exam costs $295 for ISACA members and $385 for non-members. (ISACA dues for 1998 are $95, plus a one-time new member fee of $30. A student membership is available for $47.50 for full-time students.)

Format The CISA Examination consists of 200 multiple-choice questions, administered during a four-hour session. The exam is offered only once each year, in June, and candidates must register for the exam by April. The 1998 CISA examination will be offered on Saturday, June 13, 1998. Contact ISACA at `certification@isaca.org` for a registration form. The exam is offered in the following languages: Dutch, English, French, German, Hebrew, Italian, Japanese, Korean, and Spanish.

Approximately 10 weeks after the test date, the Board will mail score reports to the candidates. A person receiving a scaled score of 75 or better will pass the examination. To ensure the confidentiality of scores, test results will not be reported by telephone, fax, or e-mail.

Resources

The ISACA Web site offers an exam bulletin, which details the test objectives and test registration procedures. Candidates receive a guide to the CISA Examination after ISACA receives the completed registration form and payment. This guide provides a detailed outline of the subject areas covered on the examination, as well as a suggested list of reference materials, glossary of acronyms, flowchart symbols commonly used on the exam, and a sample copy of the answer sheet used for the exam. For more information on this organization's certifications and courses, contact the Information Systems Audit and Control Association at:

Web	http://www.isaca.org/
E-mail	certification@isaca.org
Mail	Information Systems Audit and Control Association
	3701 Algonquin Road, Suite 1010
	Rolling Meadows, Illinois 60008
Phone	(847) 253-1545
Fax	(847) 253-1443

Microsoft Certification

The Microsoft Certified Solution Developer (MCSD) certification is one of Microsoft's premium credentials. This certification program is designed for computer professionals who want to document their ability to develop custom applications using Microsoft products and/or programming languages. There are approximately 6,700 MCSDs in the world today, and that number is climbing steadily.

Recertification or Maintenance Requirements MCSDs must take action to maintain their certifications. As Microsoft introduces new products and new versions of its operating systems, it retires the tests for previous versions. If you hold a certification that is based on a test that Microsoft is retiring, you will be informed by certified mail of the need to take a current test to maintain your certification. You will have at least six months to complete this new test or your status as an MCSD will no longer be valid.

Benefits of Certification Microsoft Certified Solution Developers receive the following benefits:

- An MCSD certificate

- Access to technical information through a secure MCSD-only Web site

- Use of MCSD logos on stationery and business cards

- Invitations to Microsoft-sponsored conferences and technical briefings

- A free subscription to *Microsoft Certified Professional* magazine

- A one-year subscription to the Microsoft Developer Network Library, which provides an informative CD each month

- A one-year subscription to the Microsoft Beta Evaluation program. Microsoft will send you free CDs each month containing beta versions of their newest software.

Microsoft Certified Solution Developer (MCSD)

To attain certification as an MCSD, a candidate must pass two core exams and two elective exams. The core exams cover the basic concepts and theory behind the architecture of Microsoft's operating systems. The elective exams concentrate on programming and database skills. Microsoft's Web site provides exam guidelines, sample tests, etc., and links to authorized training providers (see the Resources section below).

Who Needs It The MCSD certification is an excellent way to prove your worth as a programmer to your current employer or to potential employers. It can also be an excellent designation for independent consultants who want to validate their abilities for potential clients.

Requirements for Certification The certification process requires the following steps:

1. Pass the Microsoft Windows Architecture I exam (Sylvan ID: 070-160).

2. Pass the Microsoft Windows Architecture II exam (Sylvan ID: 070-161).

3. Pass two elective exams, selected from those listed in Table 11.1. If you pass two exams within the same category, only one will qualify as an MCSD elective.

TABLE 11.1: MCSD Elective Exams

Category	Sylvan ID	Exam(s)
SQL Server	070-021	Microsoft SQL Server 4.2 Database Implementation
		OR
	070-027	Implementing a Database Design on Microsoft SQL Server
		OR
	070-029	Implementing a Database Design on Microsoft SQL Server 7.0
C++	070-024	Developing Applications with C++ Using the Microsoft Foundation Class Library
Visual Basic	070-065	Programming with Microsoft Visual Basic 4.0
		OR
	070-165	Developing Applications with Microsoft Visual Basic 5.0
MS Access	070-051	Microsoft Access 2.0 for Windows-Application Development
		OR
	070-069	Microsoft Access for Windows 95 and the Microsoft Access Developer's Toolkit
MS Excel	070-052	Developing Applications with Microsoft Excel 5.0 Using Visual Basic for Applications
Visual FoxPro	070-054	Programming in Microsoft Visual FoxPro 3.0 for Windows
OLE	070-025	Implementing OLE in Microsoft Foundation Class Applications

Administrator Call Sylvan Prometric at (800) 755-3926 to register for a Microsoft exam. (See Chapter 15 for detailed information on taking tests from Sylvan.)

Fee $100 per test

Format Multiple-choice, closed-book tests. The number of questions and time limit depend on the test selected.

Resources

The Microsoft Web site offers practice tests as well as study guides that detail the objectives of each exam. Microsoft's Web site also offers a listing of Microsoft Authorized Education Centers. For more information on this organization's certification programs, contact Microsoft at:

Web	`http://www.microsoft.com/mcp/`
E-mail	`mcp@msprograms.com`
Mail	Microsoft Corporation One Microsoft Way Redmond, WA 98052-6399
Phone	(800) 636-7544
Fax	(206) 936-7329

Sun Certifications

Sun Microsystems, Inc. is the originator of the Java programming language, and is also well known for its high-performance computer systems. Sun offers two versions of its Java Development Kit (JDK). On both versions, two levels of certification are offered—the Certified Java Programmer, and the Certified Java Developer, which builds on the programmer-level certification.

Java's certification exams have earned a reputation as being challenging. Four months after the October 1996 introduction of Java's certification program, it was reported that 55 to 60 percent of the approximately 100 persons who had attempted the exam up to that time had failed to pass ("Tough Test Reveals Java Pros," Julia King, Computer World, February 3, 1997).

Recertification or Maintenance Requirements Both the Certified Java Programmer and Certified Java Developer designations apply to specific JDK version numbers, so there is no requirement for recertification on a particular version. Since your certification is tied to a certain version of a product, however, you will want become certified on the newest versions, when they become available, if you want to continue to have the most current credential in this area.

Benefits of Certification Sun Certified Java Programmers and Developers receive the following benefits:

- Logo for use on business cards and materials
- Wall certificate and lapel pin

Certified Java Programmer: JDK 1.0.2

The Sun Certified Java Programmer certification program for JDK 1.0.2 involves passing a single examination. This exam tests the breadth of the candidate's knowledge of the Java language.

Sun recommends these two instructor-led courses as preparation for the Sun Certified Java Programmer exam: Course SL-230: Introduction to Java Programming UNIX ($1195), and Course SL-270: Java Application Programming UNIX ($795).

Who Needs It   The Sun Certified Java Programmer certification is an excellent credential for Java programmers. This certification is also valuable to Web designers and administrators. It can help you demonstrate your abilities to an employer, or help you get jobs on a freelance basis.

Requirements for Certification   The certification process requires only one step:

1. Pass the Sun Certified Java Programmer for JDK 1.0.2 exam (Sylvan ID: 310-020).

Administrator   Call Sun Educational Services at (800) 422-8020 to purchase an exam voucher. You will receive the voucher by mail, as well as information on how and when to take the exam. The exams are taken through Sylvan Prometric. (See Chapter 15 for more information on Sylvan Prometric.)

Fee $150

Format   The Sun Certified Java Programmer: JDK 1.0.2 exam has 77 questions and must be completed in 135 minutes; the passing score is 70 percent.

Certified Java Programmer: JDK 1.1

The Sun Certified Java Programmer certification program for JDK 1.1 involves passing a single examination. This exam tests the breadth of the candidate's knowledge of the Java language.

Sun recommends taking one of these two instructor-led courses as preparation for the Sun Certified Java Programmer exam: Course SL-275: Java Programming UNIX ($2000) or Course SL-276: Java Programming Windows 95 ($2000).

Who Needs It   The Sun Certified Java Programmer certification is an excellent credential for Java programmers. This certification is also valuable to Web designers and administrators. It can help you demonstrate your abilities to an employer, or help you get jobs on a freelance basis.

Requirements for Certification   The certification process requires only one step:

1.   Pass the Sun Certified Java Programmer for JDK 1.1 exam (Sylvan ID: 310-022).

Administrator   Call Sun Educational Services at (800) 422-8020 to purchase an exam voucher. You will receive the voucher by mail, as well as information on how and when to take the exam. The exams are taken through Sylvan Prometric. (See Chapter 15 for more information on Sylvan Prometric.)

Fee $150

Format   The Sun Certified Java Programmer: JDK 1.0.2 exam has 60 questions and must be completed in 120 minutes; the passing score is 70 percent.

Certified Java Developer: JDK 1.0.2

The Sun Certified Java Developer: JDK 1.0.2 certification program builds on the Certified Java Programmer certification, and is comprised of two parts.

The first part is the programming assignment, which is the performance-based portion of the Developer program. The candidate accesses the Sun Educational Services Certification Database and downloads a Java program and a set of instructions. Once the assignment is completed, the candidate uploads the assignment. Then the candidate is ready for the second part of the certification program: the Sun Certified Java Developer examination.

Sun recommends this instructor-led course as preparation for the Sun Certified Java Developer exam: Course SL-300: Java Programming Workshop ($2000).

Who Needs It The Sun Certified Java Developer certification is the most advanced and respected credential for Java programmers. This certification is also valuable to Web designers and administrators. It can help you demonstrate your abilities to an employer, or help you get jobs on a freelance basis.

Requirements for Certification The certification process requires the following steps:

1. Obtain certification as a Sun Certified Java Programmer on any JDK version.

2. Complete the Developer programming assignment (see above for details).

3. Pass the Sun Certified Java Developer for JDK 1.0.2 exam (Sylvan ID: 310-021).

Once the exam is completed, the candidate's programming assignment and examination are assessed by an independent, third-party assessor within four weeks.

Administrator The procedure for the programming assignment component of the certification exam is described above.

To take the written exam, call Sun Educational Services at (800) 422-8020 to purchase an exam voucher. You will receive the voucher by mail, as well as information on how and when to take the exam. The exams are taken through Sylvan Prometric. (See Chapter 15 for more information on Sylvan Prometric.)

Fee $250 for the programming assignment. $150 for the Sun Certified Java Developer for JDK 1.0.2 exam.

Format The Sun Certified Java Developer for JDK 1.0.2 exam is comprised of 5 to 10 short essay questions that must be completed in 90 minutes.

Certified Java Developer: JDK 1.1

The Sun Certified Java Developer Program for JDK 1.1, like the Sun Certified Java Developer Program for JDK 1.0.2, builds on the Certified Java Programmer certification and is comprised of two parts.

The first part is the programming assignment, which is the performance-based portion of the Developer program. The candidate accesses the Sun Educational Services Certification Database and downloads a Java program and a set of instructions. Once the assignment is completed, the candidate uploads the assignment. Then the candidate is ready for the second part of the certification program: the Sun Certified Java Developer examination.

Sun recommends this instructor-led course as preparation for the Sun Certified Java Developer exam: Course SL-300: Java Programming Workshop ($2000).

Who Needs It The Sun Certified Java Developer certification is the most advanced and respected credential for Java programmers. This certification is also valuable to Web designers and administrators. It can help you demonstrate your abilities to an employer, or help you get jobs on a freelance basis.

Requirements for Certification The certification process requires the following steps:

1. Obtain certification as a Sun Certified Java Programmer on any JDK version.

2. Complete the Developer programming assignment (see above for details).

3. Pass the Sun Certified Java Developer for JDK 1.1 exam (Sylvan ID: 310-024).

Once the written exam is completed, the candidate's programming assignment and examination are assessed by an independent, third-party assessor within four weeks.

Administrator The procedure for the programming assignment component of the certification exam is described above.

To take the written exam, call Sun Educational Services at (800) 422-8020 to purchase an exam voucher. You will receive the voucher by mail, as well as information on how and when to take the exam. The exams are taken through Sylvan Prometric. (See Chapter 15 for more information on Sylvan Prometric.)

Fee $250 for the programming assignment. $150 for the Sun Certified Java Developer for JDK 1.1 exam.

Format   The Sun Certified Java Developer: JDK 1.1 exam is comprised of 5 to 10 short essay questions that must be completed in 90 minutes.

Resources

The Sun Web site offers an exam bulletin for each exam, which details the test's objectives. Sun's Web site also offers a listing of authorized courses. For more information on this organization's certifications and courses, contact Sun at:

Web	http://suned.sun.com/suned/
E-mail	who2contact@chocolate.ebay.sun.com
Mail	Sun Microsystems 901 San Antonio Road Palo Alto, CA 94303
Phone	(800) 422-8020
Faxback	(800) 564-4341 (code #250)

Computer Associates Certification

Computer Associates' Unicenter TNG system is an open, cross-platform enterprise management system for the control of heterogeneous networks, i.e., networks that are comprised of equipment and software from multiple vendors. Unicenter TNG is one of the most popular enterprise management software programs.

The Unicenter TNG Certification Program provides training and certification for engineers involved in the deployment and administration of Unicenter TNG.

Recertification or Maintenance Requirements Computer Associates currently has no policy regarding recertification. However, they are exploring recertification options.

Benefits of Certification In addition to industry recognition of their technical achievements, Certified Unicenter Engineers receive the following benefit:

- Use of CUE designation in advertisements or business literature

Certified Unicenter Engineer

This certification program involves taking two required courses and passing an exam on each course. The courses and exams must be taken in a specified order. Hands-on ecperience with the product is considered essential to success in passing the exam.

The basic course introduces the Unicenter TNG product. Topics covered in this course include Unicenter TNG overview and architecture; installing Unicenter TNG; Unicenter TNG agent technology; and Unicenter TNG options. The advanced course presents advanced Unicenter TNG topics, including integrating WorldView, event management, and Distributed State Machines (DSM); how to customize the WorldView GUI; and how to effectively implement management policies through manager/agent technology.

Who Needs It The Certified Unicenter Engineer is an excellent credential for network management professionals. This certification is also valuable to support and help desk personnel.

Requirements for Certification The certification process requires the following steps:

1. Complete the Unicenter TNG Basics course (Course ID: UT210). Successful completion of all hands-on labs and workshops is required.

2. Pass the Unicenter TNG Basics examination (Sylvan ID: 270-112).

3. Complete the Unicenter TNG Advanced Course (Course ID: UT220). Successful completion of all hands-on labs and workshops is required.

4. Pass the Unicenter TNG Advanced examination (Sulvan ID: 270-113).

All steps must be completed in the order listed.

Administrator Call Sylvan Prometric at (800) 859-3926 to register for a Computer Associates exam. (See Chapter 15 for detailed information on taking tests from Sylvan.)

Fee Each course costs $2125; the cost includes a voucher that lets you take the Sylvan test for free. If you fail the test and must retake it, you must pay an additional fee of $100.

Format Each test consists of 100 multiple-choice questions and must be completed in 60 minutes. Passing score is 80 percent.

Resources

For more information on this organization's certifications and courses, contact Computer Associates at:

Web	http://www.cai.com/
Mail	Computer Associates International, Inc. Rt. 206 & Orchard Road Princeton, NJ 08543
Phone	(800) 237-9273
Fax	(908) 874-7417

Hewlett-Packard Certifications

Hewlett-Packard (HP) makes a wide variety of products, from computers and laser printers to specialized medical instruments. In addition, HP makes OpenView, which is one of the most popular network management products. OpenView is a network management system for monitoring and managing networks that are comprised of equipment and software from multiple vendors.

HP's OpenView Certified Consultant designation recognizes technical competency to both sell and support HP OpenView. Three specializations are offered: UNIX, Windows NT, and a combined UNIX and Windows NT specialization.

Recertification or Maintenance Requirements To maintain their certifications, OpenView Certified Consultants are required to take a recertification exam when there is a major release of a new version of OpenView. Certified Consultants are given three months after the release of the new certification exam to update their certification status.

Benefits of Certification HP OpenView Certified Consultants receive this benefit:

- Use of the HP Certified Consultant logo

HP OpenView Certified Consultant: UNIX

Attaining this certification involves passing two tests. The first exam covers the basic operation of HP OpenView, including configuration of the computer system and the networking environment; basic knowledge of network management; configuration and installation of NNM as a stand-alone management system (non-distributed); and setting up management consoles. The second exam focuses on the implementation of OpenView on the UNIX operating system.

Who Needs It The HP OpenView Certified Consultant certification is an excellent credential for network management professionals. This certification is also valuable to support and help desk personnel.

Requirements for Certification The certification process requires the following steps:

1. Pass the Introduction to HP OpenView exam (Sylvan ID: 490-001).

2. Pass the Network Node Manager Fundamentals for UNIX exam (Sylvan ID: 490-010).

Both exams must be completed within one year of the date on which the candidate takes the first exam.

Administrator Call Sylvan Prometric at (800) 549-3926 to register for an HP exam. (See Chapter 15 for detailed information on taking tests from Sylvan.)

Fee   The HP OpenView exam costs $70. The Network Node Manager Fundamentals for UNIX exam costs $130.

Format   The HP OpenView exam consists of 27 questions and must be completed in 60 minutes. The passing score is 80 percent. The Network Node Manager Fundamentals for UNIX exam consists of two sections. It has 108 questions and must be completed in 165 minutes. To pass, the candidate must score 70 percent or higher in each of the two sections of the test.

HP OpenView Certified Consultant: Windows NT

Attaining this certification involves passing two tests. The first exam covers the basic operation of HP OpenView, including configuration of the computer system and the networking environment; basic knowledge of network management; configuration and installation of NNM as a stand-alone management system (non-distributed); and setting up management consoles. The second exam focuses on the implementation of OpenView on the Windows NT operating system.

Who Needs It   The HP OpenView Certified Consultant is an excellent credential for network management professionals. This certification is also valuable to support and help desk personnel.

Requirements for Certification   The certification process requires the following steps:

1.   Pass the Introduction to HP OpenView exam (Sylvan ID: 490-001).

2.   Pass the Network Node Manager Fundamentals for Windows NT exam (Sylvan ID: 490-020).

Both exams must be completed within one year from the date the candidate takes the first exam.

Administrator   Call Sylvan Prometric at (800) 549-3926 to register for an HP exam. (See Chapter 15 for detailed information on taking tests from Sylvan.)

Fee   The HP OpenView exam costs $70. The Network Node Manager Fundamentals for Windows NT exam costs $130.

Format   The HP OpenView exam consists of 27 questions and must be completed in 60 minutes. The passing score is 80 percent. The Network Node Manager Fundamentals for Windows NT exam consists of two sections. It has 106 questions and must be completed in 165 minutes. To pass, the candidate must score 67 percent or higher in each of the two sections of the test.

HP OpenView Certified Consultant: UNIX and Windows NT

Attaining this certification involves passing two tests. The first exam covers the basic operation of HP OpenView, including configuration of the computer system and the networking environment; basic knowledge of network management; configuration and installation of NNM as a stand-alone management system (non-distributed); and setting up management consoles. The second exam focuses on the implementation of OpenView on the UNIX and Windows NT operating systems.

Who Needs It   The HP OpenView Certified Consultant is an excellent credential for network management professionals. This certification is also valuable to support and help desk personnel.

Requirements for Certification   The certification process requires the following steps:

1. Pass the Introduction to HP OpenView exam (Sylvan ID: 490-001).

2. Pass the Network Node Manager Fundamentals for UNIX and Windows NT exam (Sylvan ID: 490-030).

Both exams must be completed within one year from the date the candidate takes the first exam.

Administrator   Call Sylvan Prometric at (800) 549-3926 to register for an HP exam. (See Chapter 15 for detailed information on taking tests from Sylvan.)

Fee   The HP OpenView exam costs $70. The Network Node Manager Fundamentals for UNIX and Windows NT exam costs $130.

Format   The HP OpenView exam consists of 27 questions and must be completed in 60 minutes. The passing score is 80 percent. The Network Node Manager Fundamentals for UNIX and Windows NT exam consists of two sections. It has 128 questions and must be completed in 180 minutes. To pass, the candidate must score 70 percent or higher in each of the two sections of the test.

Resources

The HP Web site offers self-assessment practice exams. HP's Web site also offers a listing of preparation courses. For more information on this organization's certifications and courses, contact HP at:

Web	http://www.hp.com/go/openview/
E-mail	ovtraining@fc.hp.com
Phone	(800) 225-1451
Fax	(970) 898-3647

CHAPTER

12

Organization-Based Certifications

FEATURING

- BICSI Certifications

- CNX Consortium Certifications

- CompTIA Certifications

- ICCP Certification

- Network Professional Association
  Certification

Up to this point, this book has primarily described certification programs offered by vendors—those companies that make and sell the products for which they offer certifications. While these programs are often very rigorous and difficult, some people feel that there are inherent problems with vendor-based certifications. The most significant criticism is that when a person becomes certified on a particular product, he or she does not get the full range of experience and knowledge that is required in real-world situations. The desire to address this problem was the primary motivation behind the creation of the organization-based certifications described in this chapter.

Organization-based or "vendor-neutral" certification programs are well respected in the computer and networking fields because they tend to be comprehensive and standards-based. They cover many products and concepts without promoting one vendor's products over another's. Developed by a wide range of experts in a particular field, organization-based certifications also tend to encompass a broader range of skills and abilities than vendor-based certifications. In addition, many of these certifications recognize that the role of a computer or networking professional involves a variety of professional activities and requires a set of non-technical skills, such as interpersonal and communication skills.

An additional benefit of an organization-based certification is that, at least in some cases, you can join the organization and receive member benefits such as group insurance policies, opportunities for professional development, and job referral and placement services. Most organization-based certifications do not provide the same type of benefits as vendor-based ones, such as free CDs or free access to technical support. They do, however, provide this important benefit: a widely-recognized validation of your skills and knowledge that is independent of any one vendor.

Some of the certifications covered in this chapter are among the most prestigious in the computer and networking fields. Professionals seeking these certifications include a wide range of computer professionals, from those just beginning their careers to experienced network and computer professionals.

BICSI offers the Registered Communications Distribution Designer program, which certifies experts who design and install cabling and networking for new and existing buildings. The Computer Technology Industry Association, or CompTIA, offers two important certifications: the A+ certification for computer service technicians, and the Certified Document Architect for imaging specialists. The Certified Network Professional credential—developed by the Network Professional Association—certifies networking expertise, as does the Certified Network Expert credential, which is offered by a consortium of industry representatives. The Institute for Certification of Computing Professionals (ICCP) was founded back in 1973 and offers the Certified Computing Professional credential, which covers many different aspects of computing and networking.

BICSI Certifications

BICSI, a not-for-profit organization, had its origins in 1977 when employees of the several "Baby Bell" telephone companies got together to design a program to train professionals to design and construct telecommunications infrastructures within buildings. At that time, the name BICSI stood for Building Industry Consulting Service

International. The name was chosen because each of the Bell companies had a Building Industry Consulting Service department, which concentrated on designing telecommunication wiring systems for new and existing commercial properties. Since divestiture of the Bell companies, however, these departments no longer exist as such. In the 1990's, BICSI decided to drop its full name and instead refer to itself as "BICSI: A Telecommunications Association."

BICSI currently has over 12,500 members in over 50 countries and offers training courses in several locations. BICSI's certification program—the Registered Communications Distribution Designer (RCDD) program—certifies experts who design and install cabling and networking for new and existing buildings, including telephone, cable television, and data communications circuits. Once certified, RCDDs can go on to obtain a specialization in LAN cabling.

Recertification or Maintenance Requirements The RCDD certification is valid for three years. Renewing your RCDD designation involves the following actions:

- Maintain an uninterrupted BICSI membership

- Take a minimum of 45 clock hours of training related to distribution design during each three-year period (contact BICSI for a list of approved courses)

- Submit a renewal application and $100 renewal fee

Benefits of Certification Registered Communications Distribution Designers receive these benefits:

- A registration certificate

- Use of the RCDD logo on letterheads, cards, decals, and other materials

- Access to conferences, seminars, and publications for members

Registered Communications Distribution Designer (RCDD)

Two prerequisites must be met prior to attempting the required test for the RCDD designation. First, you must be a member of BICSI (annual membership fee is $100). Second, you are expected to have at least two years of experience in cabling distribution design in commercial, campus, and multi-family buildings.

In addition, you must submit an application form detailing your experience and three letters of reference. One letter must be from your current employer; if you are self employed, you must provide a letter explaining your involvement in the design of low-voltage distribution systems. Another letter should be from a client for whom you have done design work, and one should be a personal reference. This application package must also be accompanied by a $100 nonrefundable application fee.

The test for this certification covers information on appropriate national codes as well as policies and methods of telecommunications design. See the Resources section for more information on preparing for this exam.

Who Needs It   RCDD certification is an important credential for architects, electrical engineers, consultants, interior designers, telephone company personnel, or anyone who is involved in the design and installation of low-voltage wiring infrastructure in new or existing buildings. It can also be an excellent way for independent contractors and architects to showcase their abilities for potential clients.

Requirements for Certification   The certification process requires the following steps:

1.   Meet the prerequisites: BICSI membership and two years experience.

2. Submit application package for approval (see above for details).

3. If approved, pass the BICSI RCDD exam.

You must pass the exam within one year of application approval. If you do not pass, you can retake it twice within a one-year period ($100 fee per attempt). If you fail three times, you must wait a full year before reapplying.

Administrator   BICSI administers the exam throughout the year at BICSI-sponsored conferences, and by special arrangement at BICSI's headquarters. See the BICSI Web site for details.

Fee   The exam costs $100. Additional fees include the $100 BICSI membership fee and the $100 application fee.

Format   This closed-book, multiple-choice test lasts three hours. There are 280 questions and a score of 78 percent is required to pass.

RCDD: Local Area Network Specialty

The LAN specialization can be obtained by those who already have acquired the RCDD certification. This specialty certification involves passing an additional exam that tests your ability to correctly design and install local area network cabling systems. See the Resources section that follows for information on preparing for this exam.

Who Needs It   This specialization is an excellent way to demonstrate your ability to design and install LAN cabling systems. It can be a good credential for independent contractors and architects who want to show potential clients clear evidence of their LAN knowledge and skills.

Requirements for Certification The certification process requires the following steps:

1. Obtain RCDD certification (described above).

2. Pass the BICSI LAN Specialty exam.

Administrator BICSI administers the exam throughout the year at BICSI-sponsored conferences, and by special arrangement at BICSI headquarters. See the BICSI Web site for details.

Fee $100

Format This closed-book, multiple-choice test lasts two hours. There are 115 questions and a score of 78 percent is required to pass.

Resources

The BICSI Web site offers exam bulletins that detail each test's objectives. BICSI recommends using their *Telecommunications Distribution Methods Manual* in preparing for these certifications. In addition, the BICSI Institute, BICSI's training organization, offers test preparation courses. For more information on this organization's certifications and courses, contact BICSI at:

Web	www.bicsi.org
E-mail	bicsiadm@concentric.net
Mail	BICSI 8610 Hidden River Parkway Tampa, FL 33637
Phone	(813) 979-1991
Fax	(813) 971-4311
Faxback	(800) 242-7405; ask to be transferred to the voice mail system, then press 9 to access the fax service

CNX Consortium Certifications

The Certified Network Expert (CNX) certification program was developed by a multi-vendor group called the CNX Consortium. The following companies make up the CNX Consortium: Azure Technologies, Bay Networks, Cisco Systems, Hewlett-Packard, Microtest, Network Associates, Optimized Engineering, Pine Mountain Group, The AG Group, TOYO Corporation, and Wandel & Goltermann.

This certification is designed for network professionals who are responsible for network analysis and troubleshooting. Becoming a CNX involves passing an exam on one of the following technologies: token ring, Ethernet, FDDI, or LAN cabling. The Ethernet and token ring exams are published in English, German, and Japanese, while the FDDI and LAN cabling exams are only available in English. The tests require knowledge of the use of protocol analyzers to diagnose and isolate network problems.

Recertification or Maintenance Requirements There are currently no recertification requirements for Certified Network Experts.

Benefits of Certification The main benefit of becoming a CNX is that it demonstrates your high level of networking abilities and knowledge to current and potential employers. Certified Network Experts also receive:

- A CNX certificate

- Use of the CNX logo on business cards and stationery

CNX: Token Ring

The CNX Token Ring exam requires extensive knowledge of IEEE token ring specifications. Topics covered on the exam include use of control bits such as priority, monitor count, ARI/FCI, error-detected, functional address, and source-routing-present, as well as poll/neighbor notification, station insertion and removal, soft error reporting, contention, and beaconing with fault domain isolation.

Who Needs It The CNX Token Ring certification is valuable to advanced networking professionals who want to document for current or potential employers their ability to install, maintain, and troubleshoot a token ring network. It can also be an excellent way for independent consultants and trainers to showcase their abilities for potential clients.

Requirements for Certification The certification process requires only one step:

1. Pass the CNX Token Ring exam.

Administrator Call Sylvan Prometric at (800) 269-3926 to register for a CNX exams. (See Chapter 15 for information on taking tests from Sylvan.)

Fee $250

Format The 120-minute test consists of 60 multiple-choice questions. Candidates must score 75 percent to pass.

CNX: Ethernet

The CNX Ethernet exam requires extensive knowledge of IEEE Ethernet specifications. Topics covered on the exam include similarities, differences, and areas of incompatibility between Ethernet implementations using Version 2, 802.3, SNAP, and Novell; bit patterns associated with frame corruption including propagation delay problems, reflection problems, environmental noise, and faulty hardware; and media access technology, such as preamble generation, bit jam, exponential backoff algorithm, SQE heartbeat, and jabbering.

Who Needs It   The CNX Ethernet certification is valuable to advanced networking professionals who want to document for current or potential employers their ability to install, maintain, and troubleshoot an Ethernet network. It can also be an excellent way for independent consultants and trainers to showcase their abilities for potential clients.

Requirements for Certification   The certification process requires only one step:

    1.   Pass the CNX Ethernet exam.

Administrator   Call Sylvan Prometric at (800) 269-3926 to register for a CNX exam. (See Chapter 15 for detailed information on taking tests from Sylvan.)

Fee $250

Format   The 120-minute test consists of 60 multiple-choice questions. Candidates must score 75 percent to pass.

CNX: FDDI

The CNX FDDI exam requires extensive knowledge of ANSI FDDI specifications. Topics covered on the exam include interoperation and relationships between FDDI state machine functions for PMD, PHY, MAC, and SMT, including the significance of the field in each frame;

and details and specifications of ring operation and timers involved with ring-poll, station insertion and removal, and error reporting, including physical configurations for concentrators and stations.

Who Needs It The CNX FDDI certification is valuable to advanced networking professionals who want to document for current or potential employers their ability to install, maintain, and troubleshoot an FDDI network. It can also be an excellent way for independent consultants and trainers to showcase their abilities for potential clients.

Requirements for Certification The certification process requires only one step:

1. Pass the CNX FDDI exam.

Administrator Call Sylvan Prometric at (800) 269-3926 to register for a CNX exam. (See Chapter 15 for detailed information on taking tests from Sylvan.)

Fee $250

Format The 120-minute test consists of 60 multiple-choice questions. Candidates must score 75 percent to pass.

CNX: LAN Cabling

The CNX LAN Cabling exam requires extensive knowledge of wiring systems. Topics covered include UTP, STP, ScTP, and fiber tests, including attenuation, NEXT, wiremap, length, and impedance, and their acceptable values in typical LAN cabling environments; current EIA/TIA/ISO cabling standards, link/channel models, and appropriate installation practices; and cabling requirements for common LAN networks, such as 10BASE-T, token ring, FDDI, TP-PMD, 100BASE-T, 100VGAnyLAN, and ATM.

Who Needs It The CNX LAN Cabling certification is valuable to advanced networking professionals who want to document for current or potential employers their ability to install, maintain, and troubleshoot LAN cabling. It can also be an excellent way for independent consultants and trainers to showcase their abilities for potential clients.

Requirements for Certification The certification process requires only one step:

1. Pass the CNX LAN Cabling exam.

Administrator Call Sylvan Prometric at (800) 269-3926 to register for a CNX exam. (See Chapter 15 for detailed information on taking tests from Sylvan.)

Fee $250

Format The 120-minute test consists of 60 multiple-choice questions. Candidates must score 75 percent to pass.

Resources

The CNX Web site offers an excellent pre-test guide, sample tests, and a suggested reading list. For more information on this organization's certifications and courses, contact CNX at:

Web   http://www.cnx.org/

E-Mail   webmaster@cnx.org

CompTIA Certifications

The Computer Technology Industry Association (CompTIA) is a not-for-profit organization formed in 1982 to foster cooperation in the computer industry. Today over 6,000 computer resellers, computer manufacturers, and computer service companies are members of CompTIA.

CompTIA currently offers two certifications: the A+ certification and the Certified Document Imaging Architect (CDIA). The A+ certification is designed as a benchmark for competence in basic computer repair. CompUSA, Inc., one of the largest computer resellers, requires all their service personnel to obtain A+ certification. The CDIA certification designates an advanced level of skill in working with document imaging technology and techniques.

Recertification or Maintenance Requirements As of this writing there are no maintenance requirements for either of these certifications. CompTIA does, however, update the A+ tests periodically to reflect advances in PC hardware and operating systems. The next revision of the tests is due in mid-1998 and may include a specialty test in Windows 95 (of course, Windows 98 may be on the market by then).

Benefits of Certification These differ for the two certifications. See the following sections for details on the benefits associated with attaining each certification.

CompTIA is planning the release of a new certification, the Network+. This certification is to be available in late 1998, and will cover topics of network design, installation, management, and troubleshooting.

A+ Certification

The A+ certification program targets those who want a certification that validates their competence as computer service professionals. The A+ certification is widely recognized as the standard for measuring a technician's ability to diagnose and repair computer hardware and operating system problems. Certification consists of passing a minimum of two tests: a core exam that tests general knowledge and abilities, and at least one specialty exam that tests knowledge and skills in working with a particular operating system.

The core exam covers the following topics: microcomputers, displays, storage media, printers, basic operating systems (DOS, Windows, Macintosh), modems, buses, and CD-ROMs. The test is divided into seven sections that reflect a computer repair technician's areas of job responsibility: configuration, installation and upgrading, diagnosis, repair, preventative maintenance, interaction with customers, and safety. The specialty exams focus on operating-system enviornments. The current specialty options are Microsoft Windows 3.1/DOS or the Macintosh operating system. Once candidates pass the core exam and a specialty exam, they receive a certificate that mentions the specialty module they passed, e.g., "A+ certification with a specialty in Microsoft Windows/DOS environments."

Benefits of Certification   Benefits of A+ certification include:

- Use of the A+ logo and an A+ lapel pin

- Certificate

- If 50 percent or more of a company's computer service technicians are A+ certified, the company can be designated an A+ Authorized Service Center, and be listed in CompTIA's directory

Who Needs It   The A+ certification is a great way to enter the field of computer repair and installation. This widely recognized credential indicates to a potential employer that you have the skills to diagnose and repair a broad variety of hardware and operating system problems.

Requirements for Certification The certification process requires the following steps:

1. Pass the A+ core exam.

2. Pass one of the following specialty module exams:

   - Microsoft Windows 3.1/DOS specialty exam

   - Mac operating system specialty exam

   Candidates must both pass the core exam and one specialty exam within a 90-day period.

Administrator Call Sylvan Prometric at (800) 776-4276 to register for an A+ exam. (See Chapter 15 for detailed information on taking tests from Sylvan.)

Fee Test fees are discounted for candidates employed by organizations that are members of CompTIA and for those who take more than one test at a sitting. The fees for employees of nonmember organizations are as follows: $110 for one test; $190 for two tests taken the same day; and $240 for three tests taken the same day. The same tests cost $85, $140, and $190, respectively, for employees of member organizations. To receive the CompTIA discount price, have your CompTIA membership number handy when registering for the test.

Format The 75-minute core exam has 57 questions and a passing score of 72 percent. The 60-minute Windows/DOS exam has 45 questions and a passing score of 69 percent. The 60-minute Macintosh exam has 48 questions and a passing score of 75 percent.

Certified Document Imaging Architect (CDIA)

CompTIA's CDIA credential recognizes knowledge and skill in the document imaging industry. Document imaging involves scanning and storing documents in digital form, either as images or as text, using optical character recognition software. Candidates are expected to be able to plan, design, and write specifications for an imaging system.

One test is required for this certification. It consists of eight sections designed to cover the key areas of responsibility for an imaging architect: input and capture, display, storage, communications, output, standard computing environment, integration, and management applications.

Benefits of Certification   Certified Document Imaging Architects receive these benefits:

- Use of the CDIA logo

- Listing in the CDIA central registry—a database of qualified CDIA professionals that companies consult when they are hiring document imaging personnel

Who Needs It   This certification is the *de facto* standard for knowledge and skill in document imaging. It can be valuable in obtaining a position in a wide range of companies that rely on document imaging specialists.

Requirements for Certification   The certification process requires only one step:

1.   Pass the Certified Document Imaging Architect exam.

Administrator   Call Sylvan Prometric at (800) 909-3926 to register for the CDIA exam. (See Chapter 15 for detailed information on taking tests from Sylvan.)

Fee   The testing fee is $150 for individuals employed by an organization that is a member of CompTIA, and $165 for non-members. To receive the CompTIA discount price, have your CompTIA membership number handy when registering with Sylvan Prometric for the test.

Format   The 60-minute test has 68 multiple-choice questions. A score of 77 percent is required to pass.

Resources

The CompTIA Web site offers a list of objectives and sample questions for each exam. The site also provides links to numerous self-study and instructor-led preparation courses. For more information on this organization's certifications and courses, contact CompTIA at:

Web	http://www.comptia.org
E-mail	certification@comptia.org
Mail	CompTIA 450 East 22nd Street, Suite 230 Lombard, IL 60148-6158
Phone	(630) 268-1818
Fax	(630) 268-1384

ICCP Certification

The Institute for Certification of Computing Professionals (ICCP) was founded in 1973 to develop professional standards for the computing industry. ICCP previously offered three certification programs: the Certificate in Data Processing, Certified Computer Programmer, and Certified Systems Professional. These programs have been folded into one: the Certified Computing Professional (CCP) credential. Over 50,000 individuals have obtained ICCP certification.

Candidates are expected to have at least two years of work experience prior to certification. The certification process involves passing a series of tests that cover a wide range of topics. These topics reflect the breadth of job duties that may confront the computing professional.

Recertification or Maintenance Requirements The CCP designation is valid for three years. To maintain your CCP credential, you must provide proof of 120 contact hours of professional development activities during each three-year period. These activities may include:

- Taking additional specialty or language exams

- Retaking the exams you previously passed

- Participating in educational and other professional activities

Contact ICCP for more details on ways to maintain your certification status.

Benefits of Certification Certified Computing Professionals receive the following benefits:

- A certificate

- Use of the CCP logo on business cards and stationery

Certified Computing Professional (CCP)

The CCP certification program is oriented toward experienced computing professionals. Candidates are expected to have 48 months of full-time experience in computer-based information systems before attempting this certification. Contact ICCP for further information on qualifying experience and academic alternatives to this requirement.

The certification process involves passing a core exam and meeting an additional exam requirement. The additional exam requirement can be met in several ways: by passing two specialty exams; by passing one specialty exam and two language exams; or by passing one specialty exam and holding a vendor- or organization-based certification that is on the ICCP-approved list (contact ICCP for the current list). The candidate must also agree to abide by a code of ethical conduct.

Who Needs It The CCP certification is an excellent general certification for computer professionals who perform a wide variety of tasks. It can be an excellent tool for obtaining a promotion or job offer, or it can serve as a valuable qualification for freelance consultants.

Requirements for Certification The certification process requires the following steps:

1. Meet the experience prerequisite, explained above.

2. Pass the CCP Core exam.

3. Meet the additional exam requirements as described above:

    CCP Specialty Exams (one or more as needed, explained above)

    > Management
    >
    > System Development
    >
    > Communications
    >
    > Systems Programming
    >
    > Systems Security
    >
    > Microcomputing and Networks
    >
    > Procedural Programming
    >
    > Business Information Systems
    >
    > Office Information Systems
    >
    > Software Engineering
    >
    > Data Resource Management

    CCP Language Exams (as needed, explained above)

    > Pascal
    >
    > Basic
    >
    > RPG/400
    >
    > COBOL
    >
    > C (or substitute the Learning Tree International C exam)
    >
    > C++ (or substitute the Learning Tree International C++ exam)

4. Submit a letter from a person who can verify your work experience.

5. Agree to abide by the ICCP Code of Ethics, Conduct, and Good Practice (available on the ICCP Web site).

All the required steps for the CCP certification process must be completed within a 36-month period.

Administrator To take an ICCP test, send your application and test fee to ICCP. After you have been accepted in the testing program, ICCP will give you the phone number for scheduling your test at a Sylvan Prometric center.

Fee The core and specialty exams cost $149 each; the language tests cost $79 each.

Format The Core and Specialty exams consists of 110 multiple-choice questions and must be completed in 90 minutes. The passing score for CCPs on both Core and Specialty exams is 70 percent.

The Language exams consists of 66 multiple-choice questions and must be completed in 60 minutes. The passing score for a Language exam is 70 percent.

Resources

The ICCP Web site offers sample tests and test objectives for the Core exam. In addition, the ICCP Education Foundation, in cooperation with Bird Professional Publications, offers a number of review courses. Several other organizations provide audio tapes, video tapes, and books to help prepare for the ICCP exams (see the ICCP Web site for a complete listing). For more information on this organization's certifications and courses, contact ICCP at:

Web   http://www.iccp.org/

E-mail   74040.3722@compuserve.com

Mail   ICCP
         2200 East Devon Avenue, Suite 247
         Des Plaines, IL 60018

Phone	(847) 299-4227
Fax	(847) 299-4280

Network Professional Association Certification

The Certified Network Professional credential was developed by the Network Professional Association (NPA), a non-profit association of networking professionals. NPA membership is not a requirement for certification, and the certification program operates independently of its parent organization. The CNP program is comprehensive, and consists of four focus areas: Core Fundamentals, Area of Specialty, Work Experience, and Professionalism.

Recertification or Maintenance Requirements To retain certification, CNPs are required to complete a minimum of 20 CNP units annually. These are obtained by attending training, seminars, conferences, NPA events, or working on self-study materials. In addition, CNPs are required to have a minimum of four months per year of approved work experience. There is an annual recertification fee of $100.

Benefits of Certification Certified Network Professionals receive these benefits:

- Welcome kit that includes CNP certificate, ID card, lapel pin, shirt, and resource kit

- Inclusion in the CNP referral program, which refers businesses and organizations to qualified CNPs

Certified Network Professional (CNP)

Attaining this certification involves meeting requirements in four areas: Core Fundamentals, Area of Specialty, Work Experience, and Professionalism. Skill in the first area is evaluated by an exam that tests fundamental network computing knowledge on five topics: client operating systems, microcomputer hardware platforms, network operating system fundamentals, network protocols, and network topologies. The Area of Specialty requirement is met by obtaining two vendor-based certifications. The Work Experience requirement necessitates two years of experience working in network computing. Finally, the Professionalism component requires the candidate to agree to abide by a code of ethical conduct.

Who Needs It This certification targets experienced networking professionals who have already obtained several vendor-based certifications and want to distinguish themselves by obtaining a vendor-independent certification. It can be an excellent credential for freelance trainers and consultants.

Requirements for Certification The certification process requires the following steps:

1. Meet the prerequisite of two years network computing experience.

2. Pass the CNP Core Exam.

3. Obtain a vendor certification in each of two different specialty areas selected from the following list:

   - Network Operating Systems Specialty Area:

     Certified Banyan Specialist or Certified Banyan Expert (see Chapter 7 for details)

IBM Certified Specialist AS/400 (see Chapter 4 for details)

Microsoft Certified Systems Engineer (see Chapter 7 for details)

Certified Novell Engineer or Master Certified Novel Engineer (see Chapter 7 for details)

SCO Advanced Certified Engineer (see Chapter 4 for details)

- GroupWare Specialty Area:

  Certified Lotus Professional (see Chapter 5 for details)

- Network Analysis Specialty Area:

  Certified Networking Expert (see next section for details)

- Internetworking Specialty Area:

  Certified Cisco Internetworking Expert (see Chapter 6 for details)

- Networking Hardware Specialty Area:

  Compaq Accredited Systems Engineer (see Chapter 3 for details)

  IBM Professional Server Expert (see Chapter 3 for details)

4. Agree to abide by the NPA Code of Ethics (available on the NPA Web site).

5. Submit an application for approval. An application fee is required.

Administrator   Call Sylvan Prometric at (800) 340-3926 to register for a NPA exam. (See Chapter 15 for detailed information on taking tests from Sylvan.)

Fee The Core Fundamentals exam costs $100. The application fee is $200 for NPA members and $300 for non-members.

Format The Core exam is a multiple choice test with 88 questions that must be completed in 60 minutes. Call Sylvan Prometric at (800) 340-3926 for current information on passing score.

Resources

The Certified Network Professional Web site offers a list of test objectives and sample questions. The Web site also offers a listing of training programs and references for study. For more information on this organization's certifications and courses, contact the Network Professionals Association at:

Web	http://www.cnp.org/
E-mail	darryl@rpk.com
Mail	CNP Program
	151 East 1700 Street, Suite 100
	Provo, Utah 84606
Phone	(888) 379-0910 or (801) 379-0268
Fax	(801) 379-0329

PART

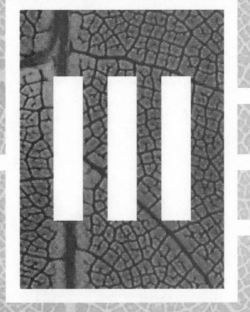

Preparing for
and Taking
Certification Tests

CHAPTER

13

Instructor-Led Training

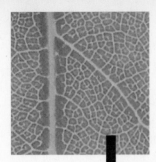

Instructor-led training can be a great way to learn the ins and outs of a product or technology and to prepare yourself for taking a certification exam. Typical courses last for two to five days and involve both lecture and lab sessions. The instructor lectures on a topic or feature of the product and then gives an opportunity for hands-on practice with the technology. Labs provide a chance to work through a variety of tasks and scenarios yourself, with the help of an instructor readily available. This allows you to try things that you might not normally want to attempt with your company's server or network.

Another advantage to taking instructor-led courses is that if you take a course from a vendor, or a vendor's training partner, you may be able to take a course that corresponds directly to a certification test. These courses offer a curriculum that is designed by the vendor to provide content that corresponds to the test objectives on the certification exam.

A disadvantage to taking instructor-led courses is that they are usually fairly expensive. A typical two-day course may cost $500 to $1500, while a five-day course may cost $1000 to $2500 or more. In many situations, however, an employer will foot the bill to send an employee to instructor-led courses.

Whether you are paying out of your own pocket, or your company is footing the bill, it is critical that you select your course provider carefully.

Selecting a Training Provider

A wide variety of course providers are available, and the market is growing rapidly. The different provider options—higher education training partners, authorized training providers, and independent training organizations—are outlined below. Regardless of the type of provider you select, there are several things to consider before you enroll in a course, including the provider's real-world experience and knowledge base, their teaching experience, and the design and level of the course.

Experience

Do the instructors have computer or networking experience outside the classroom? If so, is it current? A number of training organizations require their trainers to work as consultants in the field so they maintain current experience and have confronted and mastered unique problems and situations. University instructors may also have plenty of up-to-date experience; for example, night instructors may also be the daytime support staff for the campus network. If you make sure you take your course from an instructor who has current, real-world experience you will be more likely to get training that is practical and directly applicable to your work environment.

Certification

What training certifications do the instructors possess? If there is a training certification available for this specific product or technology, do they have it? What other certifications do the instructors possess, including both training credentials and product-related certifications? An instructor with sound instructional skills and a wide range of product and technology knowledge is most likely to offer high-quality instruction. In addition, such an instructor will be conversant with other technologies and products that are related to the topic at hand and will be equipped to provide you with a well-rounded learning experience.

Instructional Design

Does the course follow the vendor's official curriculum or one that has been approved by the vendor or organization? If not, how is the course structured?

Does the course provide only lectures or does it also involve lab components? A course that offers only lectures or has only minimal lab time won't prepare you to use a new product or technology on your own. Always look for a course that allows you plenty of hands-on time with the product or technology you want to learn to use—this is crucial to good learning.

What type of materials will you receive when you take the course? Will you take home a good text and/or lab books that you can use as a reference as you implement your new knowledge?

Advisement

It may seem too obvious to mention, but the importance of enrolling in the appropriate course cannot be overemphasized. This is a key factor in maximizing your investment; a course that is too basic or too advanced will be a waste of your time and money. A good training organization will provide some means to determine which course is appropriate for you. This may involve an interview or the completion of a questionnaire.

A variety of providers offer instructor-led courses that can lead to computer and networking certifications. The three main categories of organizations that provide this type of instruction are described below.

Colleges, Universities, and Vocational Schools

Many vocational schools, technical and community colleges, and four-year colleges and universities now offer good training opportunities at a reasonable price. We mention this option first because many people tend to overlook this alternative. Some high schools, colleges, and universities have become academic educational partners with vendors. A vocational school or college may offer the training you need as a short course; depending on the content, you might find a one- or two-day course, a weekend course, or a two- to four-week evening course that meets your needs.

It may be worth your while to seek out such opportunities in your local area, especially if you are interested in having the opportunity to get college credit as well as certification. The section in Chapter 1 (*Why Become Certified?*) entitled "Benefits for Individuals" provides some specific examples of the different types of opportunities academic education partners provide.

Authorized Training Providers

Authorized training providers are training centers that have been authorized by particular vendors to offer an approved curriculum on that vendor's product lines. Vendors are usually happy to provide you with a list of authorized training providers located in your area. There are literally thousands of authorized training provider locations across the United States and around the world (for links to authorized training providers for various vendors see http://www.certification-update.com/).

Independent Training Organizations

A number of independent training companies also provide courses throughout the country and around the world. There are literally hundreds of such organizations to choose from. The Certification Update Web site provides links to the major independent training providers (`http://www.certification-update.com/`).

A number of certification programs offered by independent providers have established a level of quality and reliability that has made them eligible to provide college credit to their participants. For example, it is possible to obtain college credit for Learning Tree International courses and ICCP Certified Computing Professional exams. The American Council of Education (ACE) in Washington, D.C. has determined college course equivalencies for these and other courses and certification programs. Approximately 1,500 colleges and universities in the United States will accept ACE recommendations for college credit.

CHAPTER

14

Self-Study for Certification

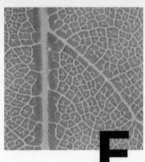

For most people, the process of obtaining certification will involve at least some amount of self-study. In some instances, self-study will be the only way to learn the information one needs to know to pass a certification test. In other cases, an individual may chose to combine some self-study with other study approaches as part of an overall plan for achieving their certification and career development goals.

NOTE   If you have not already done so, you may want to take a look at the section in Chapter 2, "Reaching Your Certification Goals," which outlines a way to construct a study plan and a timeline for reaching your study and certification goals.

Self-study has many advantages. One of the most important features of self-study is that it can be much less expensive than instructor-led study. While an instructor-led course might cost several thousand dollars, a comprehensive self-study book or video may cost less than fifty dollars.

Even if cost isn't a big issue, however, you still may find that self-study has appealing advantages in some cases. Self-study allows you to select study times that fit well with your schedule. In addition, self-study lets you work at your own pace. You can select the topics you need to work hardest on and focus your energies on those areas. And, also in contrast to being in a class, you will not have to waste any time dealing with topics that you have already mastered. These advantages—flexible scheduling and working at your own pace—can also be disadvantages for some people, of course. A successful self-study program requires a greater level of self-discipline than a program of instructor-led training.

A variety of resources can be used in a self-study program, including study guides and books, videotapes, computer-based training, online training, and practice tests.

 One of the most effective techniques you can use to check your understanding and retention of new material is to try to teach it to someone else. Try telling a colleague what you learned last night over coffee the next day. If you are not able to clearly explain the concept or process, it is time to hit the books again.

Study Guides and Books

Most certification programs offer a basic study guide and preparation materials for their exams. These can be an excellent resource for self-study and may also inform you about other helpful learning resources. And, although you may want additional learning resources, the information you get directly from the certifying entity will most accurately portray the knowledge and skills that will be evaluated on their tests.

A number of publishers, including Sybex, sell excellent books that provide entire self-study programs for specific certification tests. When selecting a text for self-study there are several things to consider:

- **Level of Presentation** Some books begin at a very basic level, while others assume that you already have a good understanding of the fundamentals. For some of the more popular certifications, a wide selection of books will be available. Take time to find a text that starts at the level that will work best for you.

- **Exercises** Does the text provide instructions for hands-on exercises that you can try out on your machine?

- **Sample questions/Sample tests** Does the text provide questions to assess your comprehension at the end of each chapter? Does it offer a sample test that you can take to determine whether you are ready for the real test? Some books include a CD-ROM that contains multiple sample tests.

- **Pointers to other sources of information** Does the book provide references to additional sources of useful information? Some texts suggest other resources on specific topics, including other books, product manuals, and online help files.

- **Endorsement** Some study guides have been endorsed or otherwise approved by the certification program they cover. This is a good indication that the book will cover the salient points of the certification you are pursuing.

Videotaped Study Programs

If you prefer the instructor-led training format, but time or money constraints prevent you from attending an instructor-led course, a videotaped course may be what you want. A videotape lacks the interaction of the classroom, but it may compensate for this with an increased use of graphics and special effects. Some videotaped programs offer supplementary items that enhance your learning process. For example, a video package may include a student workbook with step-by-step instructions on setting up the program or process you are learning.

Computer-Based Training

Computer-based training, most often in a CD-ROM format, can offer a combination of video, text, and simulation exercises. One of the advantages of this type of training format is that you can jump from one topic to another in a way that best suits your learning needs. Figure 14.1 shows a screen shot from a typical computer-based training program.

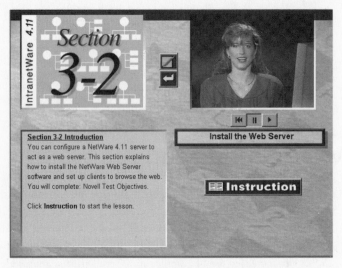

FIGURE 14.1:   Computer-based training programs allow you to navigate through multimedia presentations at your own pace. (Picture courtesy of United Education Centers, Inc. For more information on TestOut! CNE and MCSE products, contact United Education Centers at (800) 877-4889 or http://www .testout.com.)

The cost of computer-based training can vary widely, depending on the type of certification program and the subject matter. Some of the more specialized computer-based training programs can be quite expensive. Depending on the type of software license associated with a training package, you may be able to sell or trade your software when you are done with it (several providers exclusively prohibit this practice, however, so check your licensing agreement carefully).

A large number of training providers offer computer-based training programs. Check the Certification Update Web site (`http://www.certification-update.com/`) for links to some of the most well-known providers.

Online Training

Online training for certification is becoming very popular. One of the big advantages of online training is that you can network and share information with your fellow classmates. This type of training varies widely in quality and cost, and can take several formats. Available offerings range from slick multimedia presentations that students download at their convenience, to a set of e-mail lectures that are sent to the student on a preset schedule.

There are many source for online training. Some of the best-known providers include Ziff-Davis University (`http://www.zdu.com/`) and the Microsoft Online Institute (`http://moli.microsoft.com/`). There are hundreds of others as well; see the Certification Update Web site (`http://www.certification-update.com/`) for links to some of the most well-known online training providers.

Practice Tests

Practice tests, if available, are an important component of your study program. They offer an excellent opportunity for you to test your knowledge before you fork over the bucks to take the real test. A practice test can help you zero in on the areas where you need extra study. In addition, practice tests help you become familiar with the format of the exam.

A number of certification programs offer free sample tests on their Web sites. Some of these don't offer a lot of questions, however. If you want more sample tests, you may be able to buy them. Several companies are in the business of making practice tests for use by certification candidates. These tests may allow you to take multiple practice exams that contain randomly selected questions drawn from a large pool of test items. These practice exams may also provide explanations of the questions and the correct (and incorrect) answers; this can be extremely useful in understanding the concepts that are giving you trouble. See the Certification Update Web site for links to some of the most well-known providers of practice tests (`http://www.certification-update.com/`).

CHAPTER

15

Taking Your Test

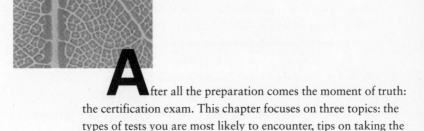

After all the preparation comes the moment of truth: the certification exam. This chapter focuses on three topics: the types of tests you are most likely to encounter, tips on taking the tests, and an overview of the three main testing center networks.

Test Formats

Typically, tests for vendor certifications have two main assessment objectives: to measure your knowledge of the vendor's product or products, and to assess your competence in using those products to accomplish specific job tasks. Many certification programs now use some type of performance-based testing. The vendors and organizations who offer certification exams want their exams to measure an individual's performance in job-related tasks, not just their ability to memorize details. It is partly this performance-based aspect of certification testing that makes certifications so significant to employers and clients.

Certification tests are typically computer-based exams that are taken at commercial testing centers or at vendor-based education centers. Different organizations and different technologies often demand different testing procedures. You may encounter a variety of test formats, including multiple-choice tests, adaptive tests, hands-on lab tests, and live-application tests. Each of these formats will be described briefly below.

Some certification programs use more than one type of testing. For example, the candidate might first take a test that is in a scenario-based, multiple-choice format. This test would assess the candidate's understanding of *when* to use a certain product or a feature of a product. This test might be followed by another type of test, such as a hands-on lab test or a live-application test. This test would assess whether the candidate knew *how* to use that product or feature of a product. In this case, depending on the nature and level of the certification sought, the candidate might be expected to perform a real task using a software program, or to plan, design, implement, maintain, troubleshoot, or upgrade a network, or to integrate a system with other systems.

Different vendors and organizations may have different names for their particular approaches to testing. You may also encounter testing that is categorized as one of the types below but is a little different from the descriptions given here. The descriptions below are intended to give you a general idea of what to expect. To be prepared for a particular certification test, it is always a good idea to take practice tests designed for that specific test.

Multiple-Choice Testing

The multiple-choice test is still the most commonly used exam format. Multiple-choice, computer-based exams are typically generated in a way that makes the test different for each test-taker. The exam program holds a large pool of several hundred or more questions. A certain number of those questions is selected for each candidate. Each candidate receives a different—but equivalent—exam.

Multiple-choice questions may be structured in different ways. You may encounter questions where more than one answer is correct. In this situation, you may be asked to select one of the correct answers; alternatively, you may be expected to select a specific number of correct answers. When you read the question, be sure to note how many responses you are being asked to select. Other questions may be of the true/false type.

At the end of a computer-based, multiple-choice exam, the computer will display a score report that indicates your score, the required passing score, and a notification of whether you passed or failed the exam. Your score report will also include a breakdown of your score in the various categories of the test. For example, a typical Microsoft Certified Professional exam will indicate your score in the following areas: planning; installation and configuration; connectivity; monitoring and optimization; and troubleshooting. The testing program will then print a copy of the score report for you to keep as evidence of your score. The testing center will emboss the score report to ensure authenticity. Your score is also automatically sent to the certifying vendor or organization.

A few organization-based certification programs use traditional paper-based multiple-choice exams. These exams are not usually administered by commercial testing centers, but rather by the organization itself.

Adaptive Testing

This type of testing will be new to many people. The first large-scale use of this testing method was done in 1991 by Drake Prometric testing centers and Novell. This computer-based test "adapts" itself to the abilities of the test-taker. An adaptive test is designed to ask only the minimum number of questions necessary to determine your level of ability. As you go through the exam, the difficulty of the next question you receive is determined by your response to the previous question. In other words, if you answer a question correctly, the next question will be more difficult. If you answer incorrectly, the next question will be an easier question. The test is continually working to determine which questions are most appropriate for your level of ability.

As you respond to each question, the testing program continually calculates an estimate of your level of ability. As the test progresses, the statistical value of that estimate becomes more accurate. The test ends when one of three things occurs: your ability has been accurately estimated; the program is at least 95 percent confident that your ability lies above the passing score; or all the questions have been given. Novell's adaptive tests use a minimum of 15 questions and a maximum of 25 questions.

The scores for adaptive tests are not simply based on the number of questions you answer correctly. Instead, the score is based on the *difficulty* of the questions you answer correctly. In the case of Novell's adaptive tests, scores will have values between 200 and 800. You will pass if your score is greater than a pre-established cut-off score.

Those who use adaptive testing believe that it is a more efficient way of testing because it saves time. It is also believed to be less stressful for the test-taker because the questions generated will, for the most part, be at a level that the candidate finds moderately challenging. Novell's Web site offers a discussion of the testing theory behind their adaptive exams (`http://education.novell.com/testinfo/theory.htm`).

Hands-On Lab Testing

Several certification programs, such as Bay Networks and Cisco, require the candidate to attend a hands-on lab exam. In these situations, you will be given appropriate equipment and software, and then instructed to complete a series of lab exercises within a given time period. At the end of the time limit, the lab proctors will inspect your work to see if you successfully completed the exercise. In addition, they will check to see if you completed the task according to standard procedures and safety practices.

These exams can be expensive and difficult. Several of the vendors and organizations that require such exams will provide you with practice exercises so that you will have a better feel for the types of activities you will be asked to perform. Some vendors provide practice exercises by mail or on the Web, while others have made arrangements to provide practice hands-on lab sessions at specially-equipped designated facilities.

Live-Application Testing

The live-application test is becoming a popular way to assess the ability of an candidate to use an application to perform a series of tasks. For example, both the Microsoft Office User certification program and the Certified Lotus Professional program use live-application testing.

This type of test is similar the to hands-on lab exam, but is usually less complex and takes less time. In a typical live-application test, the candidate sits at a computer with the appropriate application loaded and a proctor tells the candidate what task or tasks to perform. At the end of the time period, the candidate submits the work to the proctor and the proctor either grades it on-site, according to set of standard criteria, or forwards it to the certifying entity for scoring.

Test-Taking Tips

Taking a test is a stressful situation for everyone. Not only do you have to complete it within a given time limit, in a unfamiliar environment, but you may also feel stressed about not wanting to waste the money you paid to take the test. But there are a few steps that everyone can do to make taking the test a more enjoyable experience.

Prior to taking a test

1. Study well in advance. Don't schedule your exam until you are confident that you can pass it.

2. As a part of your study plan, schedule time for hands-on work with the application, operating system, or technology that you will be tested on.

3. Take advantage of any opportunity to take practice tests.

4. In the week before your exam date, spend time reviewing the test objectives, including the areas that you think you know. Don't let overconfidence allow you to miss an easy question.

5. Get a good night's sleep the night before your exam.

While taking your test

1. You will typically be given a paper and pencil for use during the exam. Some people find it valuable to jot down pertinent information from memory immediately, prior to starting to answer test questions. For example, prior to taking a TCP/IP exam you may want to memorize the formula for calculating the number of sub-networks for different sub-net masks, and then jot it down from memory at the beginning of your exam.

2. Use the paper and pencil to diagram the word problems and the presented scenarios. There will often be subtle differences between one answer and another. Make sure that you have interpreted the question correctly.

3. If your test format allows, mark the questions that you do not immediately understand and return to them later. Answer the easiest questions first and then go back and answer the questions that you skipped. This strategy will not possible with adaptive tests, however, because the answer for each question determines which question is given next.

If you do fail your test, don't feel bad. Most people fail a couple of exams during their careers. Just chalk this one up to experience and determine what you need to do in order to succeed next time.

Testing Centers

Because their tests are computer-based, testing centers typically offer certification tests on whatever day is convenient for the individual test-taker. In addition, test results are usually available on-site right after the test is completed, and they can then be sent electronically to certifying agencies. Computer-based testing can accommodate a variety of testing methods, including all of the types discussed above.

Vendor-authorized testing centers have their own policies and procedures for test registration and test taking. If you plan to take a test at a vendor's testing center, contact the vendor's education program to get more information. The addresses, phone numbers, and electronic contact information for the individual vendors are located throughout this book in the sections that describe the vendors' certification programs.

In many instances, the test you want to take will also be offered at one of the three major commercial testing centers: CATGlobal, Sylvan Prometric, or VUE. Information on each of these types of centers is provided below. Sylvan has the longest history of offering certification exams for information technology professionals, and currently offers testing for a larger number of vendors than do CATGlobal and VUE. VUE and CATGlobal have offered testing services for some time, but have only recently gotten into the business of offering certification exams for information technology vendors.

CATGlobal

Computer Adaptive Technologies, Inc. (CAT), founded in 1983, is a high-technology firm that delivers all types of computer-based testing and assessment services worldwide. CAT launched its new CATGlobal Testing Network in September, 1997. This new service allows certification candidates to schedule their own exams at CATGlobal's Web site (http://www.catglobal.com). CAT had historically offered testing at corporate and private sites; with the launching of CATGlobal, 750 public testing sites are being added.

CATGlobal testing centers offer Lotus exams and anticipate offering exams for other vendor-based certifications in the near future. For more information on taking an exam from CATGlobal, contact them at:

Web	http://www.catglobal.com/
E-mail	cat@catinc.com
Mail	Computer Adaptive Technologies 1007 Church Street Evanston, IL 60201
Phone	(800) 255-1312
Fax	(847) 866-2002

Sylvan Prometric

Sylvan Prometric, a division of Sylvan Learning Systems, Inc. operates the world's largest network of testing centers. They administer testing programs for educational institutions, professional associations, corporations, and other organizations. Sylvan offers computer-based testing services at more than 1500 locations in 80 countries. Sylvan operates two types of testing centers: Sylvan Technology Centers, which are operated by Sylvan or a franchisee, and Authorized Prometric Testing Centers, which are testing sites that are housed at training institutions, colleges, and universities. Sylvan claims that 80 percent of the population of the United States is within an hour's drive of a Sylvan testing center.

Tens of thousands of certification exams are administered by Sylvan each month. Sylvan Prometric administers testing for professional certification programs offered by a wide variety of information technology vendors and organizations. Sylvan has a different telephone number for each vendor's exams. The numbers that are specific to each vendor's exams are provided in the certification chapters in this book. To schedule an exam with Sylvan, call the vendor-specific Sylvan phone number or call one of the general telephone numbers listed below.

Tell the customer service representative which test you are interested in taking and where you would like to take it. Sylvan will tell you the locations of the testing centers available in your area and schedule it for you. Be prepared to supply the following information:

- Your name
- Your Sylvan Personal Identification Number (this is usually your social security number)
- Phone numbers (home and work)
- Your mailing address
- Test title or Sylvan ID number
- Method of Payment (voucher number or credit card)

You may schedule a test with Sylvan up to six weeks in advance, and no less than 24 hours in advance. In most cases, you may cancel or reschedule your test with no penalty if you do so at least 24 hours prior to your scheduled test time. If you schedule a test but don't take it, and don't call in time to reschedule it, you will forfeit the test fee. If you pay by credit card, you can schedule your test at the time you call

Sylvan; if you pay by check, you cannot schedule the actual test date until Sylvan receives your check. In some cases, tests are paid for with vouchers that have been issued by a vendor.

You should arrive at the test center at least 15 minutes before the test is scheduled to begin. Candidates are required to bring two forms of identification to the testing site. One must be a photo ID, such as a valid passport or a driver's license. The other must have a signature. You will be asked to sign a log book. Unless your exam specifies it, no materials will be permitted inside the test center. You will be given a pencil and some paper to use during the test; the paper must be left at the testing center when you complete your exam. Candidates are monitored by proctors during testing. For more information on taking a test from Sylvan, contact them at:

Web	`http://www.prometric.com`
Mail	Sylvan Prometric
	1000 Lancaster Street
	Baltimore, Maryland 21202
Phone	(800) 627-4276

VUE

Virtual University Enterprises (VUE) is another provider of certification exams related to information technology. VUE, a division of National Computer Systems (NCS), is based in Minnesota and has operations in The Netherlands and Australia. VUE was established in 1994 and was acquired by NCS in April, 1997.

Like CATGlobal, VUE offers real-time, Internet-based registration for testing. You can schedule, change, or cancel testing appointments and check your certification status from your own computer 24 hours a day. VUE began offering Novell certification exams at its testing centers in September, 1997 and added Sybase certification exams in early 1998. VUE anticipates offering exams for additional vendors' certification programs in the near future. For more information on taking an exam from VUE, contact them at:

Web `http://www.vue.com/`

E-mail `info@vue.com`

Mail VUE, Inc.
5001 W. 80th St., Suite 401
Bloomington, MN 55437

Phone (612) 897-7999

Fax (612) 897-1015

PART

IV

Appendices

APPENDIX

A

Related Technical Certifications

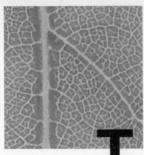

There are number of certification programs that, while not specifically designed for computer and networking professionals, may be of use for those who want a certification that validates specific technical knowledge. This appendix covers three such programs. The International Society of Certified Electronic Technicians offers a number of certifications for those involved with the repair and installation of electronic equipment, ranging from computers and electric motors to refrigeration equipment. The Institute for Interconnecting and Packaging Electronic Circuits specializes in supporting the designers and manufacturers of printed circuit boards, and offers a certification in this aspect of computer manufacture. Finally, PictureTel Corporation offers the Certified Video-conferencing Engineer to certify those responsible for the installation, repair, and support of videoconferencing systems.

International Society of Certified Electronics Technicians Certification

The International Society of Certified Electronics Technicians (ISCET) was founded in 1965, in the absence of any governmental licensing program, to address the need for certification of electronic repair service personnel. The Certified Electronics Technician (CET) program has since expanded to included two levels of certification—Associate and Journeyman—with specialties at the Journeyman level in a variety of technologies. Currently over 38,000 individuals are certified as CETs.

Benefits of Certification CETs receive a wall certificate and are eligible to join the International Society of Certified Electronics Technicians.

Associate-Level Certified Electronics Technician

The Associate-Level CET is designed for electronics technicians or students with less than four years of experience. The one required exam covers basic electronics, math, DC and AC circuits, transistors, and troubleshooting.

Who Needs It This certification is valuable to those who have experience with electronic repair but have no degree or credential to confirm their knowledge and skill.

Requirements for Certification The certification process requires only one step:

1. Pass the CET core exam test.

Administrator Certification tests are administered by ISCET members located throughout the United States. Contact ISCET for the name and address of the volunteer test administrator nearest you. Testing is arranged directly with the volunteer administrator.

Fee $50. If you fail, retaking the test costs $12.50 for the first attempt and $25 for any additional attempts.

Format   The core exam is a multiple-choice test that must be completed with a score of 75 percent or better.

Journeyman-Level Certified Electronics Technician

This certification builds on the Associate-Level program described above. If desired, a candidate for Journeyman-Level certification can take both the core CET exam and a Journeyman exam on the same day, essentially bypassing the Associate Level certification altogether. If a candidate already has Associate-Level status, he or she can become a Journeyman by taking an exam in one of eight specialty electronics areas. An individual can attain Journeyman-Level certification in multiple areas if desired.

Who Needs It   This certification is valuable to those who have experience with electronic and equipment repair but have no degree or credential to confirm their knowledge and skill.

Requirements for Certification   The certification process requires the following steps:

1. Attain Associate-Level CET certification by passing the CET core exam.

2. Pass at least one of the following Journeyman specialty exams:

   - Consumer

   - Industrial

   - Communications

   - Computer

   - Audio

- Medical

- Radar

- Video

Administrator   Certification tests are administered by ISCET members located throughout the United States. Contact ISCET for the name and address of the volunteer test administrator nearest you. Testing is arranged directly with the volunteer administrator.

Fee   If you take both the CET core exam and one Journeyman specialty exam at the same time, the total fee is $50. If you take them separately, there is a $50 fee for the core exam and a $35 fee for the first specially exam. Additional specialty exams cost $25 each.

Format   The tests are multiple-choice. Contact ISCET for details on each test.

Resources

The ISCET Web site offers more information on the certification program and the required exams. For more information on this organization's certifications and courses, contact ISCET at:

Web	http://www.iscet.org
E-mail	iscetab@aol.com
Mail	The International Society of Certified Electronics Technicians 2708 West Berry Street Fort Worth, TX 76109
Phone	(817) 921-9101
Fax	(817) 921-3741

Institute for Interconnecting and Packaging Electronic Circuits

The Institute for Interconnecting and Packaging Electronic Circuits (IPC) is a trade association comprised of over 2,300 companies that make circuit boards and interconnection components. IPC currently offers the Printed Wiring Board (PWB) Designer certification for technical professionals in this industry. IPC is planning to add additional designations to its certification program in the near future. There are currently no certification maintenance requirements for PWB Designers.

Printed Wiring Board (PWB) Designer

Attaining this certification involves passing one exam. The test assesses the candidate's knowledge of and ability to create PWBs. A PWB must be created from a schematic in such a way that the board can be easily manufactured, assembled, and tested. IPC recommends that candidates have at least five years of experience in designing PWBs before attempting the test.

Who Needs It   This certification is valuable to those involved in the design and manufacture of circuit boards.

Requirements for Certification   The certification process requires only one step:

1.   Pass the IPC Design exam.

Administrator   Call Sylvan Prometric at (800) 859-3926 to register for an IPC exam. (See Chapter 15 for detailed information on taking tests from Sylvan.)

Fee $160

Format Multiple-choice test. Call Sylvan Prometric at (800) 859-3926 for current information on length, time limit, and passing score.

Resources

The IPC Web site offers more information on the certification program and the required exam. The Web site also offers a listing of preparatory materials. For more information on this organization's certifications and courses, contact IPC at:

Web	http://www.ipc.org/
E-mail	garyferrari@ipc.org
Mail	IPC 2215 Sanders Road Northbrook, IL 60062-6135
Phone	(847) 509-9700
Fax	(847) 509-9798

PictureTel Certification

PictureTel is one of the world's leading manufacturers of video-conferencing equipment. PictureTel offers the Certified Videoconferencing Engineer (CVE) designation as a way to validate the skills of those responsible for designing, installing, and troubleshooting video-conferencing systems. CVEs are required to take a test each year to maintain their certification.

Certified Videoconferencing Engineers receive the following benefits:

- CVE Certificate of Accomplishment

- Listing in PictureTel's CVE database

Certified Videoconferencing Engineer

Attaining this certification involves passing one exam. This test assesses the candidate's knowledge of the technical aspects of a videoconferencing system in four core areas: audio, video, telecommunications network, and international standards.

Who Needs It This certification is valuable to those involved in designing and installing videoconferencing system. It can also be valuable to independent consultants who want to validate their knowledge of videoconferencing technology for potential clients.

Requirements for Certification The certification process requires only one step:

1. Pass the Certified Videoconferencing Engineer test (Sylvan ID: 1K1-001).

Administrator Call Sylvan Prometric at (888) 283-5452 to register for the Certified Videoconferencing Engineer exam. (See Chapter 15 for detailed information on taking tests from Sylvan.)

Fee $175

Format This test consists of 71 multiple-choice questions and must be completed in 90 minutes.

Resources

The PictureTel Web site offers more information on the certification program and the required exam. PictureTel's Web site also offers a listing of preparatory courses. For more information on this organization's certifications and courses, contact PictureTel at:

Web   http://www.picturetel.com

Mail	PictureTel Corporation
	100 Minuteman Road
	Andover, MA 01810
Phone	(978) 292-500

APPENDIX

B

Retired Certifications

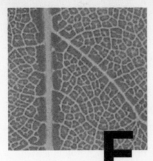

For a variety of reasons, several certification programs have recently been retired. Sometimes this happens when a company is purchased by another company or when a company simply takes a different path in its product development. In other cases, a company may decide that its program is in need of so much revision that it would be easier to scrap it entirely and start all over again. The following certifications either have been retired, or never really got off of the ground.

3COM 3Wizard

3COM's 3Wizard program was originally designed as a technical training and certification program for the company's resellers. The program had several certification levels that could be achieved by passing product-specific tests in several different technologies. This program was phased out in 1997, but will be replaced by a new program to be launched within the first six months of 1998.

Apple Certified Server Engineer

The Apple Certified Server Engineer (ACSE) certification program involved three exams that were designed to assess an individual's ability to install, maintain, and troubleshoot Apple's Workgroup Server and to manage AppleTalk-based networks. Apple required each Apple Premium Server Reseller to have at least one ACSE on staff. As is widely known, Apple has been in the process of restructuring the company to get back in the black. Apple discontinued its ACSE program in the fall of 1997 and currently has no plans to bring the program back.

Shiva Remote Access Specialist

The Shiva program was initially announced in March of 1997, but never actually materialized. When we spoke to a Shiva representative, we were told that the decision to not implement the program coincided with a change in management. Shiva currently has no plans for a certification program, but they do offer a number of classes on their remote access products.

U.S. Robotics Certified Support Professional

This certification program was phased out when U.S. Robotics was purchased by 3COM in 1997. Expect to see some aspects of this program resurrected when 3COM releases its new certification program.

APPENDIX

C

Certification Update:
A Web Resource for the Latest
Certification Information

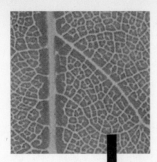

I t can be difficult to keep up with the availability and content of certification programs. Company mergers, changes in product lines and management, and other events cause some companies to rapidly change, add, or delete specific certifications within their certification programs. For example, during the three months we spent in the final preparation of this book, two certification programs by major vendors were retired, three new certification programs were launched, and four certification programs underwent major revisions and additions.

To help you keep up with the latest changes to these certification programs, we have set up the Certification Update Web site as a supplement to this book. The address is:

```
http://www.certification-update.com/
```

This companion Web site provides updates to the certification information and links to online resources that can help you meet your career and certification goals. Several vendors plan to contact us directly prior to the release of new certifications and tests; by accessing the Web site, you will have first access to this information. You will find the following areas on the Certification Update Web site:

News and Announcements Information on new certifications, and changes to certifications covered in the book.

Certification Programs Links to vendor certification programs mentioned in these pages.

Job-Hunting Resources for the Computer and Networking Professional Links to information on constructing an effective resume and conducting a job search. You will also find links to job postings around the world.

Training Resources Links to providers of computer- and instructor-based training as well as information on self-study guides and books.

INDEX

C

D

E

F

G

N

R

S

T

X

Z

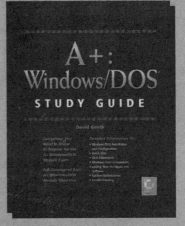

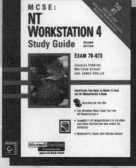